Kant's
Political
Philosophy

PHILOSOPHY AND SOCIETY
General Editor: Marshall Cohen

Also in this series:

Kant's
Political
Philosophy

Patrick Riley

Rowman & Allanheld
PUBLISHERS

The author is grateful to *Political Theory* (Sage Publications) for permitting re-use of previously published material. This includes sections I, IV and V in Chapter Seven, as well as heavily revised paragraphs from a 1973 article (now distributed throughout the book). The author is also grateful to New York University Press for permission to re-use part of his essay on Robert Paul Wolff (originally published in *Anarchism*, 1978), and to *Publius* for allowing the re-use of a 1979 article (now much revised) as Chapter Six.

ROWMAN & ALLANHELD PUBLISHERS

First published in the United States 1983 by Rowman and Littlefield,
81 Adams Drive, Totowa, New Jersey 07512.

Library of Congress Cataloging in Publication Data

Riley, Patrick, 1941-
  Kant's political philosophy.

  (Philosophy and society)
  1. Kant, Immanuel, 1724-1804—Political
science. 2. Political science—History—
18th century. I. Title. II. Series.
JC181.K4R53 1983   320'.092'4   82-573
ISBN 0-8476-6763-4   AACR2

89-13162

Printed in the United States of America

84 85 86 / 10 9 8 7 6 5 4 3 2

Printed in the United States of America

Contents

Preface

This study does not aim to provide, except incidentally, a descriptive account of Kant's political writings. Anyone seeking an intelligent précis of *Eternal Peace, Metaphysical Elements of Justice (Rechtslehre), Theory and Practice,* and *Conflict of the Faculties*—Kant's main political works—will find it in Hans Reiss's Introduction to his edition of *Kant's Political Writings.* It would be superfluous to repeat an excellent performance. The object here is quite different: it is an attempt to answer the question, what place does politics or public legal justice occupy within the Kantian critical philosophy? This question arises because Kant treats politics as very important and—simultaneously, paradoxically—holds it at arm's length. Universal republicanism and eternal peace *ought to be,* because they help to realize part of morality; but it would plainly be better if the whole world, no longer a world of particular states, were a universal ethical commonwealth living under noncoercive laws of virtue—that is, under the categorical imperative that enjoins good will or respect for persons as ends in themselves. The question then is, how could someone who believed, as Kant did, that a morally good will is the only unqualifiedly good thing on earth, argue for a republicanism and an eternal peace that at best realize some moral ends or purposes (such as peace itself) even in the total absence of good will? If politics is so very qualified a good—and sometimes, perhaps usually, a qualified evil that has historically used people as mere means—why try to make a case for it?

The question, then, is why Kant had a political philosophy at all. The attempted answer to that question will seek to place Kantian republicanism and eternal peace in the context of that reading of Kant's entire philosophy that best accommodates his politics. To anticipate, that reading is the one that holds that teleology or purposiveness is the notion that best unifies Kant's philosophy; that republicanism and eternal peace are moral ends or purposes that can be pursued politically through legal motives, even without good will; that the decisive work for a unified, politics-accommodating Kantianism is thus the *Critique of Judgment*, which is Kant's chief examination of teleology—and, in its Section 83, of a civic culture viewed as something that realizes moral ends on a legal basis. Of course there is nothing novel in taking *Judgment* to be a kind of clue to the whole of Kant. In early times that was done by Goethe, Schelling, and Hegel; later it was done by Windelband; and in more recent years *Judgment* and its theory of culture have been given primacy in valuable studies by Ernst Cassirer, Leonard Krieger, Hannah Arendt, and Yirmiahu Yovel. It is not novel, then, to read Kant through *Judgment*, but then novelty is not the purpose. The end is to find the purpose of Kant's politics within his *own* doctrine of purpose.

* * * *

I owe more than I can possibly acknowledge here to the good will of those who have helped me to understand Kant over the past twenty years.

My undergraduate introduction to Kant was through *Religion within the Limits of Reason Alone*—a happy chance, since the opening of the work contains one of Kant's finest brief accounts of his moral philosophy and particularly of his doctrine of persons as objective ends, while the final section draws a striking contrast between a potentially coercive juridical commonwealth under political laws and a purely voluntary ethical commonwealth under laws of virtue. This remarkable *summa* of Kant's practical thought I had the good fortune to learn from the late T. M. Greene, the translator of the standard edition of *Religion within the Limits*. He was a remarkable teacher, even at that very late point in his career.

During graduate work at Harvard University in the mid-1960s I was able to study Kant more fully—a study made wholly enjoyable by the efforts of Judith Shklar and John Rawls. Thanks to Mrs. Shklar I learned the then neglected *Rechtslehre* or *Metaphysical Elements of Justice*. I was assigned "Kant's Theory of Law" in her seminar on the Enlightenment, the most remarkable course I ever attended; and the wish to present that theory as carefully as possible (not a very Kantian incentive!) had the desired effect. In later years she has helped my Kant studies by commenting on manuscripts, devoting a great deal of time to conversations that mainly benefited me, and agreeing to serve on panels in which my papers were being discussed. Her constant generosity is deeply appreciated. And her knowledge of Kant is simply extraordinary, as anyone who has read her splendid Hegel book, *Freedom and Independence*, will know.

If I learned the *Rechtslehre* from Shklar, it is to John Rawls that I owe my first thorough reading of the *Fundamental Principles of the Metaphysic of Morals;* one can only hope that he will publish his very illuminating lectures on that work and on the *Critique of Practical Reason.* But *all* Kant scholars owe to John Rawls an enormous debt of gratitude for having, almost singlehandedly, revived Kant's reputation as a great political philosopher; this has been one of the incidental benefits of that magistral neo-Kantian work, *A Theory of Justice.* The mere fact that my book stresses teleology in a way that Rawls's studies do not seems to me unimportant, compared with the fact that no one would have asked me to produce such a work at all had not John Rawls brought Kant the political theorist back from near-eclipse. If Kant is once again, properly, mentioned in the same breath with Hobbes, Rousseau, and Hegel, that can be traced to Rawls's efforts. And his well-known kindness, which in my case took the form of letting me read his unpublished Kant lectures, should be even better known.

I could never have begun serious work on Kant as a political thinker without the aid of Judith Shklar and John Rawls; in later years I was helped to carry on work-in-progress by George Armstrong Kelly, the charming and generous scholar whose Kant chapter in *Idealism, Politics and History* remains much the best thing on Kant's social thought in English. Over the years I have benefited from his careful and knowledgeable, but always encouraging, remarks—most recently in September 1981, when I presented parts of Chapters I and IV at a conference in New York, and was delighted and moved by the depth and generosity of his commentary.

There are others to thank. I have enjoyed and learned from conversation with William Galston, whose *Kant and the Problem of History* I greatly respect; I am grateful for the helpful comments on my reading of Kant made by Michael Sandel after my presentation of a paper before one of his Harvard classes; I am always stimulated by exchanges with Susan Shell, since we disagree so radically over Kant interpretation but still manage to treat each other as co-members of the kingdom of ends. I am, finally, grateful to Marshall Cohen for asking me to write *Kant's Political Philosophy* and to Benjamin Barber, editor of *Political Theory,* for kindly permitting me to refashion and reuse various Kant pieces published in his journal between 1973 and 1981.

I dedicate this book to my parents, who taught me the meaning of good will long before my formal introduction to Kant.

Patrick Riley
January 1982

CHAPTER ONE

Practical Reason and Respect for Persons in the Kantian Republic

I

Strictly speaking, the respect for persons as "ends in themselves" that Kantian pure practical reason demands is fully attainable, if at all, only in the "kingdom of ends" of the *Fundamental Principles of the Metaphysic of Morals*,[1] or in the "ethical commonwealth" of *Religion within the Limits*,[2] or in the *corpus mysticum* of all rational beings of the first *Critique*,[3] and not in a mere republic, which rests on coercive laws, rather than on respect or virtue or good will.[4] So when Kant says, in the very late *Conflict of the Faculties* (1798), that if earthly sovereigns treat man as a mere "trifle" by "burdening him like a beast and using him as a mere instrument of their own ends, or by setting him up to fight in their disputes and slaughter his fellow creatures," then this is "not just a trifle but a reversal of the ultimate purpose of creation,"[5] he must be thinking of his own doctrine in *Eternal Peace*. There he states that humanity under moral laws sets a "limiting condition" to what is politically permissible[6]—a limiting condition that should somehow bear on politics, even if rulers lack the good will that would lead them to respect persons.

But what is the nature of this "somehow"? How does morality as limiting condition limit and condition Kantian politics? If a Kantian politics could be properly limited and conditioned, would persons be—if not indeed respected from moral motives—at least not used as mere means to "relative" ends? Might the notion of "objective" ends set those limiting conditions? This leads to the question whether the

1

general concept of ends could be used as a clamp to hold Kant's whole practical philosophy together. The rest of this work is an attempt to answer that question.

II

It is plainly Kant's conviction—perhaps his central political conviction—that morality and politics must be related, since "true politics cannot take a single step without first paying homage to morals."[7] At the same time, however, Kant draws a very strict distinction between *moral* motives (acting from respect for the moral law) and *legal* motives,[8] and insists that their definitions must never be collapsed into each other. This is why he argues, again in *Conflict of the Faculties*, that even with growing enlightenment and republicanism, there still will not be a greater number of moral actions in the world, but only a larger number of legal ones that roughly correspond to what pure morality would achieve if it could.[9] (At the end of time, a purely moral kingdom of ends will not be realized on earth—though it *ought* to be—but one can reasonably hope for a legal order that is closer to morality than are present arrangements.) To put the matter a little overstarkly: politics needs to reflect morality but cannot count on moral motives, only legal ones; morality must have a relation to Kantian politics without collapsing the meaning of *public legal justice* into that of *good will* and *respect for persons*. Put another way: morality and public legal justice must be related in such a way that morality shapes politics—by forbidding war and insisting on eternal peace and the rights of man—without becoming the motive of politics.

Given this tension between morality and public legal justice, which must be related but which equally must remain distinct, one can tentatively and cautiously suggest that the notion of ends may help to serve as a bridge between them. For public law certainly upholds some moral ends (e.g., nonmurder), even though that law must content itself with any legal motive. ("Jurisprudence and ethics," Kant says in the *Rechtslehre*, "are distinguished not so much by their different duties" or ends as by different "incentives.")[10] Using *telos* as a bridge connecting the moral to the political-legal realm is not a very radical innovation, since Kant himself bridged far more disparate realms, those of nature and freedom, with a notion of end or purpose (subjectively valid for human "reflective" judgment) in the *Critique of Judgment;* and then threw a further bridge from nature and freedom— now linked by a *telos* thought of as a possible supersensible ground uniting nature and freedom—to art.[11] He did all of this by arguing that nature can be "estimated" (though never known) through purposes and functions that mechanical causality fails to explain; that persons, hypothetically free, both have purposes that they strive to realize and view themselves as the final end of creation; and that art exhibits a "purposiveness without purpose," which makes it not directly moral but the "symbol" of morality.[12] Surely, then, if *telos* (sometimes confined to a "reflective" or "regulative" role) can link, or be thought of as linking, nature, human freedom, and art, it can link, much more modestly, two sides of human freedom: the moral and the legal realms.

Admittedly the "continuity" at this point is not perfect, since Kant says that purposiveness is only a "reflective" principle when it is used in estimating nature and art, while morality by contrast has "objective ends" that are "proposed by reason" and that everyone "ought to have."[13] But a possible continuity is reestablished when Kant says, rather incautiously, that there must be "a ground of unity of the supersensible, which lies at the basis of nature, with that which the concept of freedom practically contains."[14] In simpler language, an intelligence other than ours might see real purposes in nature that are as objective as the objective ends that our intelligence knows through the moral law. This could mean that *Judgment*, with its numerous teleological bridges, helps to establish the "unity of reason" that is always a central Kantian concern. (For the moment these bridges must be abridged; a full examination of them, the core of this study, will come later. Provisionally, pontification is unavoidable.)

Now, if *good will* in the purely moral realm is construed to mean never universalizing a maxim of action that fails to respect persons as ends in themselves,[15] then morality and politics/law could be connected through Kantian teleology. If all persons had a good will, they would respect all others as ends, indeed as members of a kingdom of ends, for a "rational nature" such as a person is "not an end to be effected" but an "independently existing end".[16] However, this does not actually happen, though it ought to, thanks to the "anthropological" fact that man is "radically evil."[17] Thus Kantian public legal justice is a kind of intersection between the facts of anthropology and the categorical imperative; if there were a kingdom of ends, the kingdoms of the earth would vanish. If, in sum, good will means respect for persons as ends in themselves, and if public legal justice sees to it that some moral ends (such as nonmurder) get observed, if not respected, then public legal justice in Kant might be viewed as the partial realization of what would happen if all wills were good. Beyond that, of course, Kant frequently suggests that law creates a kind of environment for good will, by bracketing out occasions of political sin (such as fear of others' domination) that might tempt, though never determine, people to act wrongly.[18] One might, indeed, say that the notion of a legal facilitation of morality does not seem very Kantian;[19] but he does say that one has a duty to remove from the world the occasions of wrong-doing ("whatever diminishes the obstacles to an activity furthers this activity itself").[20] even though one is not excused, *qua* malefactor, simply because occasions of sin are still there. Occasions are not causes.

Overall, then, Kantian public legal justice is purposively related to morality in two ways, one of them stronger than the other. In the slightly weaker sense, it simply creates legal conditions for the exercise of a good will by expanding "negative" freedom so that one can be "positively" free, or self-determining through the moral law. In the somewhat stronger sense it legally enforces (part of) what ought to be, even where good will is absent and only legal incentives are present. If in the weak sense Kantian public legal justice simply facilitates morality, in the strong sense it produces good conduct (though this conduct is only qualifiedly good because it depends on legal motives). This strong sense is illuminated by Kant himself in his unpublished commentary on Baumgarten's jurisprudence. The moral law "suffices in itself to constrain objectively" in "making known what each [person] ought to do," Kant urges in this commentary; but for "subjective constraint"—which means that each man may be "constrained to conform himself" to what he ought to do "when *motiva moralia* are insufficient"—one needs what Kant calls a *potestas executoria*, i.e., a civil state.[21] This *potestas executoria* will be instrumental to morality, or at least to some of the ends of morality, in the sense that it will see to it that what ought to happen does in fact happen. In a word, the strong sense of instrumental politics, or legality, sees to it that some of the ends of morality get enforced, even where *motiva moralia* are absent; the weak sense of instrumental politics, or politics as context, creates a state of affairs in which those *motiva moralia* themselves have a better chance to operate. On either view, public legal justice is "for" morality, is morality's instrument.

III

But why, one might reasonably ask, attempt to bridge morality and public legal justice through ends that are shared by the moral and legal realms? Does not the advantage of appealing to a Kantian teleology that links nature, freedom, and art, as well as morality and legality, pale before the plain fact that there are better and simpler bridges to be found—bridges that are at least as genuinely Kantian? The two most obvious links between morality and legality in Kant, *telos* aside, are those of *freedom* and *contract*. Before pursuing the teleological path, those other links should be glanced at.

1. Why not link morality and public legal justice in Kant mainly through freedom? After all, freedom is the *ratio essendi* of the moral law,[22] and the moral law must receive the "homage" of any "true" politics. Therefore politics must somehow pay homage to the freedom that is the essence of the moral law. Moreover, for Kant justice is the coexistence of everyone's freedom under general laws;[23] and so public legal justice, because its aim is external freedom, pays homage to a morality whose inner law is freedom. Beyond all this, Kant himself insists in *Practical Reason* that freedom is "the keystone of the whole architecture of the system of pure reason."[24] Why, then, look for a new keystone for the critical philosophy in *Judgement* if one is already given in *Practical Reason?* Why prefer the *Third Critique* to the *Second?*

This notion of freedom-paying-homage-to-freedom should indeed be stressed—but arguably not first. The reason for this is that what comes first in Kant is the moral law *qua* "fact of reason."[25] This fact of reason is, for Kant, indubitable. Freedom, by contrast, is a "necessary idea of reason" that is revealed through the moral law, but whose "objective reality" is indemonstrable.[26] Therefore one does better to start with the moral law and its objective ends, and to see politics/law as the external realizer of some of those ends (without benefit of "good will"). Besides, in politics/law one has freedom in part *because* law realizes some ends (nonmurder, nontheft, nonfraud). One is then free to do in security *(a)* what the moral law enjoins and *(b)* what is morally indifferent. None of these considerations makes freedom marginal or trivial in Kant; he remains *the* philosopher of freedom. But since he says that consciousness of our obligation under the moral law leads us to think of ourselves as necessarily free, it seems reasonable to stress that law, and its attendant objective ends, first. The decisive text is surely the following passage from *Practical Reason:*

> The question now is whether our *knowledge* of the unconditionally practical [moral] takes its inception from freedom or from the practical law. It cannot start from freedom, for this we can neither know immediately, since our first concept of it is negative, nor infer from experience, since experience reveals us only the law of appearances and consequently the mechanism of nature, the direct opposite of freedom. It is therefore the moral law, of which we become immediately conscious as soon as we construct maxims for the will, which first presents itself to us; and, since reason exhibits it as a ground of determination which is completely independent of and not to be outweighted by any sensuous condition, it is the moral law which leads directly to the concept of freedom.[27]

2. Why not link morality and public legal justice in Kant mainly through contract, perhaps through a contract between free beings, which encompasses both concepts? After all, Kant's political writings are full of quasi-Rousseauean contractarian claims ("the basic law, which can only come from the general, united will of the people, is called the original contract"),[28] and his moral philosophy has been seen by some as a "deepened" Rousseaueanism[29] in which one "gives the law to oneself" as a "legislative" member of the kindgom of ends. In this view Rousseau, placed on a proper metaphysical *Grundlegung*, and not *telos*, is the bridge uniting the whole of Kant's practical thought.

To this no simple answer can be returned; indeed, much of Chapter 4 will be given over to the attempt. But even if Kant turns out not to believe consistently that what is right, both morally and politically, is "constructed" by "autonomous" agents through a contractarian "procedure" (to use John Rawls's term),[30] it may remain true that he is a great contractarian in the special sense that he alone provides a theory of *will* adequate to underpin the voluntarism of pure contractarianism—adequate to shore up Hobbes's claim that "wills . . . make the essence of all covenants"[31] and Locke's insistence that "voluntary agreement gives . . . political power to governors."[32] Kant, in short, may have provided a groundwork for a contractarian structure that he did not fully build. (That is cryptic, but must be until the "Rousseau possibility" is fully treated later on.)

Even a bare mentioning of the "Rousseau possibility," of course, reminds one that there are two main reasonable, or at least familiar, readings of Kant's moral theory, and that those two main readings are reflected in a politics that pays homage to morals. If one stresses, as the core of Kant's ethics, the teleological notion that "a rational nature exists as an end in itself,"[33] that such a rational nature (e.g., man) is an objective end that is the "source" of the categorical imperative,[34] then one will rule out murder, and all lesser crimes, on grounds of counterpurposiveness. Public legal justice, as a reflection of morality so conceived, will be thought of mainly as enforcing objective ends. But if one stresses, in the manner of Lewis White Beck, the notion that Kant agrees with Rousseau that "obedience to a law that one has prescribed is the only real freedom," and that in Kant's hands Rousseau's "doctrine of self-government" is "deepened into a moral and metaphysical doctrine,"[35] one will surely say that the moral law is made, not "found," and by reasonable analogy that state law is also made, and not found in objective ends. All readings of Kant's politics, then, turn on a reading of his moral philosophy.

A quasi-Rousseauean contractarian reading of Kant, according to which we give the law, rather than find it, would, if correct, have an additional advantage—a very large advantage, given Kant's interest in unity and in architectonic symmetry.[36] This advantage Beck goes so far as to call Kant's "second Copernican revolution."[37] The governing idea is simple: if Kant's original Copernican revolution is the thought that our "understanding" constructs or constitutes nature, rather than reflects it, might not the second revolution be the thought that our "reason" constructs or constitutes the moral law, and then a politics flowing from it?

Now the first Copernican revolution is clearly formulated by Kant himself in the Preface to the second edition of *Pure Reason* (1787):

> Hitherto it has been assumed that all our knowledge must conform to objects. But all attempts to extend our knowledge of objects by establishing something in regard to them *a priori*, by means of concepts, have, on this assumption, ended in failure. We must therefore make trial whether we may not have more success . . . if we suppose that objects must conform to our knowledge. This would agree better with what is desired, namely, that it should be possible to have knowledge of objects *a priori*, determining something in regard to them prior to their being given. We should then be proceeding precisely on the lines of Copernicus' primary hypothesis.[38]

In the original edition (1781) of *Pure Reason*, "Transcendental Deduction," A127, Kant insists that "however exaggerated and absurd it may sound to say that the understanding is itself the source of the laws of nature," by producing a "synthetic unity" of experience out of the "manifold of sensible intuition" through the use of organizing "categories" such as "casuality," such an assertion "is nonetheless correct." For this reason "understanding is . . the lawgiver of nature." For without understanding's legislative work, "nature, that is the synthetic unity of the manifold of appearances according to rules, would not exist."[39]

The first Copernican revolution, then, treats understanding as the "lawgiver of nature," not as a passive reflection of nature. The obvious sequel, particularly for those inclined to read Kant as "deepened" Rousseau, would be to ask: if understanding gives the law to nature, might it not be the case that (our) reason gives the law to morals? And might that parallel not illuminate Kant's famous claim that Rousseau is the "Newton of the moral world?"[40] For that would mean that Newton revealed the natural law, and Rousseau the moral law.[42]

That such a reading of Kant—in which understanding and reason are given "legislative" powers to constitute two realms, nature and morals which are in turn linked only by being law-ordered—is obviously possible, is confirmed by a typical claim by Kant himself, this time in the *Critique of Judgment*. In that work's Introduction, Kant argues that

> Understanding prescribes laws *a priori* for nature as an object of sense, so that we may have a theoretical knowledge of it in a possible experience. Reason prescribes laws *a priori* for freedom and its peculiar casuality as the supersensible in the Subject, so that we may have a purely practical knowledge. [42]

All of this, if tenable, would constitute a powerful architectonic reason for viewing Kant as a contractarian (in a broad sense) who thinks that we "construct" a natural world through our understanding and a moral world through our reason. Everything, including politics, would then be the product of a universal, intersubjective, constructive capacity. Since, however, architectonic reasons have force only in proportion to the real existence of illuminating parallels, one still must wait to see how far it is true, for Kant, that our reason constructs the moral law (and then a politics and law supportive of that law). If a "legislative" reading of Kant's ethics turns out to be a weaker reading than others—say a teleological reading—then contractarian architectonic parallels will lose much of their force. But justice requires the admission that if understanding and reason are equally "legislative," that fact might supply the unity and the system that the present reading tries to find in reconceived purposiveness. *Nomos*, then, would prevail over *telos*.

IV

Having arrived at what Michael Oakeshott calls a "platform of conditional understanding"[43] (though in this case "platform of provisional understanding" might be better), one can press on to a slightly fuller, though still provisional, view of the general shape of Kant's politics. So far only very large (and therefore very abstract) systematic considerations have been taken into account: how Kantian politics relates to Kantian morals, and above all to respect for persons as objective ends; how politics as the legal realizer, via republicanism and eternal peace, of (some) objective ends fits into a larger Kantian doctrine of ends or purposes; how Kant's much-wished-for architectonic unity of reason might be found precisely in a reconstructed, critical teleology that accommodates not just moral ends (and the legal realization of some of them) but also nature and art; how teleological architectonic considerations might be thought to outweigh contractarian architectonic considerations. One must descend from these heights—which will have to be rescaled in later sections that ask what, exactly and completely, is meant by *teleology, ends, contractarianism,* and so forth, in Kant—to see some other crucial parts of his politics. Those parts can be approached, once again, through the notion of a purposiveness for which some provisional footing has been established.

V

If that footing is well grounded, then the effort to locate Kant's political theory within his complete practical philosophy necessarily involves saying something further about the notion of instrumentality; for the relation between politics and morality in his system is mainly, if not invariably, an instrumental one, and politics serves primarily to make morality, or at least moral ends, more nearly possible. (The Kantian state realizes morally important ends, but it is morally important that only ends be realized.) Kant, then, clearly subordinates politics to morality, but at the same time bases politics on "right," not on utility or happiness. As he said in his letter to Jung-Stilling (March 1789), "the laws . . . must be given not as arbitrary and accidental commandments for some purpose that happen to be desired"—such as the greater happiness of the greatest number—"but only insofar as they are necessary for the achievement of universal freedom."[44] That law-protected sphere of freedom constitutes an environment for morality, a place within which morality can take place. (How, in view of this, Charles Taylor can have urged in his imposing study of Hegel that Kantian politics "ends up borrowing from the utilitarians," that it has as its "input" the "utilitarian vision of a society of individuals each seeking happiness in his own way,"[45] is not at all easy to see. One would have thought that if Kant had succeeded in anything, if was in *not* being mistaken for Jeremy Bentham.)

There is certainly no Benthamism in Kant's well-known claim that the only unqualifiedly good thing on earth is a good will[46]—a will, one may say provisionally, that strives to act on the basis of maxims that, if made universal, would not violate the dignity of men as ends in themselves.[47] Every element of this definition—the concept of will, the idea of universality, the problem of persons as ends in themselves—is directly relevant to Kant's political philosophy. For if a good or moral will is the only unqualifiedly good thing on earth (this does not mean that everything else is thereby worthless), then politics, among other qualified goods, must be instrumental to morality; a merely powerful and stable, even glorious, state that pursues moral evil cannot be praiseworthy. This is doubtless why Kant urges, in the already-stressed passage from *Eternal Peace*, that "true politics cannot take a single step without first paying homage to morals."[48] He admits that if there exists "no freedom and no moral law based upon it, and if everything which happens . . . is simply a part of the mechanism of nature," then it is appropriate to manipulate men as natural objects in order to govern them; but that if right is to be the "limiting condition of politics," morality and politics must be conceded to be "compatible," capable of coexistence.

For Kant one has a duty to enter into a "juridical state of affairs," because moral freedom involves both the negative freedom of the will from "determination by sensible impulses" and the positive freedom of a will that determines itself through reason, through the notion of what ought to be. Negative freedom is thus instrumental to, or the condition of, positive freedom.[50] Given this, if public legal justice can remove or limit some of the objects that can incline human will to be shaped by impulse—if politics can control, for instance, a fear of violence that might lead one to violate the categorical imperative—then politics is supportive of morality because it advances negative freedom. This point is well made by Kant himself in the first Appendix to *Eternal Peace*, which shows that he took the problem of possible dangers to the "first performer" of right actions seriously.[51] He argues that government or public legal justice, by putting an end to outbreaks of lawlessness, "genuinely makes it much easier for the moral capacities of men to develop into an immediate respect for right." For everyone believes, Kant goes on, that he would always conform his conduct to what is right if only he could be certain that everyone else would do likewise; and "the government in part guarantees this for him." By creating a coercive order of public justice, then, "a great step is taken *toward* morality (although this is still not the same as a moral step), towards a state where the concept of duty is recognized for its own sake."[52]

In his late *Anthropology from a Pragmatic Point of View* (1798), Kant expands this argument. The "mania for domination," he argues, "is intrinsically unjust and its manifestation provokes everyone to oppose it. Its origin, however, is fear of being dominated by others: it tries to avert this by getting a head start and dominating them."[53] (Surely this is a perfect instance of the asocial side of "asocial sociability" that Kant describes in his *Idea for a Universal History*.)[54] But domination, he goes on, "is a precarious and unjust means of using others for one's purposes: it is *imprudent* because it arouses their opposition, and it is *unjust* because it is contrary to freedom under law, to which everyone can lay claim."[55] Government, which provides freedom under law, can manage this psychology; it can alleviate our desire to dominate others, out of fear that they will dominate us, by creating a system of public legal justice in which only law is coercive. Thus both the fact of domination and the fear of domination can be, at least, moderated by government. This may make it more nearly possible to exercise a good will, to respect the dignity of others as ends in themselves.

As was noticed earlier, a legal facilitation of morality might not seem very Kantian in spirit. It is surely this that George Armstrong Kelly has in mind when he says, in the "Kant" chapter of his remarkable *Idealism, Politics and History,* that "it should be impossible [in Kant] for citizenship or public law-abidingness to make men moral . . . a false juncture would be made between the realms of autonomous and heteronomous causation."[56] But a possible way out is to say that public legal justice is instrumental to negative freedom (e.g., freedom from fear), so that persons can be positively free by determining themselves to act from the moral law. Mere freedom from fear, taken by itself, would not be moral; but public legal justice, by restricting fear, might diminish an obstacle to moral conduct. Morality, for Kant, is objective; but we can know, from subjective facts of human "pathology," that something like fear may deter us from acting morally. Thus there can be a duty to block—legally—the effect of morality-deflecting fears and appetites. Were that not so, Kantian politics would not be possible at all. For Kantian politics tries to attain some moral ends without being able to count on moral incentives.)[57]

In Kantian politics the crucial thing is thus liberty, a liberty that, by constraining others in giving me rights, will both remove impediments to morality and allow the unrestricted enjoyment of those things that morality does not forbid.[58] The crucial thing is a harmony of my external freedom with that of others according to a universal law. Perhaps Kant's finest statement of this view is to be found in the *Critique of Pure Reason:*

> A constitution allowing the greatest possible human freedom in accordance with laws which insure that the freedom of each can co-exist with the freedom of all the others (not one designed to provide the greatest happiness . . .), is at all events a necessary idea which must be made the basis not only of the first outline of a political constitution but of all laws as well.[59]

Liberty in Kant, then, is both restrictive and permissive; liberty restricts what others can do to me by the willful exercise of their wills (things that might make it more difficult for me to be moral), and it permits the pursuit of ends that are morally indifferent.

Politics and law thus serve a high purpose in Kant's practical philosophy: they are the guarantors of those negative conditions that make respect for the dignity of men as ends in themselves more nearly possible. They make the exercise of a good will less difficult by removing impediments that could incline (though never determine) the will to act on maxims that cannot be universalized in a way that is congruent with the rights of man, and they realize some moral ends on the basis of legal motives. So if Kantian politics is only a qualified and instrumental good, and not the supreme ornament that it is in a writer such as Aristotle,[60] that instrumentality is still quite important. As Kant himself says in an already quoted passage from *Practical Reason*, "whatever diminishes the obstacles to an activity furthers this activity itself."[61] Apart from moral activity itself, then, what can be more important than furthering this activity by diminishing obstacles to that unqualified good? But that, of course, is just how Kant views public legal justice.

Legality and rightful politics generally can be instrumental to morality in this rather oblique way, because law and morals commonly require many of the same things; they both prohibit murder, fraud, and so forth. Only the incentive of obedience to the demands of practical reason differs in morality and legality; as Kant says in a now-familiar sentence from the *Rechtslehre*, "jurisprudence and ethics are distinguished . . . not so much by their different duties" or ends as by "the difference in the legislation that combines one or the other incentive with the law."[62] And on the difference between moral and legal incentives Kant is quite clear:

> What is essential in the moral worth of actions is that the moral law should directly determine the will. If the determination of the will takes place in conformity indeed to the moral law, but only by means of a feeling, no matter of what kind, which has to be presupposed in order that the law may be sufficient to determine the will, and therefore not for the sake of the law, then the action will possess legality but not morality.[63]

Both legality and morality, then, are concerned with duties or moral ends, for example a duty not to kill; and therefore adherence to the law sustained[64] by the political order is in itself and directly a duty—a "perfect duty to others"—whatever one's incentive may be. This must obviously be so, if morality and legality share a set of overlapping ends and differ only with respect to motives. But political-legal justice is still only instrumental to morality because politics can operate on the basis of any incentive to obedience; an adequate system of public legal justice, Kant says in *Eternal Peace*, is possible "even for a people of devils, if only they have intelligence, though this may sound harsh."[65] (To Kant, of course, it is not even conceivable that legal justice should try to moralize men; law is by definition external, and morality loses its meaning unless the internal recognition of duty alone is the incentive of obedience.)[66]

This certainly does not mean that Kant sets too low a value on law; and in fact he is usually criticized for giving too much weight to mere legality in his political theory, even where that legality arguable conflicts with what his own morality requires. Kant did insist, after all, that "if public legal justice perishes it is no longer worthwhile for men to remain alive on this earth,"[67] adding in the *Reflexionen zur Rechtsphilosophie* that "there must be law and justice in the world." The "civil condition," he argues in the same *Reflexionen*, "is not arbitrary, but necessary" ("der *status civilis* ist also nicht *arbitrarius* sondern *necessarius*").[68] Even if law is "necessary" rather than "arbitrary," however, that does nothing to degrade the higher status of morality in Kant's system; and even the notion of God is commonly derived by Kant from ordinary moral knowledge. In the *Critique of Pure Reason* he argues, in the manner of Plato's *Euthyphro*, that "so far as practical reason has the right to serve as our guide, we shall not look upon actions as obligatory because they are the commands of God, but shall regard them as divine commands because we have an inward obligation to them."[69] And in the *Fundamental Principles of the Metaphysic of Morals* he adds that the idea of God is derived from "the idea of moral perfection, which reason frames *a priori* and connects inseparably with the notion of a free will."[70] Given morality's supreme place it is most accurate to say that, in Kantian politics, public legal justice sets up a context instrumental to negative freedom, in which one fulfills duties (or rather the "ends" of duty) on the basis of any incentive that will yield peaceable external conduct.

Although the realms of law and morals share a set of "objective ends," the distinction between morality and legality is fundamental in Kant. Especially in his later historical writings, however, he does dare to hope that politics and morality will come closer together in a distant future—not in the sense that a moral incentive could ever become the motive for obedience to public legal justice, but in the sense that, as the world becomes increasingly "republican," as states more adequately realize what Kant calls the Idea of the original contract,[71] politics will at least no longer command what the categorical imperative absolutely forbids. Kant "predicts" that, as the human race comes closer to enlightenment, it will progressively transform the structure of politics until the state if finally "republican"—which means that every organ of the state will treat men as free, autonomous, and legally equal persons, and that everyone will either consent to law through his representatives, or will live under laws that are worthy of consent.[72] As universal republicanism emerges as the product of rational historical evolution, the political-legal context provided by states will violate morality less often; in a "cosmopolitical" structure of eternal peace whose member states freely enter into a permanent equilibrium that keeps the "intrinsically healthy resistance" of states from degenerating into violence, states will no longer force their citizens to commit immoral acts.[73] As states become more republican, as a world-order based on an equilibrium of republican states emerges, Kant argues (most carefully in the *Critique of Judgment*),[74] politics at the national and international level will increasingly become simply that uniform legal condition that gives men the chance to have the kind of will they should have, and that realizes some moral ends on a legal basis. The political order will then be parallel, though never identical, to the moral order. All of this Kant prophesies in his late but centrally important *The Conflict of the Faculties*:

> Even without the mind of a seer, I now maintain that I can predict from the aspects and signs of our times that the human race will . . . progressively improve without any more total reversals. . . . [But] the profit which will accrue to the human race as it works its way forward will not be an ever-increasing quantity of morality in its attitudes. Instead, the *legality* of its attitudes will produce an increasing number of actions governed by duty, whatever the particular motive behind these actions may be. . . . Violence will gradually become less on the part of those in power, and obedience towards the laws will increase . . . and this will ultimately extend to the external relations between the various peoples, until a cosmopolitan society is created. Such developments do not mean, however, that the basic moral capacity of mankind will increase in the slightest, for this would require a kind of new creation.[75]

This moderately hopeful view of human history—which for Kant steers a non-utopian course between "moral terrorism" (the notion of constant human decline) and "chiliasm" (the notion of constant human moral improvement)—permits him to foresee that, at the end of time, politics and morality may finally be able to co-exist. At that point politics will become what it always ought to have been: the instrument to, rather than the antagonist of, morality.[76] For Kant, if politics can (as it should) cease to be the cause of immorality, above all in the form of war, then it can champion the cause of morality, partly by translating a part of "ought" into actual existence (in the form of legality), partly by creating peaceful conditions for a good will. In either way public legal justice, stabilized at the highest level by "eternal peace," provides a "setting" for that will, which Kant himself calls a "jewel" that "shines by its own light, as a thing which has its whole value in itself."[77]

VI

Perhaps all of Kant's thoughts on politics as the instrument of morality are best summed up in Part II of his essay *On the Common Saying: "This May be True in Theory, but it does not Apply in Practice."* In that section, which is subtitled "Against Hobbes," Kant argues that while any society has a great many subsidiary social contracts that establish "unions" of many individuals for "some common end which they all share," there is *one* kind of union that is "of an exceptional nature," that is an "end in itself" that all men "ought to share," that indeed is "an absolute and primary duty in all external relationships whatsoever among human beings." This exceptional union, he argues, is the civil state or the commonwealth, a condition of "external right" that (through "coercive public laws") secures for each citizen "what is due to him" and freedom from "attack from any others." But the whole notion of "external right," Kant goes on, is derived not at all from "the aim of achieving happiness," which is a mere empirical end, but simply from "the concept of freedom."[78] And freedom secures and guarantees a sphere within which one can exercise a good will. Overall, then, Kantian public legal justice is instrumental to morality in two senses, one of them stronger than the other: in a slightly weaker sense, it simply creates *conditions* for the exercise of a good will; in a somewhat stronger sense, it legally enforces certain ends that ought to be (e.g., no murder), even where good will is absent and only legal motives are present. But, whether in a weaker or stronger sense, politics remains the instrument of the sole "unqualified" good.

This passage from *Theory and Practice*, in speaking of the state as an exceptional kind of social contract, obviously introduces the contractarian strand into Kant's politics. As was suggested earlier, one must say something about the simple fact that Kant often uses contractarian arguments in his politics, even if one thinks that he is not a contractarian in some larger, and looser, sense. Before examining some of the passages in which Kant makes Rousseau-inspired contractarian political arguments, however, a general word is needed.

Even on the strongest teleological reading of Kant's ethics, in which objective ends constitute morality and shape politics, contract can still have a place in Kant's politics. To anticipate later arguments: for Kant, citizens of a republic arguably would not consent to adventuristic wars, since they might be ruined by those wars. From the legal motive of self-love, republican citizens would dissent from war.[79] It may be, then, that a republic under the "Idea" of the contract, of everyone's consenting, yields from purely legal motives a political state of affairs that coincides with (some) moral requirements, such as eternal peace. This would merely reflect Kant's claim, already considered, that morality and law share duties (or ends or purposes), but differ over motives. A contractarian republic might—since rational citizens would have to acknowledge social practices[80]—be more likely than other forms of government to bring legality closer to morality, even if the content of that morality were found in objective ends, not made by agreement. On this view, even if Kant's moral thought were not "deepened" Rousseau, quasi-Rousseauean ideal contractarianism could still figure in the political-legal realm.

This view provides a way of integrating Kant's frequently stated doctrine of the original contract into a teleological view in which ends are "there" (as it were), not produced. If "original contract" is another way of saying "republic of consenting citizens," then Kant's contractarian utterances are fully reconcilable with his notion that morality itself requires legal enforcement of moral ends by legal means in a republic;[81] but if all ends are the *product* of actual historical contracts, then one is hard-pressed to account for Kant's "rational beings" who are already respectable "ends in themselves," not "ends to be realized" by agreement.[82] Kant's original contract, understood as the "idea" of everyone's consenting in a republic, can remain valid in Kant's politics, even if the *reason* for founding and obeying states has to do with legally realizing some moral ends, not just with keeping contracts.

It is in this light that one can, and should, read Kant's claim in *Theory and Practice* that

> An original contract . . . is in fact merely an Idea of reason, which nonetheless has undoubted practical reality; for it can oblige every legislator to frame his laws in such a way that they could have been produced by the united will of a whole nation, and to regard each subject, in so far as he can claim citizenship, as if he had consented within the general will.[83]

But one must await a full exposition of the Kantian republic (Chapter 5), to ask how far it is plausible that citizens would, through their general will, refuse to consent to some of the things (above all war) that which are forbidden by a moral law whose highest practical end—given human pathology—is peace.

VII

Kant's practical thought begins not with the general will of the citizen, but with the good will of the individual.[84] And "good will" is not something that one can choose to treat or ignore in an adequate reading of Kant's politics. For if a good will, viewed as the only unqualifiedly good thing on earth, is the core of Kantian morality; if that good will is good because it strives to act from respect for the moral law, a law that enjoins respect for persons as ends in themselves; if the moral law, in its turn, must receive the "homage" of politics; and if that homage takes the double form of (a) realizing legally some of the moral ends that a reason-governed good will "would bring forth . . . were it accompanied by sufficient physical capacities" *(Practical Reason)*,[35] and (b) providing a context of negative legal security for the flourishing of *motiva moralia;* then good will is the first link in a Kantian moral chain that provides politics with "essential ends of humanity"[86] (republicanism and eternal peace). Therefore good will must, even in a political study, be given the prominence that Kant himself gives it. To be sure, if everyone had a completely efficacious good will, there would be no Kantian politics to study: the kingdom of ends or *corpus mysticum* of rational beings would be the only kingdom, and an "ethical commonwealth" (described in *Religion within the Limits)* could embrace the whole of humanity:

> As far as we can see . . . they sovereignty of the good principle is attainable, so far as men can work toward it, only through the establishment and spread of a society in accordance with, and for the sake of, the laws of virtue, a society whose task and duty it is rationally to impress these laws in all their scope upon the entire human race . . . A union of men under merely moral laws, patterned on the above Idea, may be called an *ethical,* and so far as these laws are public, an *ethico-civil* (in contrast to a *juridico-civil)* society or an *ethical commonwealth.*[87]

What then, for Kant necessitates the juridico-civil society, which is plainly second best? Nothing but the fact that, while the ethical commonwealth is an Idea that "possesses a thoroughly well-grounded objective reality in human reason (in man's duty to join such a state)," our knowledge of "anthropology" and human "pathology" teaches us that "subjectively, we can never hope that man's good will will lead mankind to work with unanimity towards this goal."[88] (In *Conflict of the Faculties* Kant reinforces this by saying that for the "basic moral capacity of mankind" to "increase in the slightest," there would have to be "a kind of new creation or supernatural influence.")[89] But if unaided good will cannot attain its goal, that end can be partly, qualifiedly, legally attained through the republicanism and eternal peace that are most nearly parallel to the kingdom of ends. Thus the general will of the citizen has an important relation to the good will that is the sole unqualified good. General will is not good will, but they are linked by ends, by the teleological bridge that binds the whole of Kantianism together.

CHAPTER TWO

Good Will

I

No one has ever doubted that Kant begins his moral philosophy with an insistence on "good will"[1]—that is, with the idea of a "moral causality," itself independent of natural causality, that is the foundation of man's freedom and responsibility. That good will is crucial to Kant's understanding of politics is quite clear. Public legal justice is necessitated by the partial or total absence of a good will that would yield, if it could, a noncoercive ethical commonwealth under laws of virtue. Good will's absence necessitates politics' presence. And the *idea* of an ethical commonwealth generated by good will serves as a kind of utopia that earthly politics can legally approximate through peacefulness, both internal and international.[2]

Kant was by no means the first moral philosopher to insist that a good will is the only unqualifiedly good thing on earth; on this point he simply reflects and repeats St. Augustine's *De Libero Arbitrio*, Book I, Chapter 12, which argues that a good will "is a will by which we seek to live a good and upright life" and that "when anyone has a good will he really possesses something which ought to be esteemed far above all earthly kingdoms and all delights of the body."[3] (This is remarkably "pre-Kantian." Indeed, one can wonder whether Kant's kingdom of ends was not suggested by Augustine's denigration of earthly kingdoms.) But Kant, given his radical distinction between *pathology* and *morality*, could not have accepted Augustine's further notion of moral "delectation," could never have said, with Augustine, that "the man of good will" will "embrace" justice as "the object of his joy and delight."[4] The Augustinian notion of opposing higher "delectations" to lower ones, so that "concupiscence" is replaced by the love of temperance, prudence, justice, and ultimately God—by quasi-Platonic sublimated erotism (as in the *Phaedrus*)[5]—is alien to Kant, if not to, say, Pascal,[6] or even Rousseau, in some moods.[7] If, then, Kantian good will is not an Augustinian *delectatio*, or higher love, what is it? If it is not to be pathological, it must surely be the capacity to determine oneself to action through what ought to be, so that "ought" is the complete and sufficient incentive. And if what ought to be is defined as respect for persons as members of the kingdom of ends, then Kantian good will will mean "determining oneself to act from respect for persons."[8] (Respect, for Kant, is not a mere *delectatio*, a merely subjective feeling, because it is inspired by a moral law that "humbles" us, a moral law that provides objective ends—i.e., the rational beings who are ends in themselves.)[9] Surely this is a reasonable way to integrate Kant's moral philosophy; for at the outset one cannot know exactly what good will, originally an Augustinian concept, actually involves.

If, however, good will begins in Augustinianism, Kant, in insisting on will as a kind of undetermined moral causality, is still more closely related to Rousseau, who had actually used the term "moral cause" in the so-called First Version of his *Social Contract* ("every free action has . . a moral cause, namely the will which determines the act").[10] He had insisted in the *Discourse on the Origins of Inequality* that while "physics" (natural science) might explain the mechanism of the senses and even the formation of "ideas" (where ideas are Lockean impressions), it is nonetheless "in the power of willing or rather of choosing, and in the feeling of this power" that "nothing is to be found but acts which are purely spiritual and wholly inexplicable by the laws of mechanism."[21] All of this—will as moral cause, as something spiritual and not mechanically determined—Kant could and did applaud. But then Rousseau had gone on to say in *Inequality* that one must draw a line between "free agency" and "understanding"; that "if I am bound to do no injury to my fellow-creatures, this is less because they are rational than because they are sentient beings."[12] This Kant could not accept at all. In Kant's view, if the duty not to injure others rests on "sentience," then one can have duties only if one feels (and sympathizes with) the pains and pleasures of sentient beings. For Kant that is a calamitous view of morality; it makes duty a mere reflection of psychological facts (feelings) that change from moment to moment.[13]Rousseau, in Kant's view, cannot have it both ways; it cannot be the case that will is both an independent moral cause that determines moral acts, and the mere tip of an iceberg of feelings. For in the second case good will would once again become a quasi-Augustinian *delectatio*; it would not be self-determination through a rational concept.

Indeed, had Kant not been so boundlessly devoted to the "Newton of the moral world" as the moralist who had "set him straight" and taught him to "honor" mankind[14]—had Rousseau's thought been a mere *objet trouvé* that Kant stumbled across—he would have dealt with Rousseau more harshly. He might easily have said that Rousseau gets the concept of negative freedom—not being determined by mechanism—right, but without knowing why. To use the arguments from *Pure Reason*, negative freedom in Rousseau is not critically established by showing that while *phenomena* must be understood as caused, *noumena* or "things in themselves" are undetermined.[15] At best, from a Kantian perspective, Rousseau can offer an intuitive account of the *feeling* of freedom, as in *La Nouvelle Héloise:* "A reasoner proves to me in vain that I am not free, [for] inner feeling *[le sentiment interieur]*, stronger than all his arguments, refutes them ceaselessly."[16] For Kant this feeling, however eloquently expressed, must yield to the "Transcendental Deduction's" proof in *Pure Reason* that being an undetermined moral cause is conceivable.[17]

In the treatment of positive freedom, Rousseau is still more problematical from a Kantian point of view. For positive freedom in Kant means self-determination through an objective moral law ("ought"). But Rousseau is wholly sound neither on self-determination nor on "ought." He frequently undercuts real self-determination—true spontaneity or autonomy—by reducing morality to a natural, "pathological" feeling (such as sympathy), or by saying, as in the *Lettres Morales*, that "conscience" is a *sentiment involontaire* that precedes both reason and will.[18] As for "ought," that concept shifts from work to work: in the *Social Contract* it is *généralité* and the avoidance of "particularism" in one's willing;[19] in the *Profession of Faith of the Savoyard Vicar* it is an "order" that reflects the divine world order, making morality nature's "analogue"[20]; in the earlier books of *Émile* it is Stoicism or limiting one's desires to match one's power.[21] Only in the eighth of the *Lettres Écrites de la Montagne* (1764) does Rousseau get both negative and positive freedom nearly right from a Kantian perspective; there he speaks of not being determined and of *not determining others:*

It is vain to confuse independence and liberty. These two things are so different that they even mutually exclude each other. When each does what pleases him, he often does something displeasing to others; and that cannot be called a free condition. Liberty consists less in doing one's will than in not being subject to that of another; it consists again in not submitting the will of another to our own. Whoever is master cannot be free; to rule is to obey.[22]

One wonders, indeed, whether Kant hadn't this passage in mind when he said that "Rousseau set me straight . . . I learned to honor mankind."[23] Rousseau's notion in the *Lettres Écrites de la Montagne* that one should neither be subjected, nor subject others, comes closest to a Kantian negative freedom that allows one positively to respect persons as objective ends.

But if this is Rousseau's closest approach to Kant, Kant still wanted to refute Rousseau's claim that free agency is separated from understanding or reason. Against that, Kant wanted to show that a truly free will would be determined by "practical reason" itself. That is why Kant insisted in the *Fundamental Principles* that

> Everything in nature works according to law. Rational beings alone have the faculty of acting according to the conception of laws, that is according to principles, i.e. have a will. Since the deduction of actions from principles requires reason, the will is nothing but practical reason. The will is a faculty to choose that only which reason independent of inclination recognizes as practially necessary, i.e. good.[24]

Had Rousseau risen to this view of will as rational self-determination, in Kant's opinion, he would not have undermined his own distinction between physics and free agency by reducing good will to a nonrational sympathy for sentient beings. For Kant sympathy and sentience are, equally, "pathological" feelings caused by nature;[25] that being so, one does not escape from the very "laws of mechanism" that Rousseau himself rejected by placing a gulf between free agency and reason. All of this suggests what Kant actually believed: that one cannot find a real duty in sympathy, feelings of pleasure and pain, or happiness, simply because the concept "ought" cannot be extracted from these facts of pathology. The concept of moral necessity cannot be *derived* from the bare *data* of psychology.[26] (Ironically enough, Kant relies on Hume's celebrated argument about the impossibility of deriving "ought" from "is," but in a way that accuses Hume himself of falling into the same reductionistic "vulgarity" that he had warned against.)[27] Why Kant thought that "ought" could not be extracted from nature—even human nature or psychology—he made specially clear in a crucial passage from *Pure Reason:*

> That our reason has causality, or that we at least represent it to ourselves as having causality, is evident from the *imperatives* which in all matters of conduct we impose as rules upon our active powers. 'Ought' expresses a kind of necessity . . . which is found nowhere else in the whole of nature. The understanding can know in nature only what is, what has been, or what will be . . . When we have the course of nature alone in view, 'ought' has no meaning whatsoever.[28]

Because they fail to recognize reason's causality, according to Kant, writers such as Hume make fundamental mistakes in explaining how basic moral ideas such as duty and virtue are *conceivable*. Hume, of course, had argued in the *Treatise of Human Nature* that

> An action, or sentiment, or character, is virtuous or vicious; why? because its view causes a pleasure or uneasiness of a particular kind. In giving a reason, therefore, for the pleasure or uneasiness, we sufficiently explain the vice or virtue. To have the sense of virtue is nothing but to *feel* a satisfaction of a particular kind from the contemplation of a character. The very *feeling* constitutes our praise or admiration. We go no further; nor do we inquire into the cause of the satisfaction. We do not infer a character to be virtuous because it pleases; but in feeling that it pleases after such a particular manner, we in effect feel that it is virtuous.[29]

It was certainly this sort of argument that led Kant to complain, in the *Fundamental Principles*, this "those who cannot *think* believe that *feeling* will help them out, even in what concerns general laws."[30] The last clause, stressing generality, may well refer to the fact that when Hume spoke of moral pleasure as a satisfaction *of a particular kind*, he meant neither physical nor aesthetic pleasure, but a pleasure caused "only when a character is considered in general, without reference to our particular interest."[31] Of course one may wonder, as Kant doubtlessly did, where Hume gets or derives the generality, the antiparticularity, of his moral "feeling." For although Hume speaks of the "sense of virtue" as imparting "a satisfaction of a particular kind" and as pleasing "after . . . a particular manner,"[32] that particular manner must involve generality; the particular manner must be antiparticular. If it is the disinterested *generality* of a satisfaction that makes it a *moral* pleasure, then one has indeed inquired into the cause of (moral) satisfaction; disinterestedness and generality particularize moral satisfaction, as distinguished from satisfaction-in-general. But this of course is just Kant's point: one must know what counts as moral before there can be specifically moral satisfaction. This is surely what Kant has in mind in the *Lectures on Philosophical Theology*, where he insists that

> first it must be firmly established that moral duties are necessarily grounded in the nature of everyone's reason and hence that they are binding on me with apodictic certainty. For if moral duties are based only on feelings, or on the prospect of happiness . . . then well-being would already exist in the present course of things as the effect of good conduct. . . . But no sufficient ground for morality is exhibited by Hume's principle when he tried to derive all morality from particular moral feelings.[33]

Humeans, then, for Kant, do not just *derive* "ought" from "is"; they *equate* morality with feelings of a particular kind, and therefore transform morality from self-determination through a nonnatural "ought" into a purely natural desire for happiness (the wish to feel particular satisfactions). In the end, neither Rousseau nor Hume will do. Rousseau sometimes turns will into *sentiment*, and at best argues for a general will (but Kant needs a good will, a rational will);[34] while Hume insists on a generality that is ungrounded, derived from nothing, and diminishes will almost to the vanishing point to make room for feeling.[35] This is not to say that Kant, by contrast, left no room for "pathology": he thought that one might have an indirect duty to aim at happiness, if misery might lead to moral transgressions ("whatever diminished the obstacles to an activity . . . ")[36]; and he said in the *Tugendlehre* that those who reject all pleasure "on principle," even in morally indifferent cases, are moral "gymnasts."[37] But the effort to derive the concept of moral necessity from facts of psychology he always firmly rejected. To be sure, in the *Critique of Judgment* Kant finally linked morality and nature (including human nature) through the notion of a teleological "substrate"; but he was always scrupulously careful to insist that while morality has *knowable* objective ends, nature is merely "estimated" as having purposes.[38] A "supersensible" link or bridge *connecting* morality and nature Kant was willing to argue for; the attempted to extract moral necessity *from* natural facts he invariably condemned. Chapters three and four will show that this is a distinction that is also a difference.

II

Kant, then, in finding the shape of a morality whose core is to be good will, not as Augustinian *delectatio* but as rational self-determination, is determined to avoid the syncretistic moral philosophizing that blends "pathology" with bad theology:

> We need only look at the attempts of moralists . . . and we shall find at one time the special constitution of human nature (including, however, the idea of a rational nature generally), at one time perfection, at another happiness, here moral sense, there fear of God, a little of this and a little of that, in marvellous mixture, without its occurring to them to ask whether the principles of morality are to be sought in the knowledge of human nature at all . . . ; and, if this is not so—if these principles are to be found altogether *a priori* free from everything empirical, in pure rational concepts only . . .—then rather to adopt the method of making this a separate inquiry, as pure practical philosophy, or . . . as metaphysic of morals.[39]

If a pure moral philosophy is to rest on pure rational concepts that a good will takes as the motive or end of its striving, then for Kant, will itself must be defined, not as higher "delight," but as "a faculty of determining oneself to action in accordance with the conception of certain laws," or as "a kind of causality belonging to living beings insofar as they are rational."[40] A being who is able to take the conception of a law as the motive or end of his action, Kant suggests, is an intelligence or a rational being, and the moral "causality of such a being according to this conception of laws is his will."[41] He goes on to urge that freedom is the capacity of this rational will *qua* moral cause to be "efficient"—to produce moral "effects"—independent of foreign causes determining that will. Will, then, for Kant, is not a delectation or a feeling, but a kind of noumenal causality that is independent of natural causality. (Here of course Kant is deliberately calling attention to the radicalism of his position: he uses the language of causality to assert the existence of a "faculty" free of all causality.)[42]

In a moment Kant's argument on behalf of will as "uncaused causality" from the *Critique of Pure Reason* can be examined; in the meantime it is clear that if Kant can make this notion of will intelligible and plausible, he is also able to avoid reducing volition to an epiphenomenon of "pathology" and puts himself in a position to explain rationally the traditional distinctions between duty and pleasure, virtue and happiness—distinctions drawn in Plato's *Gorgias*, but not wholly successfully defended in that remarkable work.[43] For Kant's definition of will rests on a certain kind of *consciousness* (understanding the conception of a law), and on determining oneself through that conception, independently of "external" nature (extrinsic causes) or of "internal" nature ("pathology"). If one thinks of will in this way, the idea of moral responsibility begins (at least) to become intelligible. If one is the "free cause" of something of whose character he is conscious, the effect can reasonably be imputed to him—it is "his" in the strong sense.[44] But if, by contrast, will is simply—as in the case of Hobbes—the "last appetite in deliberation,"[45] one is back in the realm of "pathology." Then one's will may be the immediate or "efficient" cause of an action, but that will is no longer an uncaused "spontaneity." In arguing that will is the undetermined self-determination of a being who understands the conception of laws, Kant took himself to have rescued morality from the syncretism of his age.

In defining will as the self-determination of a rational being through the conception of a (moral) law, Kant also thought that he was doing nothing more than illuminating ordinary moral consciousness. For Kant always begins with what he takes to be the common moral concepts that everyone uses ("criticism can and must begin with pure practical laws and their actual existence"),[46] and he insists that he is providing no new moral principles at all, but merely a "transcendental deduction" of those principles, an explanation of how those principles are conceivable as "pure rational concepts" not grounded in "pathology."[47] If will-determining pure practical or moral laws are simply there—standing in need only of illumination, not of establishment or defense—then they do not require what Kant calls "justifying grounds";[48] for those justifying grounds would then have to validate the moral law, and the moral law would no longer be ultimate. If one were a utilitarian, for example, one would justify practical laws through their capacity to maximize satisfaction;[49] but Kant of course would say that maximized satisfaction cannot be made to constitute morality, because satisfaction is natural, "pathological," cannot yield an "ought." From a Kantian perspective, utilitarianism treats morality as a *means* to a "pathological" end; objective ends become the mere instruments of relative ends. This is simply to invert morality. All of this Kant tries to make clear in a specially important passage from *Practical Reason:*

> The moral law is given, as an apodictically certain fact, as it were, of pure reason, a fact of which we are *a priori* conscious, even if it be granted that no example could be found in which it has been followed exactly. Thus the objective reality of the moral law can be proved through no deduction, through no exertion of the theoretical, speculative, or empirically supported reason; and, even if one were willing to renounce its apodictic certainty, it could not be confirmed by any experience and thus proved *a posteriori*. Nevertheless, it is firmly established of itself.[50]

A critic of Kant, anxious to make an end to the kingdom of ends, would almost certainly do best to begin his attack at this point. Nietzsche, for example, could and did say, in *Beyond Good and Evil*, that what appears to "old Kant" in the guise of a moral apodictic certainty meant to guide a rational will is in reality a "desire of the heart, filtered and made abstract," and "defended with reasons discovered after the fact."[51] And perhaps Pascal's "heart" which has *ses raisons que la raison ne connait point* could be enlisted in the same critique of the critical philosophy.[52] But Kant certainly sticks to his notion that the moral law cannot find a justification beyond itself, and in doing that he merely denies what is asserted by utilitarians, Pascal and Nietzsche, separated as they are by whole worlds: they appeal to psychological facts that (for Kant) can never produce a concept of moral necessity. If we ask how "consciousness of the moral law" that should determine our will is possible, Kant insists, the answer is that "we can come to know pure practical laws in the same way we know pure theoretical principles, by attending to the necessity with which reason prescribes them to us and to the elimination from them of all empirical conditions, which reason directs."[53] If one eliminates all empirical conditions, one also eliminates utilitarianism; that much is clear. One can then no longer say, with Bentham, that right and wrong are "fastened" to the "throne" of pain and pleasure[54]—though it may remain true that one ought not to will to hurt people, because that treats them as mere means; this willing would preserve the rational kernel within the pathological shell of Benthamism. Not pain *an sich*, but voluntarily causing pain, would be wrong.

It is clear that Kant would not have been very struck by Nietzsche or Pascal. Pascal might say that the heart has its reasons, Nietzsche, that reasons arrive *ex post facto* to shore up desires of the heart (one could even add Hume's dictum that reason is the "slave" of the passions.)[55] But Kant would have asked, and did, near the beginning of the *Fundamental Principles:* what is the reason for reasons? What are they *for?* It is revealing that he poses that teleological question. What it means is that (practical) reason has the end of bringing us to will to respect persons as ends; practical reason's purpose is to lead us to the appreciation of final purposes.[56] (This is surely why Kant says, in the important 1788 essay called *On the Use of Teleological Principles in Philosophy*, that "the *Critique of Practical Reason* alone shows that there are pure practical principles, through which reason is determined *a priori*, and which therefore specify the *end* of the same [principles]," and adds that "moral philosophy" is *"eine reine praktische Teleologie* [a pure practical teleology]."[57] If all of this were not so, in Kant's view, the world would be incoherent; there would be no reason for the reasons that even a Nietzschean admits, if only after the fact. Here the key passage (from the *Fundamental Principles*) is this one:

> In the physical constitution of an organized being, that is, in a being adapted suitably to the purposes of life, we assume it as a fundamental principle that no organ for any purpose will be found but what is also the fittest and best adapted for that purpose. Now in a being which has reason and a will, if the proper object of nature were its *conservation*, its *welfare*, in a word, its *happiness*, then nature would have hit upon a very bad arrangement in selecting the reason of the creature to carry out this purpose. For all the actions which the creature has to perform with a view to this purpose . . . would be far more surely prescribed by instinct, and that end would have been attained thereby much more certainly than it ever can be by reason. . . . Nature would have taken care that reason should not break forth into practical exercise.[58]

On this teleological notion of suitable adaptation, which Kant was to work out fully only in the *Critique of Judgment*,[59] reason, which is "not competent" to guide us toward "the satisfaction of all our wants," is instead "imparted to us as a practical faculty" that is meant "to have influence on the will." (Since that will is free—an uncaused causality—Kant would agree perfectly with Heidegger's claim that "freedom is the reason for reasons.")[60] Reason then has the end of pointing out an end to a good will, namely, persons (oneself and others) as final ends.[61] Something like this must have been in Kant's mind when he asserted, in *Pure Reason*'s "Paralogisms," that "reason is . . . located in its own peculiar sphere, namely, the order of ends."[62] And it must still have been in his mind when he wrote one of the early passages of the *Fundamental Principles*—a passage that seems at first to be exclusively taken up with good will, but that briefly anticipates Kant's own distinction between objective ends and relative ones. He begins, indeed, by saying that "reason recognizes the establishment of a good will as its highest practical destination," but quickly goes on to the argument that in attaining this purpose reason "is capable only of a satisfaction of its own proper kind," namely from "the attainment of an end" that is "determined by reason only, notwithstanding that this may involve many a disappointment to the ends of inclination."[63] Reason's office, then, is to provide an *objective* purpose for a good will that might otherwise be a mere *delectatio*.

But if Kant wanted to provide a will that is free with a rational and objective end that makes it a good will (not just a "delighted" will), he did not feel entitled to use traditional ideas of freedom and will in traditional ways, as if those ideas were unproblematical and constitutive principles of theoretical reason having the same status as the principles of empiricism. This is why Kant asserts in the *Fundamental Principles* that while "freedom is only an idea of reason" whose "objective reality in itself is doubtful," nature (by contrast) is a concept of the understanding "which proves, and must necessarily prove, its reality in examples of experience."[64] This is not to say that freedom, though only the *ratio essendi* of the moral law, matters less than matter; indeed, for Kant, if the idea of will as a free or intelligent causality capable of taking ends as motives is abandoned, morality will become "empirical" (pathological).[65] And therefore

> for practical purposes the narrow footpath of freedom is the only one on which it is possible to make use of reason in our conduct . . . Philosophy must then assume that no real contradiction will be found between freedom and physical necessity of the same human actions, for it cannot give up the conception of nature any more than that of freedom.[66]

III

This last formulation recalls, and is meant to recall, distinctions drawn in the *Critique of Pure Reason*. These distinctions must be looked at, for it is in them that Kant argues for the freedom that makes morality possible ("if our will is not free . . . moral ideas and principles lose all validity");[67] and morality, as we have seen, sets the limiting condition to, and receives the homage of, politics.[68] This is why Kant says, in the *Rechtslehre*, that "the philosophical jurist" will not regard an investigation into "the ultimate principles of transcendental philosophy" as an "unnecessary subtlety in a *metaphysic of morals*," when he takes into account the difficulty of "doing justice in this inquiry to the ultimate relations of the principles of right."[69] And the truly ultimate thing is freedom, as the foundation of a morality to which politics and law pay homage.

In the "Antinomy of Pure Reason" (A 533/B 561), Kant begins by saying that freedom is "the power of beginning a state spontaneously." If there is to be true spontaneity or "absolute origination," a free act will not "stand under another cause determining it in time, as required by the law of nature."[70] Freedom as undetermined spontaneity is "a pure transcendental idea" that is not "given in any [empirical] experience."[71] (It is, of course, mainly by virtue of this argument about the nature of freedom that Kantianism is called "transcendental idealism.")[72] Kant adds, in an important aside, that the notion of spontaneity may arise, perhaps paradoxically, out of reflection on causality, spontaneity's antithesis: caused things are understood as having causes, but if one traces backward through an endless regress of causes and effects one is left unsatisfied because there is no "unconditioned" necessity. Because of this unsatisfying conditionality of everything merely caused, reason, tired of always having "one foot in the air," creates for itself "the idea of a spontaneity which can begin to act of itself."[73] The only problem is that this particular "spontaneity"—God—cannot be shown really to exist.[74] But for immediate practical purposes the essential point is that "the denial of transcendental freedom" or of spontaneity in the actions of *finite rational beings who demonstrably exist* "must . . . involve the elimination of all practical freedom."

> For practical freedom presupposes that although something has not happened, it *ought* to have happened, and that its cause, [as found] in the [field of] appearance, is not, therefore, so determining that it excludes a causality of our will—a causality which, independently of those natural causes, and even contrary to their force and influence, can produce something that is determined in the time-order in accordance with empirical laws, and which can therefore begin a series of events *entirely of itself*.[76]

There is, in Kant's view, only one way to save nature and freedom equally (for it would be fatal to expunge Newton to make room for Rousseau: to make space by denying space). That way is stated in its clearest form in the preface to the second edition (1787) of *Pure Reason*. The primary service that the *Critique* renders, Kant argues, is that of drawing a distinction between "appearances" and "things in themselves." That we can have "no knowledge of any object as thing in itself, but only insofar as it is an object of sensible intuition, that is, an appearance," means that "all possible speculative knowledge" is indeed "limited to mere objects of appearance."[77] But equally, Kant insists, "though we cannot know these objects as things in themselves," as noumena, "we must yet be in a position to think them as things in themselves," or else "we should be landed in the absurd conclusion that there can be appearance without anything that appears."[73]

All of this, in Kant's view, is epistemologically essential and interesting, but its main point is surely to make freedom possible. For he immediately goes on to say that if one fails to draw a distinction between appearances (phenomena) and things in themselves (noumena), then "all things in general, as far as they are efficient causes, would be determined by the principle of causality, and consequently by the mechanism of nature." There is only one way in which "the doctrine of morality and the doctrine of nature may each . . . make good its position," and that is by realizing that any object "is to be taken in a twofold sense, namely as appearance and as thing in itself."[79] If, Kant goes on, the *Critique* is right in its view that causality is neither a thing in itself nor a property of things in themselves, but only a category of understanding that organizes the "manifold of sensible intuition" into a unified experience; if the *Critique* is "not in error" in teaching that "the principle of causality" applies only to things considered as "objects of experience," or phenomena, and not to things in themselves, or *noumena*; then "there is no contradiction in supposing," for example, that "one and the same will is, in appearance, that is, in its visible acts, necessarily subject to the law of nature [causality], and so far not free, while yet, as belonging to a thing in itself, it is not subject to that law, and is therefore free."[80] The formula "phenomenally caused, noumenally free" is, to use Beck's accurate phrase, "hard doctrine";[81] but it would be fatally hard only if one thought that Kant was saying, with Spinoza, that freedom is an *illusion* arising out of inadequate knowledge of determining causes, that freedom is made possible only by ignorance.[82] In a way Kant is indeed appealing to the limits of our knowledge; but Spinoza would never have said that behind determined phenomenal appearance there may well be undetermined noumenal *dingheit an sich*. He would never have said, with Kant, that while "in natural science" there is "endless conjecture," in the "universal principles of morals . . . nothing can be uncertain" because those principles "must be derived from the concepts of our reason."[83]

All Kant wants to show is that there is one intelligible, if subtle, point of view from which causality can be affirmed without annihilating freedom. To be sure, as Kant at once grants, freedom is not and cannot be actually known by "speculative reason"; but freedom can be "thought" in the sense that it is "not self-contradictory, provided due account be taken of our critical distinction" between noumena and phenomena.[84] This is enough for Kant, since "morality does not . . . require that freedom should be understood, but only that it should not contradict itself."[85]

Kant has all of this in mind when he elaborates the notion of "phenomenally caused, noumenally free" later in the "Antinomy of Pure Reason" (A536/B564). The central question, he says, is whether natural causality is such that "freedom is completely excluded by this inviolable rule," or whether a thing—a human voluntary action, for instance—"may not at the same time be grounded in freedom."[86]

> The common but fallacious presupposition of the *absolute reality* of appearances here manifests its injurious influence, to the confounding of reason. For if appearances are things in themselves, freedom cannot be upheld. Nature will then be the complete and sufficient detrmining cause of every event.[87]

But if, using the method that the *Critique* reveals, "appearances are viewed not as things in themselves, but merely as representations, connected according to empirical laws," then they "must themselves have grounds which are not appearances."[88] To be sure, one "knows" of the noumenon that is the ground of appearance only that it is a conceivable *etwas überhaupt* = *X*—that it is the "intelligible cause" of *phenomena*.[89]

> The effects of such an intelligible cause appear, and accordingly can be determined through other appearances, but its [the noumenon's] causality is not so determined. While the effects [of noumenal causality] are to be found in the series of empirical conditions, the intelligible cause, together with its causality, is outside the series. Thus the effect may be regarded as free in respect of its intelligible cause, and at the same time in respect of appearances as resulting from them according to the necessity of nature.[90]

The term *intelligible cause* refers not just to a conceivable noumenal ground of all phenomena, but more exactly to Kant's argument about reason's causality in the practical sphere, in supplying will with an end ("that our reason has causality . . .")[91]. "Let us take our stand,"

Kant bravely insists, "and regard it as at least possible for reason to have causality with respect to appearances."[92] To be sure, reason's causality will *appear* as an effect in the phenomenal world: if one refrains, out of respect for a nonpathological rational imperative, from performing a wished-for murder, if one's wish never becomes one's will, there will be a gap in the phenomenal world (an absent corpse)—a gap that would have been filled had one permitted "pathology" to have its way and yielded to this unworthy *delectatio.*

> For it may be that all that *has happened* in the course of nature, and in accordance with its empirical grounds must inevitably have happened, *ought not to have happened.* Sometimes, however, we find, or at least believe that we find, that the ideas of reason have in actual fact proved their causality in respect of the actions of men, as appearances; and that these actions have taken place, not because they were determined by empirical causes, but because they were determined by grounds of reason.[93]

If the key notion is "determined by grounds of reason," then it is of course not sufficient to be merely negatively free, i.e., *not* naturally determined; negative freedom must be the foundation of positive freedom, of self-determination or will through "grounds of reason."

> Freedom ought not . . . to be conceived only negatively as independence of empirical conditions. The faculty of reason, so regarded, would cease to be a cause of appearances. It must also be described in positive terms, as the power of originating a series of event. In reason itself nothing begins; as unconditioned condition of every voluntary act, it admits of no conditions antecedent to itself in time. Its effect has, indeed, a beginning in the series of appearances, but never in this series an absolutely first beginning.[94]

The last claim is crucial, since the pure reason that can be practical in "imperatives" is "not subject to the form of time."[95] For it does not (suddenly, as it were) become the case that persons ought to be respected as ends in themselves, as the limiting condition of our willing. If a particular person begins to take this timeless moral truth as the motive of his will, then the outward manifestations of his newly moral activity will indeed have a "beginning in the series of appearances";[96] but the practical reason that serves as the ground of his will is "not itself an appearance," and is therefore not conditioned by time or causality, which bear only on appearances.[97]

Causality, then, for Kant, cannot utterly exclude freedom; causality could do that only if it were a knowable property of things in themselves. But all we can know is that phenomena are unintelligible (to us) without causality's organizing and unifying effect. This leaves noumena untouched. Practical reason necessitates our taking ourselves to be free (since "ought" implies can);[98] and pure reason cannot rule out that freedom. That is enough. It is even enough for the politics that must pay homage to a morality that is (now) possible.

Kant's theory of will and freedom—to revert to the Augustinian language of the opening of this chapter—is thus a kind of skepticized Pelagianism.[99] God is imagined by reason as "absolute originator," but only persons can be known, through the "fact of reason," as "spontaneous." A single first cause is thus replaced by as many first causes as there are wills. *All* persons must be the "intelligible causes" of their own acts; otherwise one could not speak of the acts as "their own."[100] If Kant is right, then the concept of a positively free will, self-determining through objective ends, need not be adjusted to God or causality; for God is transcendent, and causality only a category of understanding.[101] That is why Kant can avoid altogether the kind of difficulty that tortures Pascal in the wonderfully eloquent *Écrits sur la Grace:*

> The question is that of knowing which of these two wills, namely the will of God or the will of man, is the ruling one, the dominant one, the source, the principle and the cause of the other. The question is that of knowing whether the will of man is the cause of the will of God, or whether the will of God is the cause of the will of man.[102]

Pascal works out his own quasi-Augustinian answer with the expected subtlety; but Kant would say that the question cannot be answered, or indeed even asked, because God and his will are transcendent for us: the only truly spontaneous causality known by us is our own moral causality. For Kant one cannot even say, with the Molinists, that God's will "concurs" with our own, let alone causes it. As he argues in the *Lectures on Philosophical Theology* (1783–84), it is "not in the least conceivable how God might concur in our actions" despite our freedom, or "how he could concur as a cooperating cause of our will." For then "we would not be the author of our own actions, or at least not wholly so."[103] This enables Kant to say, even in a work called *Religion (within the Limits of Reason Alone)* that

> In the search for the rational origin of evil actions every such action must be regarded as though the individual had fallen into it directly from a state of innocence. For whatever his previous deportment may have been, whatever natural causes may have been influencing him, and whether these causes were to be found within him or outside him, his action is yet free and determined by none of these causes; hence it can and must always be judged as an *original* use of his will.[104]

After *Pure Reason*'s notion of *absolute origination*, one sees how literally Kant uses the term *original*. And he goes on to insist that an evil-doer

> should have refrained from that action, whatever his temporal circumstances and entanglements; for through no cause in the world can he cease to be a freely acting being. . . . It was not only his duty to have been better, it is now still his duty to better himself. To do so must be within his power. . . . Hence we cannot inquire into the temporal origin of his deed, but solely into its rational origin.[105]

From this follows quite reasonably Kant's insistence that the doctrine of inherited or transmitted original sin is the "most inept" and freedom-destroying way of accounting for the origin of evil,[106] and he goes on to amuse himself with an ironic "political" account of that origin. If one asked a university's law faculty for such an account, he says, one would be told that evil is "the legitimate consequence of succeeding to the patrimony bequeathed us by our first parents"—an inheritance "encumbered . . . with heavy forfeitures," so that "we must fulfill payment (atone) and at the end still be dispossessed (by death) of the property. How just is legal justice!"[107] But the theological faculty, Kant insists, would give a still more "political" account; it would

> regard this evil as the personal participation by our first parents in the *fall* of a condemned rebel, maintaining either that we ourselves then participated (although now unconscious of having done so) or that even now, born under the rule of the rebel (as prince of this world), we prefer his favors to the supreme command of the heavenly ruler.[108]

Small wonder that the political authorities of Kant's day disliked and temporarily suppressed such grimly ironical accounts of the origin of evil.[109] For Kant, genuine evil arises neither from God nor Adam nor Satan, but from the fact that a free person "does not will to withstand" inclinations contrary to the moral law "when they tempt him to transgress":[110] the Fall is our own creation.

> The source of evil cannot lie in an object *determining* the will through inclination, nor yet in a natural impulse; it can lie only in a rule made by the will for the use of its freedom, that is, in a maxim. . . . If this ground itself were not ultimately a maxim, but a mere natural impulse, it would be possible to trace the use of our freedom wholly to determination by natural causes; this, however, is contradictory to the very notion of freedom.[111]

This is simply a more popular way of restating the doctrine of transcendental freedom from *Pure Reason*. Since that freedom of will makes possible the morality some of whose ends are to be legally realized through republicanism and eternal peace, it is not surprising that Kant should insist that a "philosophical jurist" will applaud the inquiry into "the ultimate principles of the transcendental philosophy" that underpin the "ultimate relations of the principles of right."[112]

It was, doubtless, because Kant took this inquiry to be a "necessary subtlety" that he himself sometimes drew a deliberate parallel between his argument on behalf of transcendental freedom and the case he wanted to make for eternal peace. Just as the possibility of freedom-underlying-morality cannot be disproved in *Pure Reason,* so, too, for Kant the possibility of eternal peace cannot be disproved; and since one has a duty to try to realize eternal peace (as politics' supreme "homage" to morals), it must be possible to move toward it by "infinite approximation." Hence the title *Zum Ewigen Frieden* ("Toward Eternal Peace").

> If a person cannot prove that a thing [such as eternal peace] exists, he may attempt to prove that it does not exist [through the "antinomies" of existence and nonexistence]. If neither approach succeeds . . . he may still ask whether it is in his interest to assume one or the other possibility. . . . We can have a duty to act in accordance with the idea of such an end [peace] . . . provided there is no means of demonstrating that it cannot be realized.[113]

This parallels exactly the argument about freedom in *Pure Reason:* neither proof nor disproof is possible, and therefore practical (not theoretical) interests gain the upper hand.[114] If something ought to be, and its possibility cannot be refuted, then it must be. If one had a purely good will, that "ought" would serve as one's end, one's complete incentive; but even legally that end can be approximated. Even in the absence of good will, one can move toward eternal peace.

IV

Kant, then, builds his moral philosophy on a good will that is neither an Augustinian *delectatio,* a Hobbesian "last appetite," a Rousseauean *sentiment,* or a Humean "feeling . . . of a particular kind."[115] Kantian will is an uncaused causality, a moral cause, an undetermined power of spontaneous self-determination or of absolute origination, which is shaped neither by external nature, internal nature, or divine causality or concurrence. It is a doctrine of absolute freedom and absolute responsibility, of taking rational ends as the motives of one's actions, that might have permitted some of Kant's great predecessors to be more coherent. Had Hobbes, for example, been a transcendental idealist and not a determinist, one could attach more meaning to his celebrated dictum that there is "no obligation on any man"—such as the duty to observe a social contract—that "ariseth not from some act of his own."[116] For Kant the expression act of his own is meaningless unless there is a power of absolute origination: that is why he says in *Practical Reason* that "I cannot conceive how those who persist in seeing space and time as attributes belonging to the existence of things in themselves can avoid the fatalism of actions."[117] From Kant's perspective a Hobbesian falls precisely into fatalism by viewing will as an "appetite" caused by perception of a natural world whose first cause reduces everything else to a mere effect.[118] That "fatalism" is then fatal to Hobbes's own political doctrines: before it can be true that "wills . . . make the essence of all covenants" (*Leviathan*, Chapter XL),[119] there must actually *be* a will which is truly efficacious. But for that one needs "absolute origination": persons must be *their own causes.*

For one to conceive of a rational being having a causality that is not caused, one must, in Kant's view, draw the now-familiar distinction between "a world of sense and the world of understanding."[120] With respect to the "mere perception and receptivity of sensations" to which a Hobbesian gives "fatal" weight, one must indeed understand himself as belonging to the world of sense; but insofar as one is capable of initiating rational "pure activity" through the conception of a law, he must count himself as belonging to the intellectual world.[121]

> A rational being . . . has two points of view from which he can regard himself, and recognize laws of the exercise of his faculties . . . first, so far as he belongs to the world of sense, he finds himself subject to laws of nature (heteronomy); secondly, as belonging to the intelligible world, under laws which, being independent of nature, have their foundation not in experience but in reason alone.[122]

If one belonged exclusively to the world of understanding, then for Kant, all of his actions would conform to the principle of "autonomy of the free will"; if one were entirely a creature of sense, then only a will caused by desire and inclination would be possible. Since, however, beings such as human beings, who are "finite rational beings," recognize themselves as "subject to the law of the world of understanding, that is, to reason," this law is an imperative for them.[123] They *ought*, in their own view, to act from principles given by a reason that "has causality"—a reason that is "located in its own peculiar sphere, namely, the order of ends."[124]

But what are the precise outlines of the order of ends, an order that provides a rational motive to a good will and that (if a telological reading of Kant is supportable) also throws a bridge from morality to legality, and then further spans from practice generally to nature and art? (The *complete* order of ends, including objective and relative ends, ends known "determinantly" and those known "reflectively," would apparently be called "the totality of all ends" *(das Ganze aller Zwecke)* in the language of *On the Use of Teleological Principles in Philosophy.)*[125] One must next move on to a full and careful consideration of the ends that a spontaneous good will takes as its motive—ends that may be partly realizable, if the ethical commonwealth that ought to be our Creation fails to materialize, through republicanism and eternal peace.

CHAPTER THREE

Persons as Ends in Themselves: A Content for Morality, a Limiting Condition of Politics

I

Kant has argued in the *Fundamental Principles of the Metaphysic of Morals* that the only unqualifiedly good thing on earth is a good will.[1] Most of that work is given over, as has been seen, to a treatment of will as the capacity to determine oneself to action in accordance with principles and reasons that one understands, above all the notion that something "ought" to be done.[2] In understanding will as the capacity for self-determination through reason, Kant avoids reducing volition to an Augustinian *delectatio*, or to a Hobbesian "last appetite," or to a Rousseauean *sentiment*, and provides men with a "faculty" that permits them to be viewed as the causes of the moral effects that they produce.[3] And this notion of will as noumenal or intelligent causality does much to shape Kant's political thought: his notion that men are free agents capable of willing what ought to be the case serves as the "limiting condition" of a politics, outlined in *Eternal Peace*, that should respect men as moral causes and not simply manipulate them as unfree objects.[4]

However, one may still ask, what is it that the good will *qua* intelligent, moral causality, actually wills? What is the relation of good will to what ought to be and of both of these to the "universality" that Kant calls the "objective principle" of the "categorical imperative"?[5] And how do all of these notions relate to the Kantian idea that persons are "ends in themselves" who ought to be respected and not treated as mere means to some arbitrary purpose, which serves as

37

a further limiting condition of what should happen in Kantian politics? To answer all of these questions adequately one would have to work out a wholly consistent interpretation of every element of Kant's practical philosophy—a task obviously impossible here, even if it were possible in principle. But perhaps a little light can be thrown particularly on the notion of persons as ends in themselves, who ought to be respected in the maxims of action that, according to Kant, we will as universal laws;[6] and it will at least be shown that when Kant speaks of the "rights of man" in his political writings he is usually referring to the notion that persons are ends who ought to be respected and not simply using a catch-phrase without philosophical foundations. The "rights of man" are better grounded in Kant's teleological argument about men *qua* ends than in the arguments of any other political philosopher.[7] Before arriving at this view, however, one must consider the objection, first advanced by Hegel, later by J. S. Mill, that there is no coherent notion of ends in Kant that could serve as the content of categorical imperatives and as the limiting condition of politics. To that objection one must turn first of all.

II

At least since the time of Hegel, the most common objection brought against Kant's moral philosophy—and, by implication, against as much of his political theory as flows from that philosophy—has been that it is abstract, formal, has no content, and, on the most extreme view, can justify the universalization of anything, however intrinsically evil. A recent version of this complaint is to be found in W. B. Gallie's "Kant's View of Reason in Politics" (1979), which claims that Kant "appears to equate morality with an arbitrary list of abstract rules of conduct, whose only bond of union is their guarantee by the principle of noncontradiction."[8] To be sure, Kant insisted in all of his major "practical" works on the importance of the universal form of the moral law, on the necessity of removing all "matter" from that law. This is clearest, perhaps, in the *Critique of Practical Reason*, where Kant argues that the moral law is the sole determining principle of a pure will, but that, since this law is purely formal, "it abstracts as a determining principle from all matter—that is to say, from every object of volition."[9] He adds, again in *Practical Reason*, that "since the material of the practical law . . . cannot be given except empirically, and since a free will must be independent of all empirical conditions (i.e., those belonging to the world of sense) and yet be determinable, a free will must find its ground of determination in the law, but independently of the material of the law. But besides the latter there is nothing in a law except the legislative form. Therefore, the legislative form . . . is the only thing which can constitute a determining ground of the [free] will."[10]

Not the smallest of Kant's reasons for insisting that "the mere legislative form of maxims is the sole sufficient determining ground of a will,"[11] of course, was that he wanted to relate *Practical Reason* as strongly as possible to the transcendental idealism of *Pure Reason*. This he did by arguing

> Since the mere form of a law can be thought only by reason and is consequently not an object of the senses and therefore does not belong among appearances, the conception of this form as the determining ground of the will is distinct from all determining grounds of events in nature according to the law of causality, for these grounds must themselves be appearances. Now, as no determining ground of the will except the universal legislative form can serve as a law for it, such a will must be conceived as wholly independent of the natural law of appearances in their mutual relations, i.e. the law of causality. Such independence is called *freedom* in the strictest, i.e. transcendental, sense. Therefore, a will to which only the legislative form of the maxim can serve as a law is a free will.[12]

Of course, Kant's concern to avoid sense and causality in morality might also be satisfied if objective ends (as determining grounds of will) are just as noumenal, just as spontaneity-preserving, as "legislative form."[13] And one thinks of that because the various formulations of the categorical imperative in the *Fundamental Principles* increasingly insist on a moral content—on the dignity of persons as objective ends in themselves, as members of a "kingdom of ends" who ought never to be used merely as means to "relative" ends.[14] This increasing stress on teleological considerations as the *Fundamental Principles* unfolds leads to the obvious question, how can Kant's insistence on legislative form as the *sole* determining ground of a free will be reconciled with his teleological claims about respecting persons as objective ends, while at the same time respecting every strand of Kant's thought, including his politics?

The simplest answer is, it cannot. And that, in effect, is the answer returned by Hegel in a series of works, including the early *Natural Law* and *Glauben und Wissen* (both from 1802–3), the slightly later *Phenomenology*, and the late *Philosophy of Right*.[15] The early essay on *Natural Law* is in some ways the most interesting, since it first accuses Kant of "formalism" in ethics, then goes on to find him a formalist in politics as well. Hegel begins by characterizing Kant's ethical "formalism": Kantian "practical reason," he insists, is the complete abstraction from all content of the will; to introduce content is to establish a heteronomy of choice. But what is precisely of interest is to know *what* right and duty are. We ask for the content of the moral law, and this content alone concerns us. But the essence of pure will and pure practical reason is to be abstracted from all content. Thus it is a self-contradiction to seek in this absolute practical reason a moral legislation, which would have a content, since the essence of this reason is to have none.[16]

If, Hegel goes on, this Kantian "formalism" is to "be able to promulgate a law," some matter, some content, must be found; but Kant, Hegel complains, reduces content to another kind of formalism, namely formal universality, or the notion that "a maxim of thy will shall count at the same time as a principle of universal legislation."[17] But, Hegel immediately insists, any and "every specific matter is capable of being clothed" with "universality";[18] one *can* will universally, for example, that those who have had monetary deposits entrusted to them simply keep them, if one is willing that such deposits should universally cease to exist. There is no contradiction, Hegel argues, in the nonexistence of deposits, or in the universal willing of their nonexistence; it is only contradictory to will that there be deposits *and* that there not be deposits.[19] But one cannot extract the notion that "deposits ought to exist" from the bare logical ideas of universality and noncontradiction. Kantian ethics "work," for Hegel, only if one "smuggles" content (life, property, etc.) into Kantian universality.[20] At the end of *Natural Law* Hegel insists that just as Kant is an ethical formalist who tries to squeeze moral content out of logical concepts, so too in his politics Kant escapes into the "abstractions and formalisms" of "the shapelessness of cosmopolitanism . . . the void of the Rights of Man, or the like void of a league of nations or a world republic."[21] For Hegel these are indeed formalisms because they are "filled with exactly the opposite of ethical vitality . . . of absolute ethical life."[22]

That same ethical life, of course, is given its main justification in the *Philosophy of Right*, but at least that work is somewhat more generous to Kant than is *Natural Law*. For in the *Philosophy of Right* Hegel starts by praising Kant for revealing "the pure unconditioned self-determination of the will as the root of duty";[23] that much of Kant is compatible with Hegel's own assertion that "right and the science of right" must begin with "the position of the free will."[24] Soon enough, however, the complaints of *Natural Law* reappear, and it turns out that Kant's notion of universalizing moral maxims contains "no principle beyond abstract identity and the 'absence of contradiction.' " Hegel goes on to insist that "a contradiction must be a contradiction of something": if one wills murder as a universal law, that will indeed "contradict" life,[25] but that says nothing about the value of life. Universalized murder is bad only if life is good. But Kant, in Hegel's view, clings to the vacuum that nature is said to abhor: he is barred *by his own formalistic principles* from showing that anything is (simply) good, and so all he can show is that if murder is universalized then life will vanish. But that "if" reduces the so-called categorical imperative by a cruel irony to something merely hypothetical ("if . . . then . . ."). And the only way out of this dilemma, for Hegel, is to pass from the "empty formalism" of Kantianism and its "dry leaves that never were green,"[26] to the ethics outlined in the *Philosophy of Right:* to the state as realized freedom, the satisfying "object" of our subjective will.[27] For an obsession with contentless Kantian duty might, in Hegel's view, lead to the political consequence that morally self-satisfied "beautiful souls" would, by virtue of the doctrine that the only unqualifiedly good thing on earth is a good will, treat the state as something "external" and "other," rather than as the concrete embodiment of rational freedom.[28]

Later Hegelians and Hegelo-Marxists have continued to press the charge of contentless formalism against Kant. Bradley insists in *Ethical Studies* that Kant's moral philosophy "has been annihilated by Hegel's criticism,"[29] and Georg Lukács argues in *The Young Hegel* that Hegelian ethics is "incomparably richer" and "more dialectical" than "Kant's narrow formalism, his crabbed appeal to the conscience and the sense of duty of the isolated individual."[30] To be sure, philosophers wholly removed from Hegelianism have brought roughly comparable charges. John Stuart Mill, for example, insists in *Utilitarianism* that

> Kant . . . whose system of thought will long remain one of the landmarks in the history of philosophical speculation, does . . . lay down a universal first principle as the origin and ground of moral obligation. It is this: 'So act, that the rule on which thou actest would admit of being adopted as a law by all rational beings.' But, when he begins to deduce from this precept any of the actual duties of morality, he fails, almost grotesquely, to show that there would be any contradiction . . . in the adoption by all rational beings of the most outrageously immoral rules of conduct. All he shows is, that the *consequences* of their universal adoption would be such as no one would choose to incur. . . . To give any meaning to Kant's principle, the sense put upon it must be, that we ought to shape our conduct by a rule which all rational beings might adopt *with benefit to their collective interest.*[31]

The objections of Hegel and Mill would have the most serious weight, if it could be shown that Kant really falls into the effort to derive moral substance from bare logic. But it is at least arguable that when Kant declines, especially in *Practical Reason*, to admit any "matter" into the moral law, he is trying to exclude empiricism from morality, to exclude "pathological" impulses of pleasure and happiness as motives for adhering to that law. A Kantian free will, as was seen in Chapter Two, determines itself through the moral law, "not only without the cooperation of sensible impulses, but even to the rejection of all such."[32] It is possible that Kant's determination to exclude sensible motives from ethics led him to overstate a part of his case in such a way as to make the dignity of persons as ends in themselves sometimes seem to be a matter that also had to be excluded from moral consideration. However, this can scarcely be what Kant intended, for he insists in the *Fundamental Principles* that the teleological notion of treating persons as ends is merely a different formulation of the first version of the categorical imperative, which requires only that moral maxims be formally universalizable.[33] Thus there is good reason to believe that Kant did not view respect for the dignity of persons as ends in themselves as sensible or "pathological": had he thought so he could not conceivably have said that all of his formulations of the categorical imperative are "at bottom" the same.[34] And this teleological strand in Kant's practical thought is of central political importance, if it is correct to view Kantian "public legal justice" as instrumental to the "legal" realization of ends that good will would attain if it were completely efficacious.

III

Kant's claim that persons are ends in themselves is found in its best-known form in the *Fundamental Principles of the Metaphysic of Morals.* He begins by drawing a distinction between two kinds of ends, which he calls "relative" and "objective," and goes on to say that ends in general serve the will as the "objective ground of its self-determination."[35] The arbitrary ends that a rational being proposes to himself "at pleasure" are merely relative, since those ends change as "pathological" desires and interests change. But if, Kant insists, there "exists something whose existence has in itself an absolute worth," something which, as an end in itself, can be a "source of definite laws," then such an objective end could be the "source of a possible categorical imperative."[36] These distinctions between *kinds* of ends lead Kant to the assertion—made provisionally in dogmatic form— that "man and generally any rational being exists as an end in himself, not merely as a means to be arbitrarily used by this or that will, but . . . must be always regarded at the same time as an end."[37]

He begins to convert dogmatism into "criticism" by saying that if there is to be a categorical imperative, it must be a moral law which "being drawn from the conception of that which is necessarily an end for everyone because it is *an end in itself*, constitutes an objective principle of the will." This principle must be based on the idea that "[a] rational nature exists as an end in itself."[38] In strictness, Kant's argument about rational natures as objective ends is "intersubjective" rather than "objective": men necessarily, he says, think of their own existence as an end in itself, but every other rational being conceives its existence in the same way, "so that it is at the same time an objective principle from which as a supreme practical law all laws of the will must be capable of being deduced."[39] Following this, Kant reformulates the categorical imperative, which at first had insisted only that one's maxims be willed as universal laws, to read: "So act as to treat humanity, whether in thine own person or in that of any other, in every case as an end withal, never as means only."[40]

Kant continues by saying that the idea of men as ends in themselves is not derived from mere "experience," because that idea does not "present humanity" as an arbitrary and optional end, self-proposed "at pleasure," that may or may not be adopted. "Humanity" is rather the "supreme limiting condition of all our subjective ends."[41] He then introduces a distinction between objective and subjective principles that is probably at the root of Hegelian objections:

> The objective principle of all practical legislation lies . . . in the rule and its form of universality which makes it capable of being a law . . . ; but the subjective principle is in the end; now by the second principle, the subject of all ends is each rational being inasmuch as it is an end in itself. Hence follows the third practical principle of the will . . . the idea of the will of every rational being as a universally legislative will.[42]

Here Kant seems to put the objective principle above the subjective one. But, since it is the "subjective" end—men as ends in themselves—that provides universal maxims with a non-arbitrary "content," the subjective element of this formulation must be given full weight if criticisms such as Hegel's and Mill's are to be answered.

Kant proceeds to relate his argument about ends to his theory of volition. The reformulated categorical imperative is a "law of one's own giving," but not in terms of a mere "interest" such as happiness. He argues that the moral laws to which a man is subject are given by his own will—a will that is "designed by nature to give universal laws."[43] Such a will, which determines itself through laws that recognize objective ends is, for Kant, autonomous. But a will that makes merely contingent ends the maxim of its action is, by contrast, heteronomous.[44]

The notion of the will as universally "legislative" in terms of objective ends leads, Kant then suggests, to the idea of a "kingdom of ends." He defines such a "kingdom" or "realm" as a "systematic union of rational beings by common objective laws." In quasi-Rousseauean language, Kant says that a rational being belongs to such a kingdom as a member when he is subject to its laws, and that he belongs to it as a "sovereign" when, "while giving laws, he is not subject to the will of any other."[45] In such a kingdom of ends, which is only an "ideal," he continues, everything has either a value or a dignity: anything that has mere value can be replaced by something of equivalent value, but that which is the condition of anything's having a value—that is, humanity itself—has dignity.[46] (Of course, this quasi-Rousseauean passage is at the basis of Beck's view that Kant is "deepened Rousseau"—as will be seen.)

Kant then summarizes his position in a way that it is essential to examine, since it shows why his critics have been able to tax him with "contentless formalism." He insists that all of the formulations of the categorical imperative "are at bottom only so many formulae of the very same law."[47] All maxims that conform to the categorical imperative, he says, are characterized by

1. A *form*, consisting in universality; and in this view the formula of the moral imperative is expressed thus, that the maxims must be so chosen as if they were to serve as universal laws of nature.
2. A *matter*, namely, an end, and here the formula says that the rational being, as it is . . . an end in itself, must in every maxim serve as the condition limiting all merely relative and arbitrary ends.
3. A complete characterization of all maxims by means of that formula, namely, that all maxims ought, by their own legislation, to harmonize with a possible kingdom of ends.[48]

The difficulty with this three-part formulation is clear enough: what Kant calls a "matter" in item 2 (above) is called "subjective" in adjoining passages. Also, immediately below the formulation he says that while it is better to start from the formula of the categorical imperative—the principle of universality—it is "useful" to consider the other factors as well (that is, the matter or end of a maxim and the complete characterization of all maxims), so that the moral law can be brought "nearer to intuition."[49] Kant's moral thought is problematical mainly if one regards even objective ends in themselves as something injected into the "higher" notion of formal universality merely in order to "gain entrance" for morality, intuitively conceived, and if one considers it merely "useful" (though not essential) to take account of ends as well as of formal universality. And Kant himself sometimes seems to invite this. Since, however, he also insists on the idea of an "independently existing end" that one must "never act against" and on the "dignity of man as a rational creature,"[50] it is at least arguable that the three elements of a moral maxim are all necessary, and that no one of them is alone sufficient. This reading, while not absolutely decisive, is shored up by the key paragraph of Kant's late and little-read *Tugendlehre* (1797).

> Since there are free actions, there must also be ends to which, as objects, those actions are directed. But among those ends there must be some which are at the same time (i.e., by their very concept) duties. For if there were no such ends, and since no action can be without an end, all ends for practical reason would always be valid only as means to other ends, and a categorical imperative would be impossible. Thus the doctrine of morals would be destroyed.[51]

This passage, which insists that there must *finally* be an end that is not a mere means to some further end, is Kant's final thinking on humanity as an objective end. If what is "subjective" in a maxim (the end) is as important as what is "objective" (the form), and is indeed an essential aspect of a "completely characterized" maxim, then Kant's moral philosophy, however problematical, is no arid "formalism." Although Kant's proof of the validity of an objective end in itself is intersubjective rather than (as he hopes) objective, the argument is at least persuasive, if not as decisive as Kant may have wished. (To go beyond *persuasiveness*, one must await the full account of all "ends" in the *Third Critique*; one should suspend judgment until one reads *Judgment*.)[52]

IV

It will have been obvious that there is a tension, so far understressed, in Kant's formulations of the categorical imperative. For in one vein he tells us that the categorical imperative is "drawn from the conception of that which is necessarily an end for everyone because it is an end in itself"[53] (this may be styled the *teleological* vein); in another vein he tells us that the categorical imperative is a "law of one's own giving" as an "autonomous being"[54] (this may be called the *contractarian* vein). This tension leads to an obvious question: if "objective ends"—above all the person as a "limit" never to be acted against— are provided by reason, in what sense can it be true that we give the law to ourselves, out of our own reason, insofar as we are autonomous legislators in the kingdom of ends? Does reason point out or reveal objective ends, as seems to be the case when *Pure Reason* asserts that reason "frames for itself," with "perfect spontaneity," a moral "order"?[55] Or does our reason construct objective ends for us, through autonomous human legislative activity? In short, is Kant closer to the Plato who supplies "excellent practical principles," [56] or to the Rousseau who is the "Newton of the moral world"?[57] This is obviously a crucial question. If reason *(selbst)* could be said to "propose" objective ends that we "ought to have" *(Religion within the Limits),*[58] and if the objective end is the rational being viewed as a "limit" to all relative ends, then the whole content of morality (and therefore of public legal justice) simply *follows*—murder and war, for example, would be counter-purposive, would contradict reason's objective ends.

On this the *Fundamental Principles* are not as clear as one could wish. At one point Kant says that "all rational beings come under the law that each of them must treat itself and all others never merely as means, but in every case at the same time as ends in themselves. Hence results a systematic union of rational beings by common objective laws, that is, a kingdom which may be called a kingdom of ends."[59] Now this argument, given the word "hence," certainly seems to rest on Kant's teleological view that "a rational nature exists as an end in itself."[60] But, by obvious contrast, Kant says, apropos of "any rational being," that it is "just the fitness of his maxims for universal legislation that distinguishes him as an end in himself"[61]—i.e., being an end in oneself *arises out of* the capacity for universal legislation. This reinforces the passage where Kant says that all previous moral philosophy "failed" because it did not see that "the laws to which he [man] is subject are only those of his own giving."[62] Once again the obvious question must be, does a teleological argument about objective ends provide a source for the categorical imperative? Is rational nature as an end in itself the content of the moral law, insofar as the moral law, *qua* "fact of reason," enjoins respect for persons?[63] Or are persons ends because, or insofar as, they "give the law to themselves," à la Rousseau?

A passage in the *Fundamental Principles* perfectly illustrates Kant's difficulties on this point:

> What then justifies virtue or the morally good disposition in making such lofty claims? It is nothing less than the privilege it secures to the rational being of participating in the giving of universal laws, by which it qualifies him to be a member of a possible kingdom of ends, a privilege *to which he was already destined by his own nature as being an end in himself, and on that account legislating in the kingdom of ends [wozu es durch seine eigene Natur schon bestimmt war, als Zweck in sich selbst]* (emphasis added).[64]

Here, as is evident, the argument shifts from the rational being's participating in the "giving" of universal laws—a *Gesetzgebung* that qualifies him to be a member of the kingdom of ends, to the rational being's "already" *(schon)* being destined by his own nature *qua* end in himself for such membership, and on that account legislating in the kingdom of ends.

One might, of course, say that these strands converge: that a Kantian being legislates *in the light of,* and *limited by,* objective ends. But then what is left for legislation? If most wrongs are ruled out on grounds of their counter-purposiveness, their violation of our "perfect duty" to persons as ends in themselves;[65] and if, on the positive side, reason points out, as in the *Tugendlehre*, "ends which are duties"—one's own (moral) perfection and the happiness of others;[66] what *can* legislation do but attempt to govern the realm of the morally indifferent? But only "ethical gymnasts," in Kant's own phrase, try to make the morally indifferent morally consequential.[67]

V

Kant's difficulties with the relation of the universal form of the moral law to the *telos* of that law emerge very clearly in the opening parts of *Religion within the Limits.* Kant begins the Preface to the First Edition by asserting that morality's laws are binding "through the bare form of universal legality of the maxims," that morality "requires absolutely no material determining ground of free choice, that is, no end, in order . . . to know what duty is." On the contrary, Kant insists, "morality is perfectly able to ignore all ends, and it ought to do so."[68] This looks almost like a categorical imperative enjoining the *ignoring* of purposiveness. When Kant goes on to give an example of this (morally necessary) shunning of ends as incentives, he considers whether "in order to know whether I should (or indeed can) be truthful in my testimony before a court," it is "necessary for me to search for an end which I might perhaps propose to achieve with my declaration." He concludes that whoever, in order to give true testimony, needs to "look about him for some kind of end, is by this very fact, already contemptible."[69] It will be recalled, nonetheless, that in the *Fundamental Principles* Kant makes a distinction between relative ends, which one proposes to oneself at pleasure, and objective ends which could be the "source of a categorical imperative." In the passage about giving true testimony, from *Religion*, Kant is plainly complaining of "looking about" for *relative* ends, such as a useful reputation for honesty. For in a slightly later footnote Kant begins by saying that "an end is always the object of an inclination, that is, of an immediate craving for possession of a thing through one's action," but then quickly adds, despite his own "always," that "an objective end (i.e., the end which we ought to have) is that which is proposed to us by reason alone."[71] Such an end is precisely *not* self-proposed at pleasure.

At this point Kant says nothing further about objective ends; but slightly later he throws doubt on the adequacy of formal universality alone as the sufficient characterization of moral law. For he says that "from the fact that a being has reason it by no means follows that this reason, by the mere representation of the fitness of its maxims to be laid down as universal laws, is thereby rendered capable of determining the will unconditionally, so as to be practical of itself." The "most rational moral being in the world" might, Kant goes on, "still stand in need of certain incentives . . . to determine his choice."[72] The incentive that Kant has in mind, as something (apparently) not deducible from universal legality, is "the absolutely imperative moral law which proclaims that it is itself an incentive and, indeed, the highest." However, were this law "not given to us from within, we should never by any ratiocination subtilize it into existence or win over our will to it."[73] Here, then, as in *Practical Reason*, what comes first is the moral law as a fact of reason located within us; one cannot, as it were, construct that law simply and exclusively by appeal to its fitness for universal law. What this means, or might mean, is that universal form is only an *element* in a "completely characterized" moral law. On this view, a teleological one, the moral law is universal because it has "apodictic certainty" for the universe of rational beings.[74]

Perhaps the resolution of the tension between *telos* and *nomos* in Kantian practical thought lies in taking *au pied de la lettre* Kant's own insistence that all the versions of the categorical imperative are "at bottom" only so many "formulae" of "the very same law."[75] And the most important passage in the *Fundamental Principles* illustrating that sameness is surely this one:

> Rational nature is distinguished from the rest of nature by this, that it sets before itself an end. This end would be the matter of every good will. But since in the idea of a will that is absolutely good without being limited by any condition (of attaining this or that end) we must abstract wholly from every end *to be effected* (since this would make every will only relatively good), it follows that in this case the end must be conceived, not as an end to be effected, but as an *independently* existing end. Consequently it is conceived only negatively, that is, as that which we must never act against, and which, therefore, must never be regarded merely as means, but must in every volition be esteemed as an end likewise. Now this end can be nothing but the subject of all possible ends, since this is also the subject of a possible absolutely good will; for such a will cannot without contradiction be postponed to any other object. This principle: So act in regard to

every rational being (thyself and others) that he may always have a place in thy maxim as an end in himself, is accordingly essentially identical with this other: Act upon a maxim which, at the same time, involves its own universal validity for every rational being. For that in using means for every end I should limit my maxim by the condition of its holding good as a law for every subject, this comes to the same thing as that the fundamental principle of all maxims of action must be that the subject of all ends, that is, the rational being himself, be never employed merely as means, but as the supreme condition restricting the use of all means—that is, in every case as an end likewise.[76]

Here it is worth noticing that Kant has subtly altered the formal requirements of the categorical imperative, converting the original "Act only on that maxim whereby thou canst at the same time will that it should become a universal law" into "act upon a maxim which, at the same time, involves its own universal validity for every rational being." The addition of "validity for every rational being" obviously adds a bit of nonheteronomous teleological flesh to the bare bones of universality. (But it adds nothing that Kant had not already expressed in his insistence that "since moral laws ought to hold good for every rational creature, we must derive them from the general concept of a rational being.")[77] That added teleological flesh is fattened when Kant goes on to say, only a little later, that "the mere dignity of man as a rational creature without any *other* end or advantage to be attained thereby, in other words, respect for a mere idea," must serve as "an inflexible precept of the will."[78] Although other ends are ruled out, *one* end—man as a rational creature—is ruled in. He is the objective end who limits the pursuit of relative ends. It may well be, then, that Kant himself would have been astonished to find that he was a partisan of "contentless formalism"; he might well have said that anyone who read the entire *Fundamental Principles* would have seen ends from which to infer the content of morality.

Even in the *Critique of Practical Reason*, which insists most strongly on abstracting all matter from morality and on formal universality as the core of morality, Kant sometimes reformulates his formula in a way that admits persons as objective ends. In a key passage he insists that

The rule of judgment under laws of pure practical reason is: Ask yourself whether, if the action which you propose should take place by a law of nature of which you yourself were a part, you could regard it as possible through your will. Everyone does, in fact, decide by this rule whether actions are morally good or bad. Thus people ask: If one belonged to such an order of things that anyone would allow himself to deceive when he thought it to his advantage, or felt justified in shortening his life as soon as he was thoroughly weary of it, or looked with complete indifference on the need of others, would he assent of his own will to being a member of such an order of things? . . . If the maxim of action is not so constituted as to stand the test of being made the form of a natural law in general, it is morally impossible.[79]

In this passage Kant begins and ends with universality; but in the middle he asks whether one could will universal maxims with complete indifference to the needs of others (a sin of omission) or that allow deceit (a sin of commission). Surely this supports the view that the reason one cannot will universalized deceit or indifference is that persons would then be treated as mere means to a relative end, namely one's mere *wish* to deceive or neglect them. If that is so, then it should not be surprising that, even though it is the least teleological of his great moral works, Kant ends *Practical Reason* with the claim that "in the order of ends man (and every rational being) is an end in himself, i.e., he is never to be used merely as a means for someone (even for God) without at the same time being himself an end, and that thus the humanity in our person must itself be holy to us."[80]

Universality and teleology are drawn even more tightly together in the *Lectures on Philosophical Theology* (1783–84), written and delivered during Kant's "critical" period.[81] In the *Lectures*, indeed, Kant argues that

Since morality makes possible a system of all ends, it gives to the rational creature a value in and for himself, by making him a member of this great kingdom of ends. The possibility of such a universal system of all ends depends solely on morality. For it is only insofar as all rational creatures act according to these eternal laws of reason that they can under a principle of community and together constitute a system of all ends. For example, if all men speak the truth, then a system of ends is possible among them; but if only one should lie, his end is no longer combined with the others. Hence the universal rule for judging morality of an action is always this: If all men did this, could there still be a combination of ends?[82]

In this extremely important passage, universal form and objective ends are virtually identified. But even the more careful (and authentic) *Practical Reason* makes a roughly comparable argument. That established, one must now consider how far objective ends are simply "given" by reason itself.

VI

Everything, then, turns on how far Kant thought that reason itself— not just our quasi-Rousseauean "legislative" reason—gives or provides or proposes objective ends that could be the source of the categorical imperative. This should be treated, in the first instance, by examining those passages in *Pure Reason* in which Kant speaks of reason's "causality" in the moral sphere.

In the "Transcendental Dialectic" of *Pure Reason*, beginning at A327/B384, Kant starts to discuss reason's practical causality. "I understand by idea a necessary concept of reason to which no corresponding object can be given in sense experience," Kant begins. "Thus the pure concepts of reason now under consideration are transcendental ideas." Those concepts are "not arbitrarily invented"; they are "imposed by the very nature of reason itself."[83] Now "no object adequate to the transcendental idea can ever be found within [sense] experience," and for this reason the transcendental ideas are problematical in our understanding of nature: "the absolute whole of all appearances," for example, is only an idea"; since we can never represent it in an image, "it remains a problem to which there is no solution."[84] In the moral realm of freedom, by contrast, "the practical idea is . . . always in the highest degree fruitful, and in its relation to our actual activities is indispensably necessary."[85] (This, Kant insists, was especially clear to Plato, who realized that "our reason naturally exalts itself to modes of knowledge which so far transcend the bounds of experience that no given empirical object can ever coincide with them, but which must nonetheless be recognized as having their own reality, and which are by no means mere fictions of the brain." Plato, Kant adds, "found the chief instances of his ideas in the field of the practical, that is, in what rests upon freedom"; and in this he was right since "it is only by means of this idea that any judgment as to moral worth" is possible. And if, Kant concludes, we "set aside" the "exaggerations" of Platonism, such as the tendency to think of ideas as things which have to be "laboriously" recalled by reminiscence, Plato's "spiritual flight" from nature to the "architectonic ordering" of the world "according to ideas" [principles of morality, legislation and religion] is "an enterprise which calls for respect and imitation.")[86]

Reason in the practical sphere, Kant continues, is "indeed, exercising causality, as actually bringing about that which its concept contains."[87] One is not yet told, to be sure, what reason's concept actually contains, and so as yet there is no source for the categorical imperative; so far there is simply the assertion that while the employment of "ideas of reason" in theoretical inquiry is problematical, their employment in the practical sphere is morally fruitful and "indispensably necessary."

These questions resurface in the "Antinomy of Pure Reason"

(A547/B575), after the resolution of the third antinomy has made a person's self-determination through reason noncontradictory by drawing a necessary distinction, already examined in Chapter 2, between phenomenal determination and noumenal self-determination. Kant again takes up reason's "causality," saying inter alia that reason is something that "we distinguish in a quite peculiar and especial way from all empirically conditioned powers."[88] He then offers a paragraph so important—both positively for his own practical philosophy, and negatively for his critique of eudaemonism and utilitarianism—that it ought to be cited in full, even though it was briefly examined while treating Hume in Chapter Two:

> That our reason has causality, or that we at least represent it to ourselves as having causality, is evident from the *imperatives* which in all matters of conduct we impose as rules upon our active powers. *'Ought'* expresses a kind of necessity and of connection with grounds which is found nowhere else in the whole of nature. The understanding can know in nature only what is, what has been, or what will be. We cannot say that anything in nature *ought* to be other than what in all these time-relations it actually is. When we have the course of nature alone in view, 'ought' has no meaning whatsoever. It is just as absurd to ask what ought to happen in the natural world as to ask what properties a circle ought to have.[89]

The negative consequences, for both moral and political thought, are what is immediately clearest. If "ought" is a concept "pronounced by reason," as Kant says elsewhere, and whose "necessity" (moral necessity) cannot be found in the whole of nature, then eudaemonism and utilitarianism are automatically wrong in trying to extract moral necessity from natural facts (happiness and the desire for happiness). For Kant a utilitarian has nothing but the course of nature in view; but in that course "ought" has no meaning whatsoever.

Even this negative achievement—showing that eudaemonism and utilitarianism attempt the (in principle impossible) derivation of "ought" from facts of nature—is consequential; but of course Kant's main aim is to show positively that reason has causality in the form of moral imperatives.[90] Here the real difficulties begin, and much turns on which words are given decisive weight. Thus one reading of A547/B575 might be this:

> That *our* reason has causality, or that *we* at least represent it *to ourselves* as having causality, is evident from the imperatives which in all matters of conduct *we* impose as rules upon *our* active powers (emphasis added).[91]

This choice of words for emphasis might be represented as correct if one reads the *Fundamental Principles* as saying that autonomous rational beings give the law to themselves and are ends in themselves *because of* their legislative capacity. The text (or at least part of it) will bear this reading, but another reading of this passage is possible:

> That our *reason* has causality, or that we at least represent it to ourselves as having casuality, is evident from the *imperatives* which in all matters of conduct we impose as *rules* upon our active powers (emphasis added).[92]

Here the notion is that reason provides rules (out of itself, so to speak); the stress is on the law, not on our legislating.

Unfortunately, the remaining relevant passages in *Pure Reason* fail to make clear which reading is more authentic. The following crucial paragraph, for instance, might be accommodated within either reading:

> Reason does not here [in morality] follow the order of things as they present themselves in appearance, but frames for itself with perfect spontaneity an order of its own according to ideas, to which it adapts the empirical conditions, and according to which it declares actions to be necessary, even though they have never taken place, and perhaps never will take place. And at the same time reason also presupposes that it can have causality in regard to all these actions.[93]

The same is true of the very important passage in the "Canon of Pure Reason," near the end of the first *Critique:*

> Reason . . . provides laws which are imperatives, that is, objective laws of freedom, which tell us what ought to happen . . . therein differing from laws of nature, which relate only to that which happens. These laws are therefore to be entitled practical laws.[94]

In this passage reason is said to *provide* laws which are imperative, but even this could be read to mean that our legislative reason, by giving laws, provides imperatives.

What makes one doubly cautious in discussing reason's practical "causality" in Kant is that John Rawls has recently published a remarkable article, "Kantian Constructivism in Moral Theory," which casts grave doubts on the notion that (impersonal) reason could simply "provide" imperatives. Rawls begins with the notion that Kant is the most important of "constructivists" in moral theory—that is, that in Kantian morality there is a "procedure of construction in which rationally autonomous agents subject to reasonable conditions agree to public principles of justice," so that right is the "constructed object" of a correct procedure, not something "found" or "seen".[95] He then goes on to argue that Kantian "constructivism" can best be understood by contrasting it with "rational intuitionism":

> Rational intuitionism may be summed up by two theses: first, the basic moral concepts of the right and the good, and the moral worth of persons,

are not analyzable in terms of nonmoral concepts . . .; and, second, first principles or morals (whether one or many), when correctly stated, are self-evident propositions about what kinds of considerations are good grounds for applying one of the three basic moral concepts, that is, for asserting that something is (intrinsically) good, or that a certain action is the right thing to do, or that a certain trait of character has moral worth. These two theses imply that the agreement in judgment which is so essential for an effective public conception of justice is founded on the recognition of self-evident truths about good reasons. And what these reasons are is fixed by a moral order that is prior to and independent of our conception of the person and the social role of morality. This order is given by the nature of things and is known, not by sense, but by rational intuition.[96]

Now Kant, on Rawls's view, was no rational intuitionist. It is clear to everyone, Rawls argues, that Kant "would have rejected Hume's psychological naturalism as heteronomous"; but it is "less obvious" that for Kant rational intuitionism is also heteronomous. The reason that it is less obvious is that Kant is in agreement with the rational intuitionists that "the basic moral concepts are conceptually independent of natural objects."[97] But it "suffices" for heteronomy, Rawls goes on, that moral principles "obtain in virtue of relations among objects the nature of which is not affected or determined by the conception of the person."[98] Kant's ideas of autonomy (as against rational intuitionism), Rawls insists, requires that

there exists no such order of given objects determining the first principles of right and justice among free and equal moral persons. Heteronomy obtains not only when first principles are fixed by the special psychological constitution of human nature, as in Hume, but also when they are fixed by an order of universals or concepts grasped by rational intuition, as in Plato's realm of forms or in Leibniz's hierarchy of perfections.[99]

Thus, Rawls concludes, while in rational intuitionism there is only a "sparse notion of the person" (*qua* knower of "already fixed" moral truth), in Kantian constructivism "a relatively complex conception of the person plays a central role." And it is these persons who, as "agents of construction," construct practical principles as their "object."[100] Presumably this refers to Rawls' claim in *A Theory of Justice* that for Kant "moral principles are the object of rational choice," so that "moral philosophy becomes the study of the conception and outcome of a suitably defined rational decision."[101] To be sure, since Rawls's Kantian choosers are "free and equal rational beings," they do not fall into what Rawls calls "radical choice" by "sheer fiat," as in Nietzsche and existentialism; choice is reasonably constrained by the free, equal, and rational nature of choosing beings, as well as by "preference for primary goods" and by "highest-order interests."[102] But none of these constraints is "given" in a rational intuition, although Rawls does say that his constraints "seem reasonable."[103] For Rawls "Kant's main aim is to deepen and to justify Rousseau's idea that liberty is acting in accordance with a law that we give to ourselves."[104] Rawls adds that his reading of Kant as "deepened" Rousseau can be confirmed by Lewis White Beck's *Commentary on Kant's Critique of Practical Reason*.[105] Beck himself, in an essay written for the 200th anniversary of the *Critique of Pure Reason* ("Was haben wir von Kant gelernt? " *Kant-Studien* 1981, I), argues that Kant's ethics is a "development" of Rousseau's insistence that "l'obéissance á la loi qu'on s'est préscrite est liberté," that Kant learned from "Rousseau's model" that "the only law that I can respect is the law that I give to myself."[106] Obviously this is an important view; it would provide a provenance for Kant's moral *and* political theory.

One questions with trepidation the conclusions of two of the most important living students of Kant's practical philosophy. But it is at least possible—here returning specially to Rawls—that Kant's un-doubted devotion to Rousseau did not utterly exclude every conceivable rational intuition. Certainly Rawls is wholly right in saying that Kant would not try to ground morality in "relations among objects the nature of which is not affected or determined by the conception of the person."[107] Kant would not, for example, in the manner of Leibniz, try to relate moral truth to the other "eternal verities" of mathematics and logic. In an important letter from 1696, Leibniz insisted that

> eternal truths are the fixed and immutable point on which everything turns. Such is the truth of numbers in arithmetic, and of figures in geometry. . . . That postulated, it is well to consider that order and harmony are also something mathematical and which consist in certain proportions: and that justice being nothing else than the order which is observed with regard to the good and evil of intelligent creatures, it follows that God, who is the sovereign substance, immutably maintains justice and the most perfect order which can be observed.[108]

Perfect order, then, for Leibniz, is the substrate of justice as much as of mathematics (although Leibniz coupled this quasi-Platonic view, ultimately traceable to the *Republic* and the *Euthyphro*, with a Christian notion that justice is the "charity of the wise)."[109] It was certainly Leibniz's conviction that "justice follows certain rules of equality and of proportion which are no less founded in the immutable nature of things, and in the ideas of the divine understanding, than the principles of arithmetic and geometry" (*Opinion on the Principles of Pufendorf*, 1706).[110]

But if Kant plainly would not countenance relations (e.g., mathematical relations) among objects that are not "affected or determined by the conception of the person" as the source or even analogon of ethics, what about *the conception of the person itself?* Where does this, to put it plainly, come from? Personality, for Kant, as distinguished from humanity, always means moral personality, the capacity of being moral or at least of willing the moral;[111] personality is revealed through the moral law. But the moral law, in the language of *Practical Reason,* is a, or rather *the,* "fact of reason";[112] and that "fact" is (at least arguably) a "rational intuition." As Kant insists, in a passage already briefly examined,

> The moral law is given, as an apodictically certain fact, as it were, of pure reason, a fact of which we are *a priori* conscious, even if it be granted that no example could be found in which it has been followed exactly. Thus the objective reality of the moral law can be proved through no deduction, through no exertion of the theoretical, speculative, or empirically supported reason; and even if one were willing to renounce its apodictic certainty, it could not be confirmed by any experience and thus proved *a posteriori.* Nevertheless, it is firmly established of itself.[113]

(To be sure, Kant argues in the last part of the *Fundamental Principles* that we shall never *understand* how pure reason can be practical, but that is another matter.)[114]

Every reading of Kant must rest somewhere. Rawls and Beck, both of whom deny that consciousness of the moral law *qua* "fact of reason" is "given" in a rational intuition, rest with "deepened" Rousseau; but a good case can be made for resting on the moral law, not as something constructed but as something "there." The argument, laid out in schematic form, is roughly this: (1.) Criticism (Kant's critical philosophy) "can and must" begin with "pure practical laws" and their "actual existence."[115] The "pure practical" or moral law is a "fact of reason."[116] Or, as Kant puts it in *Pure Reason,* "I assume that there really are pure moral laws which determine completely a priori (without regard to empirical motives, that is, to happiness) what is and is not to be done, that is, which determine the employment of the freedom of a rational being in general; and that these laws command in an absolute manner" ("Canon of Pure Reason," A807/B835).[117] (2.) "*All* moral conceptions have their seat and origin completely a priori in the reason" (*Fundamental Principles,* Abbott, p. 29) and therefore "the conception of an objective principle, insofar as it is obligatory for a will, is called a command (of reason), and the formula of the command is called an imperative" (ibid., p. 30).[118] (3.) An imperative is called categorical "if it is conceived as good in itself and consequently as being necessarily the principle of a will which of itself conforms to reason" (ibid., p. 32).[119] (4.) But categorical imperatives or (applied) moral laws "ought to hold good for every rational creature," and therefore "we must derive them from the general concept of a rational being" (ibid., p. 29).[120] (5.) A rational being, in its turn, "necessarily" regards its own existence as an end in itself, and what is true of a rational being is true of every rational being (ibid., p. 46).[121] (6.) Therefore, rational beings, as ends in themselves, furnish the content of moral laws, since these must be derived from "the general concept of a rational being."[122] Thus one begins with moral law as "fact of reason"; the content of the moral law is then derived from the general concept of a rational being, and this links up with Kant's insistence that "a rational nature exists as an end in itself."[123]

Now if the general concept of a rational being *qua* end in itself is arguably the content of the moral law as sole "fact of reason"—and this seems to be the most reasonable reading of Kant—neither the moral law itself nor the public legal justice which realizes some moral ends can be viewed as the constructed object of a contractarian procedure. But perhaps the gap between Rawls's and Beck's Kant as "deepened" Rousseau, and the present teleological reading, is smaller than it seems. After all, Rawls does say that it suffices for heteronomy that moral principles "obtain in virtue of relations among objects the nature of which is not affected or determined by the conception of the person."[124] That formulation would logically permit Rawls to allow as nonheteronomous (autonomous) a recasting that says that as long as a "conception of the person" does indeed "affect or determine" the "relations among objects," this would count as a "moral principle." The Rawlsian "conception of the person" (which needs to be "found" somewhere) could be based on Kant's notion of "the general concept of a rational being."[125] But Rawls seems, in strictness, to allow no antecedent object to affect or determine the rational deliberations of "agents of construction": constructing practical principles, he argues, is not like "seeing" truth.[126] In this, however, there is a problem: Rawls's agents of construction are characterized as free;[127] but Kant insists (always) that freedom is known only *through* the moral law, and that would seem to mean that unless there were a moral law we would not think of ourselves as free.[128] That supports *beginning* with the moral law, then finding the law's content in the rational being as self-conceived end in itself; it supports the teleological reading.

Certainly this is not absolutely conclusive. Someone unsympathetic to Kant might say that he never made it clear (or perhaps did not know) whether the moral law is, plainly speaking, "found" or "made."[129] But a fairly strong presumption in favor of finding the moral law (*in* rational beings as objective ends) has been established; that presumption is strengthened by a further consideration best brought out by H.B. Acton in his brief but helpful *Kant's Moral Philosophy:*

> 'Making' [moral law] . . . imports a notion of production or manufacture that is foreign to Kant's intention. It also carries an implication of beginning to exist which is at variance with Kant's view of the moral law. At one place in the *Fundamental Principles,* it is true, Kant does say that *the will* can regard itself as author of the law. But . . . elsewhere he makes a point of denying that the giver of the moral law, its legislator, can be its author. . . . In the *Lectures on Ethics,* which were delivered in 1780–82, not long before he wrote the *Fundamental Principles* . . . he says that 'no being, not even the divine being, is an author of moral laws, since they do not originate from choice but are practically necessary. If they were not necessary it could also be that lying would be a virtue.'[130]

That passage from the *Lectures* links Kant to Plato's view, in the *Euthyphro,* that morally necessary things are the *motive,* not the *effect,* of even a divine will.[131] Since the *Lectures* are both precritical and based on student notes, they cannot serve as the foundation of an entire interpretation. But they can legitimately be used to shore up an already strong teleological reading of Kant's ethics. The advantage of such a teleological reading is that it is congruent with—indeed provides the justification for—Kant's claim that "a rational nature exists as an end in itself."[132]

VII

Nothing, however, supports a teleological reading as well as teleology itself; and since Kant's teleological claim that "a rational nature exists as an end in itself" is fully expounded in the second half of the third *Critique,* one should turn to that work. Indeed, one of his most subtle and imaginative defenses of the idea of men as ends in themselves is to be found in the *Critique of Judgment.* In Part II of that work, which is concerned with, inter alia, the possibility of purposiveness in an apparently mechanical world, with showing that while purposiveness cannot be shown actually to exist in a way that satisfies the "determinant" judgment, it can at least be presupposed by human "reflective" judgment in its effort to make the world intelligible to itself,[133] Kant urges that while the purposes of things in the natural world (e.g., the "purposes" of plants or animals) are imputed by us to those things (which certainly cannot themselves conceive purposes), man is the ultimate purpose of creation on earth because "he is the only being upon it who can form a concept of purposes, and who can by his reason make out of an aggregate of purposively formed things a system of purposes."[134]

This argument, which has an obvious relation to Kant's distinction between acting according to laws and acting according to the *conception* of laws—that is, having a will[135]—is also related to the argument in the *Fundamental Principles of the Metaphysic of Morals* about the way in which all men necessarily conceive themselves (that is, as "ultimate ends").[136] While this is, strictly speaking, again an intersubjective rather than an objective proof, since purposiveness is only subjectively necessary for men, it does have considerable force: the idea of a rational nature as an end in itself, or of the dignity of a person (a being capable of conceiving worth and purpose) as an end in himself, is not an arbitrary premise. It is a conception that defines the kind of being who would be capable of *understanding* what is at issue in Kant's own (or any) moral philosophy. If Kant is right in believing that "lower" beings cannot conceive worth or purpose or final ends (let alone conceive of themselves as unconditioned ends), and that the idea of God is deduced out of the concept of moral perfection (rather than the reverse), then men-as-persons, as partly moral beings, will be the only unconditioned thing in nature, and will have to serve as ends in themselves if there are to be any such things.[137] This is why Kant can say, again in the *Critique of Judgment,* that it is not open to us, in the case of man as a moral agent, to ask the question, for what end does he exist? "His existence," Kant argues, "inherently involves the highest end."[138] This is true, Kant grants, only if nature is considered as a teleological system, in which one mounts from things that are conditioned (caused) to that which is unconditioned. Everything in a purposive nature is caused, except man as noumenon, for his will is an uncaused causality and hence "qualifie[s] him to be a final end to which all of nature is teleologically subordinated."[139] What this means is that for Kant not God, but the moral law, which only men certainly know and (sometimes) follow, is the final cause of creation considered as teleological; man would thus be an end in himself because he is the only being capable of conceiving and following the sole unconditioned end (what "ought" to be) that can be known.[140]

However, someone might ask, why should Kant insist on teleological judgment at all? This leads to the larger question, why would anyone want to appeal to the notion of *telos?* Since Aristotle, as is well known, it has been usual to say that any earthly thing can, perhaps must, be viewed from four perspectives: one can inquire into the form of a thing, into its matter, into its efficient cause, and into its final cause or end or *telos*.[141] Kant, in a sense, preserves all this, but in a novel way. Since he wants to steer a minimalist course between any dogmatic assertion of the demonstrable reality of the four types of Aristotelian causality, and a Humean skepticism that would convert these four perspectives into mere questions of human habit or custom, he transforms the dogmatic slumber of the Aristotelians into critical philosophy.[142] That is, he certainly does not dispense with form, or matter, or efficient causality, or *telos*, but neither have any of these an absolute reality as things in themselves. Form and matter, on the Kantian view, become elements of appearance or the phenomenal world (at least where form informs and shapes matter);[143] causality (efficient causality) becomes a category of understanding that the mind employs in producing a "synthetic unity of apperception" out of the "manifold of sensible intuition";[144] and purposiveness or teleology becomes a possible mode of interpreting the world, once one assumes that causality is not the sole principle of explanation.[145] The old Aristotelian categories are transformed: they are still "there," but in a minimalist way that mediates between the dogmatic assertion of the reality of Aristotelian interpretive perspectives and the skeptical denial of any reality whatever to those perspectives.

To be sure, some philosophers try to reduce the Aristotelian four-part canon to something smaller. Hobbes, for example, frequently attempts to rest the whole of his thought on material and causal factors, interpreting the whole world (including the human world) as ceaseless motion set off by God *qua* first cause.[146] Despite Hobbes's supposed materialism, however, one can wonder whether only matter matters; even in *Leviathan* one can reasonably ask what the "social contract" and "sovereignty" are *for*; and it turns out that their purpose is the termination of war and the creation of legal conditions for the pursuit of "felicity."[147] So even the most famous advocate of a "politics of motion" (in Spragens's phrase)[148] appeals to teleological notions, despite a clear aversion to Aristotelianism.

This leads to the further question, would moral and political thought be possible at all without teleological notions? One could, perhaps, say that the "form" of a Kantian state is republican: that the "matter" of that state is citizens who are not mere subjects; that the "cause" of such a state is a (hypothetical) contract that produces something that is not naturally there; would one then draw up short at asking what such a state is *for*? Is it not, according to Kant, for the purpose of creating a public legal justice that will realize some of the ends of morality on a merely legal basis, and that will (perhaps) create a context for morality by removing certain "occasions of sin," such as fear of others' domination?[149] It is exceedingly difficult, perhaps impossible, to imagine a politics without a purpose, or, to recognize Burke's point, to imagine a politics that does not try to meet an indescribably complex network of purposes.[150] Is it not the worst (and most dangerous) sort of legal positivism to say that the state is just "there," but that nothing can be said about the purpose that it ought to pursue? There is nothing odd, then, in Kant's notion that a state has a *telos*, just as morality has its end.

But if there is nothing odd or eccentric in Kant's claim that everything can be "estimated" in light of a hypothetical teleology that is humanly valid for the reflective judgment, though not objectively valid for the determinant judgment,[151] how does this relate to his different and distinguishable claim that the whole of nature can be estimated as "teleologically subordinated" to man as the final end of creation?[151] That Kant himself believed in teleological subordination is plain in several parts of *Judgment*, notably Sections 86 and 87:

> Now, supposing we follow the teleological order, there is a *fundamental principle* to which even the most ordinary human intelligence is obliged to give immediate assent. It is the principle that if there is to be a *final end* at all, which reason must assign a priori, then it can only be *man*—or any rational being in the world—*subject to moral laws*. For—and this is the verdict of everyone—if the world only consisted of lifeless beings, or even consisted partly of living, but yet irrational beings, the existence of such a world would have no worth whatever, because there would exist in it no being with the least conception of what worth is.[152]

Against this, someone could say that there is no irresistible connection between teleology and teleological subordination (in which "higher" things have more worth than "lower" ones). Teleology need not take a "vertical" form; it could be "horizontal," such that while everything indeed has its end and its as-if-intelligently-designed structure, still everything is on a plane with everything else. Then the chain of being would be stretched *across* creation, and not begin in its depths and finally attain its heights, whether that height is God or man.[153] Before, however, considering the radical proposal that the chain of being runs from side to side, connected by links that are equations, let us ask the more modest question of whether it was an innovation on Kant's part to end a teleologically subordinated creation with man as final end.

There is, perhaps, no innovation here if one thinks of the Greek notion that "man is the measure of all things."[154] But there is innovation, very certainly, if one thinks of two millenia of Christianity intervening between Protagoras and Kant. If, for instance, one picks an important Christian philosopher from the seventeenth century, such as Malebranche, one finds a very clear notion of teleological subordination, but one with God as its end. "God is wise, and he thus loves that which is most lovable: that is to say he loves himself more than all other things," Malebranche argues in the *Conversations Chrétiennes* (1677); "thus God is the end of creation, and that is why our [human] minds and wills are made to love God."[155] It is almost as if Kant were replying to this very formulation, for he tells us that man "considered as a moral agent" is the end of creation.[156] It is reasonably clear why he thinks this: God's actual existence is problematical, but the categorical imperative that moral agents ought to follow has "undoubted" necessity, and there is nothing demonstrably extant beyond or above that objective end. Kant's notion of the ultimacy of humanity, conceived through a minimalist teleology, is eccentric, then, only with respect to orthodox Christianity—although in his day that "only" was not as slight a matter as it is now, and led to his being forbidden to publish on religious subjects for some years.[157]

Kantian humanism soon enough became fashionable, though not always expressed in Kantian ways. There is a very clear notion of teleological subordination of nature to man in a number of important nineteenth century works—works that, with Kant, decline to mount allegedly higher rungs of a ladder of being to reach a God whose existence is either problematical or illusory. In his *Utilitarianism* J. S. Mill, despite an opening anti-Kantian salvo seen earlier in this chapter, declares flatly that it is "better to be Socrates dissatisfied than a pig satisfied," and that the pain of exercising higher faculties is worth bearing (even though utility remains the "ultimate appeal on all ethical questions").[158] And in his essay "The British Rule in India," Marx expresses rather plainly a quasi-Kantian view of teleological subordination in his furious indictment of Hindu "superstition":

> We must not forget that these little [Indian] communities . . . subjugated man to external circumstances instead of elevating man to be the sovereign of circumstances, that they transformed a self-developing social state into never changing natural destiny, and thus brought about a brutalizing worship of nature, exhibiting its degradation in the fact that man, the sovereign of nature, fell down on his knees in adoration of Hanuman, the monkey, and Sabbala, the cow.[159]

"Sovereign of nature," of course, is Kant's very phrase in the *Critique of Judgment*.[160]

Still, one can ask whether a Kantian notion of teleological subordination is as persuasive as it was influential. One can always ask whether the Kantian notion that a rational nature is an end in itself is not a vestigial Platonic prejudice that views reason as higher than appetite and passion. Is it not very unfair indeed to say that plants cannot be ends in themselves, simply because they cannot conceive the concept of *telos?* Is it right to make the possibility of conceiving a thing the foundation of a being's "having" that thing? Does Kant do well in arguing that earthly things can be estimated as having "intrinsic finality" (i.e., an as-if-intelligently-designed structure),[161] but do badly in urging that all earthly things save man also have an "extrinsic finality" (i.e., being "for" the use of higher beings)?[162] Does Kant give vegetables a raw deal? Does he fail to fawn on flora? Cannot a dingo be *an sich?* "We may ask," as Dr. Johnson says—adding, with him, that "no created wisdom can give an adequate answer."[163]

VIII

This brief beginning of a glance at the *Critique of Judgment* only proves that a full examination of that work is necessary. For if the *Fundamental Principles* insist that persons are objective ends whom we must never act against;[164] if the political writings speak of a legal realization of some moral ends through republicanism and eternal peace;[165] if *Judgment* itself finds that nature cannot be interpreted by finite human reason without teleological notions such as purpose and function, and that art exhibits a "purposiveness without purpose" which makes it morality's *analogon;*[166] and if it is that same *Judgment* that shows how far there are "bridges" between these various Kantian realms, and that tests the strength of those bridges; then the *Third Critique,* which relates all Kantian ends, is the *summa* of Kantianism.[167] In the belief that this is so, a large-scale treatment of the work must now follow as the heart of a teleological reading of Kant.

CHAPTER FOUR

Civic Culture and the Legal Realization of Moral Ends in the *Critique of Judgment*

I

One does not look to the second half of the *Critique of Judgment* just to find support for a teleological reading of the *Fundamental Principles*—though that work's concept of a rational nature that is an end in itself[1] coincides, as will be seen, with the "person" who is the final end of creation and the limiting condition of rightful politics in Sections 84–86. One looks to *Judgment* for something broader as well: a unifying notion that will draw together the realms (especially nature and morality) of the critical philosophy. For if *telos*, appropriately reconceived, could link nature, morality, politics, art, and even history, then that would serve Kant's always important architectonic ends.[3] (This was seen clearly by Goethe, who argued in his essay "Einwirkung der neueren Philosophie" that the *Critique of Judgment* brings together the "most diverse interests . . . [with] . . . artistic and natural production handled the same way; the power of aesthetic and telological judgment mutually illuminated [by] each other.")[4] If reconceived teleology illuminates the whole of Kant, then it is reasonable to think that it illuminates a part of Kant—the *Fundamental Principles*, say, and its notion of objective ends.

This claim can be substantiated, of course, only by working one's way through the various strands of *Judgment*—those dealing with nature, morality, politics, art, and history—that are linked through *telos*. While treating some of those strands, particularly Kant's notion of nature and natural "purpose", the larger teleological design (culmi-

64

nating in civic "culture") may briefly recede from view; only at the end will the purpose of treating all Kantian ends be wholly obvious.

II

Even in the *Critique of Pure Reason,* which concerns itself in large measure with justifying Newtonian science by rescuing efficient causality from the skeptical grasp of the Humeans,[5] the notion of purposiveness or final causality is not utterly absent. Indeed, in the Appendix to the "Transcendental Dialectic" (A687/B715), Kant insists that the "highest formal unity, which rests solely on concepts of reason, is the purposive *[zweckmässige]* unity of things. The speculative interest of reason makes it necessary to regard all order in the world as if it had originated in the purpose of a supreme reason." Such a teleological principle, Kant goes on, "opens out to our reason, as applied in the field of experience, altogether new views as to how the things of the world may be connected according to teleological laws, and so enables it to arrive at their greatest systematic unity."[6] To be sure, Kant adds, an attempted teleological understanding of the "things of the world" may culminate in "error": but as long as teleology is used in a "merely regulative" way (never as a "constitutive" principle of theoretical reason), "the most that can happen would be that where we expected a teleological connection *(nexus finalis)* we find only a mechanical or physical connection *(nexus effectivus)*." Then we simply fail to find additional unity, but do not "destroy the unity [of efficient casuality] upon which reason insists in its empirical employment." If the merely regulative usefulness of *telos* is kept in mind, then it can "aid us in securing the highest possible systematic unity, by means of the idea of the purposive causality of the supreme cause of the world."[7]

In this Appendix to the "Transcendental Dialectic," the notion of teleology as a reflective principle has been mainly confined to understanding the things of the world (such as the function of bodily organs in medical studies).[8] But the notion of the "unity of reason" suggests a larger vista; and since one already knows that reason exercises "causality" through moral imperatives ("that our reason has causality . . is evident from the imperatives which, in all matters of conduct, we impose as rules"),[9] it is not unreasonable to expect that Kant will (finally) say something about a possible unity of reason in its theoretical and practical employment. This expectation is not disappointed; for in the "Architectonic of Pure Reason" (A832/B860), he insists that "in accordance with reason's legislative prescriptions, our diverse modes of knowledge must not be permitted to be a mere rhapsody, but must form a system. Only so can they further the essential ends of reason."[10]

Unity and the *essential ends of reason* are fully taken up at A840/B868, where Kant discusses "what philosophy prescribes as regards systematic unity . . . from the standpoint of its essential ends."

> Essential ends are not as such the highest ends; in view of the demand of reason for complete systematic unity, only one of them can be so described. Essential ends are therefore either the ultimate end or subordinate ends which are necessarily connected with the former as means. The former is no other than the whole vocation of man, and the philosophy which deals with it is entitled moral philosophy. On account of this superiority which moral philosophy has over all other occupations of reason, the ancients in their use of the term "philosopher" always meant, more especially, the *moralist;* and even at the present day we are led by a certain analogy to entitle anyone a philosopher who appears to exhibit self-control under the guidance of reason, however limited his [speculative] knowledge may be.[11]

The idea that the moral vocation of man is the ultimate end of reason prefigures, albeit a bit obscurely, the notion of the *Fundamental Principles* that a rational being is the sole objective end.[12] Kant then goes on to say that philosophy (or the "legislation of human reason") "has two objects, nature and freedom, and therefore contains not only the law of nature, but also the moral law, presenting them at first in two distinct systems [nature's causality and reason's causality] but ultimately in one single philosophical system."[13]

But *Pure Reason,* despite its own insistence on unity and one single philosophical system, does little to illustrate that unity and system, apart from the claim that the highest unity is the "purposive unity of things." Still, that notion of a unifying purposiveness, which is underdeveloped in *Pure Reason,* can serve as a bridge to the *Critique of Judgment,* the work that avowedly links nature and freedom, nature's causality and reason's causality. *Judgment* actually provides the unity-through-purposiveness that *Pure Reason* stresses but does not wholly supply. Perhaps it was precisely this that Goethe had in mind when he insisted, in comparing *Pure Reason* and *Judgment,* that "both works, springing up out of a single spirit, mutually explain each other."[14]

III

The Introduction to *Judgment,* indeed, takes up where *Pure Reason* had stopped. "The function of prescribing laws by means of concepts of nature [e.g., causality]," Kant begins, "is discharged by understanding, and is theoretical." But the function of prescribing laws "by means of the concept of freedom is discharged by reason and is merely practical." Understanding and reason, then, for Kant, "have two distinct jurisdictions over one and the same territory of experience"; but one can still wonder how it happens that "these two different realms do not form one realm."[15] It certainly *seems* that "between the realm of the natural concept" and the "realm of freedom" there is "a great gulf fixed . . . just as if they were so many separate worlds, the first of which [reason] is powerless to exercise influence on the second [nature]."[16] Indeed it was Kant himself, in the most famous passage of his entire philosophy, later to be abbreviated on his own tombstone,[17] who insisted on a gulf between separate worlds:

> Two things fill the mind with ever new and increasing admiration and awe, the oftener and the more steadily we reflect on them: the starry heavens above me and the moral law within me . . . The former begins at the place I occupy in the external world of sense, and it broadens the connection in which I stand into an unbounded magnitude of worlds beyond worlds and systems of systems and into the limitless times of their periodic motion, their beginning and their continuance. The latter begins at my invisible self, my personality, and exhibits me in a world which has true infinity but which is comprehensible only to the understanding . . . The former view of a countless multitude of worlds annihilates, as it were, my importance as an animal creature . . . the latter, on the contrary, infinitely raises my worth as that of an intelligence by my personality, in which the moral law reveals a life independent of all animality and even of the whole world of sense.[18]

But if the concept of separate worlds can yield the most beautiful passage in the *Second Critique*, it has become intolerable in the *Third*. For *Judgment* insists that reason is "meant" to bear on nature: "that is to say, the concept of freedom is meant to actualize in the sensible world the end proposed by its laws; and nature must consequently also be capable of being regarded in such a way that in the conformity to law of its form it at least harmonizes with the possibility of ends to be effected in it according to the laws of freedom."[19]

Here Kant is not thinking merely of the distinction between phenomena and noumena, or of the notion that "ought" implies "can"; he is also putting forward the much more radical thought that "there must be . . . a ground of the unity of the supersensible that lies at the basis of nature [the *noumenon*, the thing in itself] with what the concept of freedom contains in a practical way."[20] But the only conceivable noumenal "ground" underlying both nature and morality is *telos*; nature can be estimated teleologically by our reflective judgment, and may actually have real purposes knowable determinantly by a nondiscursive, "intuitive" intelligence, such as a divine intelligence; while morality (freedom) is "meant to actualize . . . the end proposed by its laws."[21] Purpose, then, might be the substrate or substratum unifying nature and freedom.

That Kant is actually suggesting something of this kind becomes clearer in the last section (IX) of the Introduction to *Judgment*. He begins by recasting his earlier argument about the law-prescribing functions of understanding and of reason:

> Understanding prescribes laws *a priori* for nature as an Object of sense, so that we may have a theoretical knowledge of it in a possible experience. Reason prescribes laws *a priori* for freedom and its peculiar causality as the supersensible in the subject, so that we may have a purely practical knowledge. The realm of the concept of nature under the one legislation, and that of the concept of freedom under the other, are completely cut off from all reciprocal influence that they might severally (each according to its own principles) exert upon each other, by the broad gulf that divides the supersensible from phenomena. The concept of freedom determines nothing in respect of the theoretical cognition of nature; and the concept of nature likewise nothing in respect of the practical laws of freedom. To that extent, then, it is not possible to throw a bridge from the one realm to the other.[22]

But *Judgment*, Kant goes on, "with its concept of a purposiveness of nature, provides us with the mediating concept between concepts of nature and the concept of freedom—a concept that makes possible the transition from the pure theoretical [legislation of understanding] to the pure practical [legislation of reason]."[23] For through the concept of purposiveness "we cognize the possibility of the final end [morality] that can only be actualized in nature and in harmony with its laws." To be sure, this is only conceivable on the assumption that the "supersensible substrate" of nature—the noumenal *etwas überhaupt* = X that is the ground of the phenomenal in *Pure Reason*—is "undetermined" (determinism applies to phenomena), so that this substrate can be shaped "through the intellectual faculty," that is, through purpose.[24] But reason uses the same principle of purposiveness in "its practical law"; therefore *Judgment* "makes possible the transition from the realm of the concept of nature [which is teleologically estimated] to that of the concept of freedom [and morality's objective ends]."[25]

This transition from nature to morality via *telos* is perhaps even more striking in the First Introduction to *Judgment* (suppressed because of its length), where Kant says that "a teleological judgment compares the concept of a natural product as it is with what it *ought* to be." Thus we judge, Kant goes on, that the eye "ought to be adapted for seeing," and that "this 'ought' contains a necessity which is clearly differentiated from the physico-mechanical [type], wherein a thing is possible under laws of the efficient causes alone."[26] Surely Kant realized that in making this passage exactly parallel to the famous one in *Pure Reason* ("*ought* expresses a kind of necessity . . . which is found nowhere else in the whole of nature")[27] he was drawing nature and morality exceedingly close together: perhaps too much so, for in the published Introduction the passage is omitted, and nature and morality are joined only by a teleological substrate, not by an explicit "ought." On this point, at least, the published version is superior, for it is only through reflective judgment that we read purposiveness into nature (as will be made clear shortly),[28] while practical reason by contrast has objective ends that we ought to follow.[29] That is why Kant can say, in the main body of *Judgment*, that "reason cannot command one to pursue an end that is recognized to be nothing but a fiction";[30] purpose in nature is not a mere "fiction," to be sure, but neither is it—determinantly—*known*.

This reading of the Introduction to *Judgment* is supported by two specially important passages from the last half of the work, "Teleological Judgment." In the first passage (Section 87), Kant draws a parallel between physical teleology (ends in nature) and moral teleology (persons as the final end of creation), and goes on to argue that just as in the study of nature "we have a physical teleology" valid for human reflective judgment, so too "we find a moral teleology" in ourselves and still more in "the general concept of a rational being endowed with freedom of its causality."[31] (It is surely no accident that the key phrase, "the general concept of a rational being," echoes the *Fundamental Principles'* assertion that we must "derive" the moral law from "the general concept of a rational being.")[32] Kant adds that in "moral teleology" our own relation to an end (a moral end) is "determined *a priori*, and consequently cognized as necessary."[33] This passage provides additional evidence that when Kant speaks in *Judgment*'s Introduction of the "unity of the supersensible" that "lies at the [noumenal] basis of nature" with "what the concept of freedom contains in a practical way,"[34] he is thinking of *telos*. Otherwise it would make no sense to use the deliberately parallel terminology of *physical teleology* and *moral teleology*.

The second important supporting passage follows in Section 88, where Kant complains that "speculative philosophy" has failed to find what the *Critique of Judgment* apparently has found: speculative philosophy "undertakes to connect the ethical end with physical ends by means of the idea of a single end"; but that "single end," undetected by speculative philosophy, seems to be that possible (though by us unknowable) *telos* that "lies at the basis of nature" and in the "content" (which *is* knowable) of "the concept of freedom."[35]

If, to say it again in passing, *telos* can bridge the gulf between nature and freedom, it can certainly and obviously bridge narrower chasms (such as that between morality and law, which in any case already share ends or duties and diverge only over incentives).[36] Thus the Introduction to *Judgment* ties together *Pure Reason*'s concern with "purposive unity," the *Fundamental Principles'* notion of "objective ends," and the main body of *Judgment* itself, which insists on *telos* in estimating nature and art, and views civic culture as the "ultimate end of nature").[37] If this general view of Kantianism is admissable, then *telos* is not a mere "bridge": it more nearly resembles a foundation, a *Grundlegung*.

This is clearest of all, perhaps, in the remarkable Section 57 of "Aesthetic Judgment," which extends and completes the Introduction. Kant begins by saying that we are compelled, "whether we like it or not, to look beyond the horizon of the sensible, and to seek in the supersensible the point of union of all our faculties *a priori*"; that unless we find that union in purposiveness "we are left with no other expedient to bring reason into harmony with itself."[38] The crucial passage appears several pages later, where Kant makes it clear that, if the *Critique of Judgment* is right, "three ideas then stand out in evidence":

> Firstly, there is the supersensible in general, without further determination, as the substrate of nature; secondly, this same [supersensible] as principle of the subjective finality of nature for our congitive faculties; thirdly, the same again, as principle of the ends of freedom, and the principle of the common accord of these ends with freedom in the moral sphere.[39]

Finally, in a nearby sentence, Kant speaks of the "supersensible substrate of humanity"—which integrates man, morality, nature, and art into a single substratum.[40]

No other passage, anywhere in Kant, makes it so clear that it is precisely a supersensible purposiveness that links the "realms" of Kantianism. And it is not just *a* supersensible link; Kant says "the same" and says it twice. Since the supersensible in morality is reason—a reason whose "peculiar sphere" is "the order of ends"— and since Kant speaks of "the same" supersensible as linking morality, nature and art, he must suspect that reason and reason's ends are the universal substrate. But Kant, unlike Hegel, cannot claim to *know* this; only practical reason's "causality" is fully known, through the moral law, and the purposiveness of nature and art is only a kind of "analogy" to morals.[42] Surely, however, it is Section 57 of *Judgment* that brings Kant closest to the Hegelian dictum that "reason is not so powerless as to be incapable of producing anything but a mere ideal . . it is the infinite complex of things."[43]

IV

Once the Introduction to *Judgment* is left behind, the main body of the *Third Critique* is divided into two parts, "Aesthetic Judgment" and "Teleological Judgment." Much of "Aesthetic Judgment" has little immediate bearing on Kant's practical thought, except for the crucial Section 57 and the section, to be taken up later, in which Kant insists that, though the beautiful is not "for" anything beyond *ars gratia artis,* the beautiful is nonetheless the "symbol" of morality.[44] But "Teleological Judgment" bears much more directly on Kantian politics, law, and history—chiefly because Kant tries to enclose those practical things within "culture" viewed as the "ultimate end of nature" and hence as link between nature and moral freedom ("not nature, nor yet freedom").[45]

Before arriving at culture understood as the ultimate end of nature, however, Kant considers the more general notion of ends *in* nature. He is driven to the idea that nature must be estimated as having ends mainly by the facts of biology; Newtonian physics can make do with "mechanical causality," but "organized beings" (organisms) must be explained otherwise.

> It is . . . quite certain that we can never get a sufficient knowledge of organized beings and their inner possibility, much less get an explanation of them, by looking merely to mechanical principles of nature. Indeed, so certain is it, that we may confidently assert that it is absurd for men even to entertain any thought of so doing or to hope that maybe another Newton may some day arise, to make intelligible to us even the genesis of but a blade of grass from natural laws that no design has ordered. Such insight we must absolutely deny to mankind.[46]

Indeed, Kant adds in Section 77, it is "utterly impossible for human reason, or for any finite reason . . . to hope to understand the generation of even a blade of grass from mere mechanical causes . . . *Judgment* finds the teleological nexus . . . quite indispensable for the possibility of an object like this."[47] This is not to say that an infinite reason might not be able to conceive organisms on purely mechanical lines (or, alternatively, on purely teleological lines); but the notions of *purpose, end* and *design* are unavoidable for finite reason. "It is one thing to say," Kant argues, that "the production of certain things of nature [i.e., organisms or physical ends] is only possible through the agency of a cause that pursues designs in determining itself to action." It is entirely different, however, to say that "by the peculiar [i.e., finite] constitution of my cognitive faculties the only way I can judge of the possibility of those things [physical ends] . . . is by conceiving for that purpose a cause working designedly," by analogy to "the causality of an understanding."[48] The first statement would be an objective one valid for the determinant judgment; the second a subjective one valid for human reflective judgment. It is only the second that Kant argues for, since "strictly speaking we do not *observe* the ends of nature as designed. We only read this conception into the facts as a guide to judgment in its reflection upon the products of nature. Hence these ends are not given to us by the Object."[49]

To be sure, Kant insists, it may well be that an "infinite reason" would see, not tension or incompatability between mechanical and teleological explanation, but a higher unity. It is for us "an open question," Kant argues, whether "in the unknown inner basis of nature itself" a "mechanical" and a "final" nexus may not "cohere in a single principle."[50] This not inconceivable "higher principle of nature," uniting mechanical and final causality, is indeed (because "transcendent") unavailable to "the narrow capacity of our under-standing"; all we *can* know is that for the understanding of "organic products of nature" we must "subordinate" mechanical explanation "to a teleological principle."[51] Otherwise the as-if-intelligently-de-signed internal structure of a blade of grass will be incomprehensible to us. Here the decisive passage is the final part of Section 78:

> It is an open question, and for our reason must always remain an open question, how much the mechanism of nature contributes as means to each final design in nature. Further, having regard to the above-mentioned intelligible principle [substrate] of the possibility of a nature in general, we may even assume that nature is possible in all respects on both kinds of law, the physical laws and those of final causes, as universally consonant laws, although we are quite unable to see how this is so. Hence we are ignorant how far the mechanical mode of explanation possible for us may penetrate. This much only is certain, that no matter what progress we may succeed in making with it, it must still always remain inadequate for things that we have once recognized to be physical ends. Therefore, by the constitution of our understanding we must subordinate such mechanical grounds, one and all, to a teleological principle.[52]

Just how carefully Kant is treading in this passage becomes clear if one contrasts it with a superficially similar "dogmatic" one from Rousseau's *Institutions Chymiques*, a 1747 paraphrase of Boerhaave's *Elementa Chemiae* in which the "Newton of the moral world" briefly turns into the Rousseau of the physical world:

One would have to know the structure of the universe better than we do in order to determine which are the first and the most general of these laws [of nature]; perhaps they are all reducible to a single one; more than one great man has suspected it, and Newton nearly explained all the phenomena of nature through the sole principle of attraction . . .

The heavenly bodies move; we don't know how, and by which principles; the sun sends us its healthful rays each day to preserve life and movement on earth, [and] without it everything in nature would perish. But neither the sun, nor all the stars, nor all the fire, nor all the movement which exist in the universe, is capable of producing the least of all plants, or the lowest of all insects; this abyss of generation in which all philosophers were lost long ago is still, today, the despair of the incredulous, [and] the construction of an organized body through laws of motion alone is a chimera which one must abandon to those who pay themselves in words. [53]

Some parrallels with Kant are striking enough: Rousseau stresses the limits of our knowledge, and the impossibility of explaining an "organized" body through physics. But he also seems to say that one can *know* that mechanical causes could never generate an organism, while Kant says, more cautiously, that such generation is incomprehensible *to us*, but is also beyond refutation. Despite this, the Rousseau and the Kant passages resemble each other rather strongly; Rousseau's botanical studies and Kant's biological reflections lead to roughly comparable teleological conclusions.

V

Through Section 81 of "Teleological Judgment," Kant has been considering mainly "intrinsic purposiveness," the as-if-intelligently-designed *internal* structure of an "organized being" or "physical end" (such as a plant or an animal).[54] But he has not yet considered what he calls "extrinsic finality," by which he means the purposiveness that exists "where one thing in nature subserves another as means to an end."[55] In "extrinsic purposiveness," in a word, one asks what "intrinsically purposive" organized beings are *for*. This distinction between means and ends—reminiscent, by what one is tempted to call design, of the *Fundamental Principles* distinction between treating beings as ends or merely as means"[56]—allows Kant to begin to talk about ends in nature that are merely means to "higher" ends, and about those ends (namely persons) who are "inherent" or "final" ends (ends that therefore transcend mere nature).

Kant begins by arguing, in Section 82, that "we may either say that the end of the real existence of a natural being" is "inherent in itself," so that such a being "is not merely an [organized] end, but also a final end" or we may say that " the final end lies outside" a natural being, so that it is "at the same time a means" to something, or someone, beyond itself.[57] But if, Kant goes on, "we go through the whole of nature," we fail to find "any being capable of laying claim to the distinction of being the final end of creation." Even if we could find an "ultimate end of nature," Kant adds, that ultimate end could never "in its character of a natural thing . . . be a final end."[58]

Here a distinction has been drawn, at first rather obscurely, between a "final end of creation" and an "ultimate end of nature."[59] But it turns out that this distinction, however linguistically fine, is absolutely central to a correct understanding of *Judgment,* and more particularly to an understanding of *Judgment's* significance for Kantian politics. It is only by moving ahead to Section 83, however, that one begins to see what the distinction means.

At the beginning of this section Kant asserts that "we have shown" that "there is ample ground" to make us "estimate man as not merely a physical end," like a plant or an animal, but also as "the ultimate end of nature, and the one in relation to whom all other natural things constitute a system of ends."[60] This, of course, is a reference to Section 82, where Kant had argued that if one begins with "lower" forms of existence, one can always ask what "the vegetable kingdom" is "for"; that the plausible answer is that vegetables are "for" the sustenance of herbivorous animals; that the herbivora in their turn are means to the end of the existence of the carnivora; that "at last we get down to the question, what is the end and purpose of these and all the preceding natural kingdoms." And the answer is,

> for man, we say, and the multifarious uses to which his intelligence teaches him to put all these forms of life. He is the ultimate end of creation here upon earth because he is the one and only being upon it that is able to form a conception of ends, and from an aggregate of things purposively fashioned to construct by aid of his reason a system of ends.[61]

For a moment, as is evident, Kant forgets his own crucial distinction between "ultimate end of nature" and "final end of creation," and fuses them in the hybrid phrase "ultimate end of creation." What matters centrally at this point, however, is that Kant is speaking of man's intelligent and purposive, but nonmoral, *use* of things (plants, animals) that are "organized ends," but "at the same time" mere means. (That Kant is not yet thinking of morality is clear in his phrase "multifarious uses.") If man did nothing more than arrange and use organized ends for his own relative ends, he would indeed be the "titular lord of nature," but not yet "the final end of creation."[62] And if man never went beyond the titular lordship of nature, he would exercise, as Gerard Lebrun has wittily said, nothing more than a cosmic *droit du seigneur.*[63]

But the working out of the concept of the final end of creation—that is, man under moral laws—does not really appear until Sections 84– 87; and since Section 83 is of decisive importance not just for Kant's teleology, but more particularly for his politics, it needs a fuller examination. If, at the beginning of this section, one knows that man is the ultimate end of nature in the sense that he is its organizing titular lord, one may still ask, as Kant does, what the end or purpose of man's connection with nature is. That is, one can still ask for what (ultimate) purpose man organizes and employs nature.[64]

Before enlarging on the human employment of nature, however, Kant draws a distinction between the kinds of connection that man could conceivably have with nature. It turns out that the connection "must either be of such a kind that man himself may be satisfied by means of nature and its beneficence," or else it is "the aptitude and skill for all manner of ends for which he may employ nature both external and internal. The former would be the happiness of man, the latter his culture."[65]

Culture, or the capacity to take ends as one's motive, will soon emerge as the key notion of Section 83, but Kant first discusses happiness along familiar lines. One already knows from the *Funda- mental Principles* that happiness cannot be (directly) a moral princi- ple;[66] in Section 83 of *Judgment* one learns that it cannot even be the "ultimate end of nature." For Kant gives a harrowing account of happiness-destroying natural miseries that almost rivals Pascal's *Pen- sées.*[67] It is not just that man is the victim of "external nature," so that he is ravaged by "destructive operations—plague, famine, flood, cold, attacks from animals great and small." What is still worse is that his own "inner nature"—his psychology or, as Kant will have it "pathology"—"betrays him into further misfortunes" such as "the oppression of lordly power" and the "barbarism of wars," so that the human race has "ruin," not happiness, to look forward to.[68] Indeed, Kant insists, the "value of life for us, measured simply by what we enjoy . . . by happiness, is easy to decide. It is less than nothing."[69]

But one already knows, if he has read Section 4 of "Aesthetic Judgment," that "only by what a man does heedless of enjoyment, in complete freedom and independently of what he can procure pas- sively from the hand of nature, does he give to his existence, as the real existence of a person, an absolute worth."[70] It may still be, however, that between the absolute worth of a person under moral laws (or man as the final end of creation) and mere nature viewed as a disappointing fountain of never-materializing happiness, there is a mediating thing—no longer mere nature, but not yet the realm of personality—that helps to convey man from a lower to a higher realm. That is, nature may have, in addition to a low end—happiness that it holds out in imagination but withdraws in reality—a high end that runs up against the edge of the moral sphere. Or, in Kant's own words,

> We must seek out what nature can supply for the purpose of preparing him [man] for what he himself must do in order to be a final end, and we must segregate it from all ends whose possibility rests upon conditions that man can only await at the hands of nature.[71]

The real ultimate end of nature, then, is not an illusory and elusive happiness that one passively awaits; it is "what nature can effect" relative to the "final end" (the moral end) that lies outside nature itself, beyond nature itself. If nature couldn't serve a moral end beyond itself, it would be, for Kant, a ruinous connection that rational beings would shun; for natural inclinations are such that "it must be the universal wish of every rational being to be wholly free of them."[72] It is because man is not wholly free of inclinations, because of his connection with nature, that the kingdoms of the earth must legally realize some of the ends of the kingdom of ends. Even for Kant, nature must be redeemed: not by grace, to be sure, but by morality.[73] Nature redeems itself by overcoming nature; culture, nature's ultimate end, transcends the relative ends of natural inclination. This is why Kant can ask, and then answer, the question he poses in the *Reflexionen zur Anthropologie:* "Why do we grant so little worth to the existence of reasonable and happy beings, who however make no progress in culture? [It is because] they seem only to fill up an empty spot in creation *[das Leere der Schöpfung auszufüllen].*"[74]

But what is the high or ultimate end of nature, which approaches the final end of creation—an approaching that would not have been conceivable at all had not nature's and morality's ends already been shown to be possibly linked by a teleological substrate?

> The production in a rational being of an aptitude for any ends whatever of his own choosing, consequently of such a being in his freedom, is *culture.* Hence it is only culture that can be the ultimate end which we have cause to attribute to nature in respect of the human race. His individual happiness on earth, and, we may say, the mere fact that he is the chief instrument for instituting order and harmony in irrational external nature, are ruled out.[75]

What then are the "elements" of culture, and in what sense does culture as a whole convey man to the borders of a higher realm? These two questions Kant answers in order.

He begins by separating culture into "skill" and "the discipline of the inclinations."[76] Skill mediates between mere nature (*qua* source of "enjoyment") and the objective ends of morality; it does this by developing a general capacity for "the furthering of ends of all kinds." As it facilitates the pursuit of "all kinds" of ends, it does not aim directly or exclusively at the moral end; but it at least develops a nonnatural, nonpassive "aptitude for ends."[77] This aptitude is something *positive*. The "discipline of inclinations," by contrast, is *negative*; just like the "negative freedom" of the *Fundamental Principles*,[78] discipline consists in the liberation of the will from the "despotism of desires whereby . . . we are rendered incapable of exercising a choice of our own."[79] ("Incapable" is of course too strong.) As long as we are "enchained by impulse," we are less likely to take as our motive "the ends of our reason."[80] This last claim links "skill" and "discipline"; skill develops an "aptitude for ends" (generally), and discipline lets us take the "ends of reason" as *our* ends.

In an extended and brilliant passage that follows immediately, Kant manages to relate all of his main political, moral and historical ideas to "culture" (with its branches of skill and discipline). Skill, whose ultimate end is to further an aptitude for ends, "can hardly be developed in the human race otherwise than by means of inequality among men."[81] This permits Kant a set of reflections which concedes much to Rousseau, but which draws positive conclusions from Rousseau's negative ones. The majority of men, Kant argues, work "in a mechanical sort of way" to provide the "necessities of life for the ease and convenience of others who apply themselves to the less necessary branches of culture in science and art." Kant will not say that the practitioners of the less necessary branches are as moral as they are cultured (even though it will soon appear that culture, linking nature and freedom, is the bridge for passing from the lower to the higher). Indeed, the cultured "keep the masses in a state of oppression, with hard work and little enjoyment," even if some higher things ultimately "trickle down." Before this state of affairs gets better it gets worse, for with the arrival of "superfluous" culture—luxury—misfortunes "increase equally on both sides." (Here Rousseau is partly clung to, partly tranformed: superfluity and luxury are cast in a bad light, but they "equally" afflict poor and rich. The former suffer the "force of domination from without," but the latter are gnawed by "seeds of discontent within.")[81] The whole enterprise of civilization, Kant says in a passage that cannot have failed to strike Freud, amounts to "splendid misery";[82] but what redeems that misery is the fact that antagonistic social relations (perfectly expressed in *Idea for a Universal History* as "asocial sociabil-

ity")[83] provide the occasion for the springing up of a "civil community"—a community that will legally realize some moral ends even in
the absence of good will.[84] Thus antagonism in Kant is parallel to the
felix culpa of Christianity: both are bad things that make good ones
possible.

> The formal condition under which nature can alone attain this its real end
> is the existence of a constitution so regulating the mutual relations of men
> that the abuse of freedom by individuals striving one against another is
> opposed by a lawful authority centered in a whole, called a *civil community*.
> For it is only in such a constitution that the greatest development of natural
> tendencies can take place.[85]

In addition to a purely legal or "lawful" civil community, Kant
adds, what is needed above all is "a cosmopolitan whole";[86] here he
encapsulates in a single paragraph much of *Eternal Peace*, published
five years after *Judgment*, and a kind of working up of Section 83 into a
full treatise. The "cosmopolitan whole" would be

> a system of all states that are in danger of acting injuriously to one another.
> In its absence, and with the obstacles that ambition, love of power, and
> avarice, especially on the part of those who hold the reins of authority, put
> in the way even of the possibility of such a scheme, *war* is inevitable.
> Sometimes this results in states splitting up and resolving themselves into
> lesser states, sometimes one state absorbs other smaller states and en-
> deavors to build up a larger unit. But if on the part of men war is a
> thoughtless undertaking, being stirred up by unbridled passions, it is
> nevertheless a deep-seated, maybe far-seeing, attempt on the part of
> supreme wisdom, if not to found, yet to prepare the way for a rule of law
> governing the freedom of states, and thus bring about their unity in a
> system established on a moral basis.[87]

("Moral basis" can only mean that the "end" or purpose of "eternal
peace" is a moral end: within mere culture, as an "aptitude for the
furthering of ends of all kinds," a moral *motive* cannot be counted on.
Even "devils," as will be recalled, must be able to consent to peaceful
conditions from "interested," or even vicious motives.)[58]

Having injected the notions of "civil community" and "eternal
peace" into the bare notion of "skill"—by showing that varying skills
lead to inequality, inequality to misery, misery to antagonism, and
antagonism to the necessity of a legal order, both domestic and
foreign—Kant goes on to work out the idea of "the discipline of the
inclinations." This passage is supremely important, for it more than
any other is *Judgment* links nature, morality, law and art. The natural
inclinations, Kant begins, are "very purposively adapted to the
performance of our essential functions as an animal species"; but

when those inclinations become overly refined they generate "luxury," "food for vanity," and "insatiability."[89] So far Rousseau was right; what he did not wholly see was that culture tends "more and more to prevail over the rudeness and violence of inclinations that belong more to the animal part of our nature."[90] Thus Rousseau cannot have been wholly right, either about the mere perniciousness of the arts and science in the *First Discourse,* or about law as a mere rich man's confidence trick in the *Second Discourse.*[91] Indeed Kant says, in a passage that is obviously an answer to Rousseau's *Discourses,* that

> fine art and the sciences, if they do not make man morally better, yet, by conveying a pleasure that admits of universal communication and by introducing polish and refinement into society, make him civilized. Thus they do much to overcome the tyrannical propensities of sense, and so prepare man for a sovereignty in which reason alone shall have sway.[92]

In his remarkable essay "Conjectural Beginning of Human History," which anticipates *Judgment,* Kant boldly asserts that even Rousseau himself, properly understood, sometimes draws a comparable distinction between culture and nature:

> The assertions of the celebrated J. J. Rousseau . . . are often misinterpreted and do, indeed, have an appearance of inconsistency. In his *[Discourse] on the Influence of the Sciences* and his *[Discourse] on the Inequality of Man* he shows quite correctly that there is an inevitable conflict between culture and the human species, considered as a natural species of which every member ought wholly to attain his natural end. But in his *Emile,* his *Social Contract* and other writings he tries to solve this much harder problem: how culture was to move forward, in order to bring about such a development of the dispositions of mankind, considered as a *moral* species, as to end the conflict between the natural and the moral species. . . . This conflict is in fact altogether unresolved, because culture, considered as the genuine education of man as man and citizen, has perhaps not even begun properly, much less been completed.[93]

If this completion is to be hoped for, through an historical process of "infinite approximation" involving many painful "reversals,"[94] one must first establish a Kantian civil community: for in Kant art, science and a "lawful" constitution are instrumental to negative freedom, to transcending the "tyrannical propensities of sense."[95] Of course law or public legal justice also has a directly moral end which art and science do not. Nonetheless, art is (as Section 59 of "Aesthetic Judgment" argues) the symbol of morality; like law, it contributes to negative freedom.

Now, I say, the beautiful is the symbol of the morally good . . . We shall bring out a few points of this analogy, while taking care, at the same time, not to let the points of difference escape us.
(1) The beautiful pleases *immediately* (but only in reflective intuition, not, like morality, in its concept). (2) It pleases *apart from all interest* . . . (3) *The freedom* of the imagination . . is, in estimating the beautiful, represented as in accord with the understanding's conformity to law (in moral judgments the freedom of the will is thought of as the harmony of the latter with itself according to universal laws of Reason). (4) The subjective principle of the estimate of the beautiful is represented as *universal*, i.e., valid for every man . . . the objective principle of morality is set forth as also universal, i.e., for all individuals . . . and, besides, as cognitive by means of a universal concept [the moral law].[96]

And Kant adds that aesthetic taste, even if only analogous to morality, makes possible "the transition from the charm of sense to habitual moral interest."[97] If he were not thinking of this transition, it would be hard to understand why he should end "Aesthetic Judgment" with an otherwise inexplicable closing passage on "social life regulated by laws," a passage that anticipates the theory of culture in "Teleological Judgment," Section 83, and that insists that the "pleasure which taste declares valid for mankind in general and not merely for the private feeling of each individual" is "the true propaedeutic for laying the foundation both of taste" in the "development of moral ideas and the culture of moral feeling."[98] Culture then, like *telos* itself, is a bridge: it is, for Kant, "not nature, nor yet freedom."[99]

VI

Surely, then, Kant's culture—including legality, peace, art and science—is mid-way (as it were) between nature and freedom. At least culture is instrumental to negative freedom; it overcomes (if only legally or, in art, aesthetically) the dominion of sense, and thus prepares the way for positive freedom, for self-determination through "ought," through "objective ends." Thus Section 83 of *Judgment* is parallel to the First Appendix to *Eternal Peace*; both argue for quasi-moral "veneers" that are not themselves wholly moral but are morally important, morality's instruments.[100]

It seems, then, that Yirmiahu Yovel cannot be wholly right when he asserts, in *Kant and the Philosophy of History*, that "even to the best of states cannot be attributed a moral value per se."[101] That "per se" is obscure; in a revealing footnote Yovel supports himself by quoting *Conflict of the Faculties*, which had said that a good political order can be attained "without the moral foundation of mankind having to be enlarged in the least," without "an ever-growing quantity of morality with regard to intention."[102] Yovel pays insufficient attention to those last four words; Kantian politics must indeed make do with mere legal intentions, but it must (at the same time) somehow pay homage to morals and its ends. Yovel, however, usually will not allow Kant's moral philosophy to *have* any ends ("human reason must abide only by those universal rules it sets up by itself");[103] therefore, "true politics" has no "objective" moral ends to which it *could* "pay homage." Thus Yovel, like Lewis White Beck in Chapter 3, sometimes transforms Kant into "deepened" Rousseau: the moral law is made, not found.[104] The great strength of Yovel's book is that it shows, better than any work of recent years, how important *Judgment* is for an understanding of Kant's political and historical thought; the great weakness is that the book suddenly diminishes the weight of purpose at the most important point of all—in the *Fundamental Principles'* account of "objective ends."[105] In Yovel one is left with a formalistic Kant in ethics who is also a teleological Kant in politics and history; an opportunity to find the complete unity of Kant slips away.

On the present radically teleological reading of all of Kant, by contrast, politics can pay homage to some of the ends of morality, if not to its incentives, and it can also supply the negative freedom that will facilitate self-determination through objective ends. Yovel, despite the real value of his book, drives politics too far back into mere nature; he doesn't sufficiently stress Kant's notion of culture as a mediator between nature and morality.

But if the realm of culture brings one to the perimeter of a higher realm, the moral, what is the character of the moral realm itself? That of course one already knows in large measure; Section 84 of Judgment is the *Fundamental Principles'* kingdom of ends reexamined (now in a teleological context linking *all* ends.)[106] To be sure, there is not a perfectly smooth transition from culture to morality; as Yovel has strikingly put it, "the final end of creation [man under moral laws] is not discovered by a reflective judgment but is imposed on reality by practical reason. In this sense it is a break in the continuity of the third *Critique*."[107] This, presumably, refers—or could reasonably refer—to Kant's claim in "Aesthetic Judgment" that the "absolutely good" or morally good involves a necessity "resting upon concepts *a priori*"; that the morally good is "not a mere claim, but a command upon every one to assent"; that the morally good "is not ascribed to nature but to freedom, and that in a determinant and not merely a reflective judgment."[108] But this, like Yovel's insistence on the nonmoral character of the state, can be exaggerated; after all, the Kantian state, though it belongs in the realm of culture, legally enforces some moral ends—

ends that Yovel underrates, or rather vacillates on, since he sometimes insists on our "constituting" moral laws, but sometimes speaks
of the "final end" as "imposed by practical reason."[109] If culture is the
high end of nature, nature itself is connected (at the level of its
supersensible substrate) with the *purposiveness* of practical law. So the
transition from civic culture to the moral final end of creation is *as
smooth as it could be*, given that culture at best promotes moral ends by
legal (or sometimes aesthetic) means.

A final end of creation, part 84 begins (always supposing the "final
nexus in the world to be real")[110] is an end "that does not require any
other end as the condition of its possibility." Such a final end "is not
an end which nature would be competent to realize or produce . . .
because it is one that is unconditioned."[111] (By contrast, in nature—at
least *qua* "thing of sense," not as culture—there is nothing that is not
conditioned.)[112]

> Now we have in the world beings of but one kind whose causality is
> teleological, or directed to ends, and which at the same time are beings of
> such a character that the law according to which they have to determine
> ends for themselves is represented by them themselves as unconditioned
> and not dependent on anything in nature, but as necessary in itself. The
> being of this kind is man, but man regarded as noumenon. He is the only
> natural creature whose peculiar objective characterization is nevertheless
> such as to enable us to recognize in him a supersensible faculty—his
> *freedom*—and to perceive both the law of the causality and the object of
> freedom which that faculty is able to set before itself as the highest end—
> the supreme good in the world.[113]

It is not open to us, Kant goes on, in the case of man "considered as
a moral agent," to ask: "For what end *(quem in finem)* does he exist?
His existence inherently involves the highest end." And in virtue of
his being the "highest end," man is entitled (positively) to "subject
the whole of nature," or at least is entitled (negatively) not to be
"subjected to any influence" on nature's part. For without man "the
chain of mutually subordinated ends would have no ultimate point of
attachment."[114]

All of this is amplified in Section 86, where Kant draws together the
whole of what he has said about physical and moral teleology.

> There is a judgment which even the commonest understanding finds
> irresistible when it reflects upon the existence of the things in the world
> and the real existence of the world itself. It is the verdict that all the
> manifold forms of life, co-ordinated though they may be with the greatest
> art and concatenated with the utmost variety of purposive adaptations . . .
> would all exist for nothing, if man, or rational beings of some sort,

were not to be found in their midst. Without man, in other words, the whole of creation would be a mere wilderness, a thing in vain, and have no final end. Yet it is not man's cognitive faculty, that is, theoretical reason, that forms the point of reference which alone gives its worth to the existence of all else in the world—as if the meaning of his presence in the world was that there might be some one in it that could make it an object of *contemplation*. For if this contemplation of the world brought to light nothing but things without a final end, the existence of the world could not acquire a worth from the fact of its being known.[115]

It is already clear that "worth," or at least *absolute* worth, cannot rest on the happiness or enjoyment that Section 82 had earlier shown to be chimerical:

> It is not by well-being, not by enjoyment, whether bodily or mental, not, in a word, by happiness, that we value that absolute worth. For the fact that man, when he does exist, makes happiness his own final purpose, affords us no conception of any reason why he should exist at all. . . . It is the worth which he alone can give to himself, and which consists in what he does—in the manner in which and the principles upon which he acts in the freedom of his faculty of desire [will], and not as a link in the chain of nature [that matters]. In other words a good will is that whereby man's existence can alone possess an absolute worth, and in relation to which the existence of the world can have a *final end*.[116]

The last sentence is of course problematical, since if one respected only persons who actually have a good will, one might be left with no one to respect; it must then be the case that one should respect those who are *capable* of good will, that is, all persons.[117] This alteration is suggested by Kant himself in Section 87, where he says that "if there is to be a final end at all, which reason must assign *a priori*, then it can only be man—or any rational being in the world—*subject to moral laws*." Kant goes on to add, "I say deliberately, *under* moral laws. It is not man in accordance with moral laws, that is to say, human beings living in conformity with such laws, that is the final end of creation." For this "would be to assert more than we know."[118] We *know* (from the *Fundamental Principles*) what ought to be, and (from *Practical Reason*) that this "ought" is a "fact of reason";[119] we do not know (as *Pure Reason* insists) whether anyone has ever actually done what he ought to have done, simply from a moral incentive.[120]

With this alteration in mind, one can move to Kant's final thoughts on *telos* as a unifying principle culminating in man under moral laws, found in *Judgment's* final section, "General Remark on Teleology":

> For reasons asks: for what end do all these things of nature exist which exhibit art-forms? And for what end does man himself exist—man with

whose consideration we are inevitably brought to a halt, he being the ultimate end of nature, so far as we can conceive? Why does this universal nature exist, and what is the final end of all its wealth and variety of art? To suggest that it was made for enjoyment, or to be gazed at . . . cannot satisfy reason. For a personal worth, which man can only give to himself, is pre-supposed by reason, as the sole condition upon which he and his existence can be a final end. In the absence of this personal worth—which alone admits of a definite conception—the ends of nature do not dispose of the question.[121]

But the concept of ends generally does dispose of a very large question, namely the one that Kant poses at the outset of *Judgment*: why do the different realms of the critical philosophy "not form one realm"?[122] By the end of the *Third Critique*, after teleology has been transformed from a "dogmatic" into a "critical" principle, the outlines of that single realm begin to emerge. It is a single realm in which politics, law and eternal peace, as facets of a culture that also embraces art and science, fit into a remarkably comprehensive scheme based on "purposive unity" as the "highest" unity. It is in *Judgment* above all that the place of politics in Kant's philosophy is wholly clear.[123]

VII

Once one sees that a Kantian civil community or system of public legal justice fits into the realm of culture (viewed as the transition from nature to the moral sphere), certain passages in the overtly political writings—*Eternal Peace*, the *Rechtslehre*—take on a quality, a strong relation to the three *Critiques*, that one would not have seen without an appreciation of "Teleological Judgment."

In Section 55 of the *Rechtslehre*, for example, Kant is discussing "what right the state has *as against its own subjects* to employ them in a war on other states, and to expend or hazard their possessions or even their lives in the process." To decide this question, he uses distinctions drawn in *Judgment*, which had been published seven years before the *Rechtslehre*. He begins by pointing out that a country may produce "various natural products" (such as potatoes) which, though they are "nature" from one point of view, are also "artifacts of the state . . . because of their very abundance." For food production would not be what it is "if there were no state or proper government in control."[124] The question then is, are citizens in any sense artifacts or products of the state as well?

Now one can say that vegetables (e.g., potatoes) and domestic animals, in quantity at least, are *made* by human beings, and that they may therefore be used, expended or consumed (i.e., killed) at will. One might therefore appear justified in saying that the supreme power in the state, the sovereign, has the right to lead his subjects to war as if on a hunt, or into battle as if on an excursion, simply because they are for the most part produced by the sovereign himself.[125]

This "legal" argument—of which, Kant says sarcastically, monarchs are "no doubt dimly aware"[126]—is valid in the case of potatoes and animals, which can indeed be the property of human beings, and therefore mere means to human ends. But, Kant insists,

It is absolutely impermissible to apply it to human beings themselves, particularly in their capacity as citizens. For a citizen must always be regarded as a co-legislative member of the state (i.e., not just as a means, but also as an end in himself), and he must therefore give his free consent through his representatives not only to the waging of war in general, but also to every particular declaration of war. Only under this limiting condition may the state put him to service in dangerous enterprises.[127]

All of this is simply Sections 83–86 of *Judgment* applied to a particular political case and fused with Kant's argument that rational citizens in a republic would ordinarily dissent from war, not consent to it.[128] This passage, indeed, is the perfect illustration of a point made provisionally in Chapter 1: that citizens in a Kantian republic, acting under the "Idea" of the social contract (the idea of everyone's consenting or dissenting), might well choose moral ends—above all eternal peace—from purely legal motives (such as the desire not to suffer from dangerous enterprises).

Another example—this one drawn from *Eternal Peace*—will prove the point. In the First Appendix to that work, in an argument considered at the outset of this study, Kant argues that if "there is neither freedom nor any moral law based on freedom, but only a state in which everything that happens or can happen simply obeys the mechanical workings of nature," politics would be "the art of utilizing nature [the facts of human psychology] for the government of men." This political reliance on nature would then be "the whole of practical wisdom," and the "concept of right" would be "only an empty idea," not even a "limiting condition" restricting what politics can do.[129]

This distinction between *nature* and *right*—where *nature* means the mere mechanical workings that cannot even explain a blade of grass and not the high nature of culture—is really a development of a point made in "Teleological Judgment," Section 90, in which Kant had argued against false "analogies" between government and physics: "on the analogy of the law of the equality of action and reaction in the mutual attraction and repulsion of bodies I am able to picture to my mind the social relations of the members of a commonwealth regulated by civil laws."[130] However, although one can picture a commonwealth in this way—and Kant knew that both Hobbes and Locke had used analogies drawn from physics[131]—one ought not to, since one cannot really transfer properties between essentially dissimilar things. One must know when Newton should yield to Rousseau.

For, Kant goes on in *Eternal Peace*, if one thinks of politics as mere nature, not even as culture, as mediator, one will commit mistakes at best and crimes at worst. This will come about mainly by claiming that human nature makes a rightful politics impossible. "Moralizing politicians," as contrasted with "moral politicians," Kant says, will "try to cover up political principles which are contrary to right, under the pretext that human nature is incapable of attaining the good which reason prescribes as an idea.[132] And in that way moralizing politicians "make progress impossible, and eternalize the violation of right."[133] (Kant puts a comparable thought still more strongly in *Conflict of the Faculties*, when he says that "our politicians" tell us to "take men as they are, and not as the world's uninformed pedants or good-natured dreamers fancy that they ought to be." But, Kant goes on, the expression " 'as they are' ought to read 'as we have made them by unjust coercion, by treacherous designs which the government is in a good position to carry out.' ")[134]

Kant uses this same sort of analysis—an analysis that leads to his most radical political thoughts (which are then softened and moderated elsewhere)[135]—to illuminate the second of the three maxims that he thinks moralizing politicians use to cover their crimes: "act first and justify your actions later . . . if you are the perpetrator [of crime], deny it ; . . . divide and rule."[136] The second of these, for Kant, plainly involves an illegitimate appeal to a low nature:

> If you have committed a crime, for instance, in order to lead your people to desperation and thence to rebellion, deny that the guilt is yours. Maintain instead that it arose from the intransigence of the subjects; or if you have seized control of a neighboring people, say that the very nature of man is responsible, for if he does not anticipate others in resorting to violence, he may count on it that they will anticipate and overpower him.[137]

These maxims, of course, amount precisely to a politics that does not "pay homage to morals." This is why (still in the First Appendix to *Eternal Peace*) one should never give a "hearing" to those "political moralists" who "produce the very evil they predict" by insisting that the "natural mechanism" of human pathology makes rightful politics an impossibility. For such people "put men into the same class as other living machines, which only need to realize consciously that they are not free beings for them to become in their own eyes the most wretched of all earthly creatures."[138]

Again, all of this is *Judgment* applied; it is Section 83's insistence on the distinction between nature as mechanism and nature as culture (bordering on morality), used to throw light on the false politics that pays homage only to expediency. (Surely W. B. Gallie calls the First Appendix "the most badly organized and over-abstract précis of philosophical argument that [Kant] ever perpetrated," turning *Eternal Peace* into "a fantastic literary farrago," simply because he does not see that that Appendix *is* an application of *Judgment*.)[139] And so it is no accident that precisely this part of *Eternal Peace* ends with the central claim that "true politics cannot take a single step without first paying homage to morals."[140] This must, as we know, refer to the *ends* of morals; and in *Judgment* those ends are brought into coherent relation to all other Kantian ends.[141]

VIII

To be sure, there has always been disagreement about the worth of Kant's effort to find a teleological substrate that bridges nature, morality and art—even when it is kept in mind that *only* morality (with freedom as its *ratio essendi*) has "objective" ends (some of which are then "legally' realized), that nature and art are only "estimated" teleologically by "reflective" judgment. Hegel insisted in *Glauben und Wissen* (1802–3) that the *Critique of Judgment* is "the most interesting point in the Kantian system," but then accused Kant, in effect, of suppressing his own better knowledge. Kant knew, Hegel insists, that "the substratum of nature" (as well as of art) is "intelligible," even that it is "rational and identical with all Reason"; but he perversely stuck to his idea that finite human intelligence cannot attain a divine being's intuitive knowledge of the rational substrate.[142] According to Hegel, Kant briefly glimpses reason as the universal substrate of morality, nature and art, but then wantonly "corrupts" the "highest Idea" by "exalting . . . finite cognition" above it.[143] (As for the practical reason that appears in Kantian morality, Hegel sticks to his usual view that the categorical imperative is a "tyranny" of practical reason *qua* duty over human nature, whose "formalism" determines "nothing.")[144] For Hegel the *Critique of Judgment* is that part of Kant that is closer to the truth, "the only interesting aspect"; therefore its failure is all the "harder" to endure.[145] (In *Glauben und Wissen*, of course, Hegel says not a word about Kantian politics as the legal realization of moral ends; for he thought that Kant had failed to recognize *real* ends, and that to view the state as a mere legal superstructure—possibly even erected by "devils"—was a failure to see the state as the "prodigious transfer" of reason from the "inner" to the "external" world. Surely Hegel's insistence in the *Philosophy of Right* that "what stands between reason as self-conscious mind, and reason as an actual world before our eyes . . . is the fetter of some abstraction"[146] is directed at Kant as much as at anyone. For Hegel the Kantian antithesis between legality and morality, between the juridical commonwealth under coercive laws and the ethical commonwealth under laws of virtue, must be "canceled and preserved"; that is why Hegel calls the state an "ethical institution.")[147]

In post-Hegelian times *Judgment* has received mixed notices. Nietzsche, whose loathing of Kant is well known, may have been thinking of the Kantian notion that a state or civil community is the key aspect of culture when he asserted in *Twilight of the Idols* that

> Culture and the state—one should not deceive oneself about this—are antagonists: '*Kultur-Staat*' is merely a modern idea. One lives off the other, one thrives at the expense of the other. All great ages of culture are ages of political decline: what is great culturally has always been unpolitical, even *anti-political*.[148]

What Nietzsche means by "culture" is clarified by the figures that he goes on to treat as "spirits" who "count from a European point of view": Goethe, Heine, Wagner, Hegel, Schopenhauer.[149] Clearly for Nietzsche politics is unworthy to count as part of real culture: "if one spends oneself for power, for power politics, for economics, world trade, parliamentarianism, and military interests—if one spends in *this* direction the quantum of understanding, seriousness, will, and self-overcoming which one represents, then it will be lacking for the other direction."[150]

To be sure, the notion that it is mistaken to count politics as a branch of culture was not Nietzsche's deepest complaint about Kant, or even about the *Critique of Judgment*; the fatal error of the *Third Critique* is that of believing that mankind under moral laws is the final end of creation. *Judgment* is plainly the work being attacked in Sections 705–707 of *The Will to Power*, and Nietzsche begins the assault on the *The Third Critique* with a swipe at the close of the *Second*—the stars-above-me, moral-law-within-me passage.

> I see above me, glittering under the stars, the tremendous rat's tail of errors that has hitherto counted as the highest inspiration of humanity. "All happiness is a consequence of virtue, all virtue is a consequence of free will . . ."
>
> The "conscious world" cannot serve as a starting point for values. . . . In relation to the vastness and multiplicity of collaboration and mutual opposition encountered in the life of every organism, the *conscious* world

of feelings, intentions and valuations is a small section. We have no right whatever to posit this piece of consciousness [man] as the aim and wherefore of this total phenomenon of life . . . it is a piece of naiveté to posit pleasure or spirituality or morality or any other particular of the sphere of consciousness as the highest value—even perhaps to justify "the world" by this means.

This is my basic objection to all philosophic-moralistic cosmologies and theodicies . . . one kind of means has been misunderstood as an end; conversely, life and the enhancement of power has been debased to a means.[151]

For Nietzsche, then, Kant is generally wrong; he is more particularly wrong in trying to "justify" the world through moral consciousness and in treating life as a means to the end of duty; he is most particularly wrong in letting politics have a place in a culture whose *real* content is the "creative mastery" of a Goethe or a Heine.[52] Given Nietzsche's transvalued—ultimately purely aesthetic—values, the *Critique of Judgment* offers not the highest unity but the highest falsehood. For Nietzsche beauty is not the mere symbol of morality; it is the crystallization of the life and power to which everything is a means.[153]

Nietzsche's aestheticism—the worst thing of which he can be fairly accused[154]—leads to a kind of inverted Rousseaueanism. Rousseau fears that art and science will corrupt morality and citizenship;[155] Nietzsche that morality and citizenship will corrupt art and science and turn the correct distinction between good and bad into the false distinction between good and evil.[156] Kant keeps in balance what Rousseau and Nietzsche drive to brilliant extremes: against Nietzsche, public legal justice is the core of culture (but not at the expense of the artistic genius celebrated in "Aesthetic Judgment");[157] against Rousseau, art and science make a civilizing contribution without being directly moral.[158] (One is sometimes tempted to think, with Rickert, that Kant is *the Kulturforscher*.)[159]

If Nietzsche was unpersuaded that politics counts as culture, and still more by Kantianism in general, his eminent near-contemporary, the historian of philosophy Wilhelm Windelband, called the *Third Critique* "the highest synthesis of the critical philosophy: the application of the category of practical reason to the object of the theoretical . . . a looking at nature from the point of view of purposiveness or adaptation to ends."[160] In speaking of purposiveness as a "point of view" usable in "looking at nature," Windelband keeps close to Kant himself, and is able to avoid Hegel's charge of suppressing better knowledge. Windelband goes on to note that "the category of practical reason"—purposiveness or ends—is not just "applied" to the estimation of nature in *Judgment*, but also is "everywhere authoritative in [Kant's] construction" of "right" in "the community of men."[161] And the celebrated Kant scholar H. J. Paton was not far from Windelband when he said, in 1938, that *Judgment* "may be regarded as the coping stone of the Critical Philosophy. Only when its teaching has been understood can we be in a position to grasp fully the relation between Kant's speculative philosophy and his ethical philosophy, and to follow the structure of his system as a whole."[162]

However, the most recent *Judgment* scholarship has been less favorable: in his remarkably thorough study entitled *Kant and the Claims of Taste* (1979), Paul Guyer notes that Kant's "indeterminate idea of a supersensible substratum" that somehow bridges art, morality and nature is something that a "skeptic" will view with "suspicion," and seems to speak for himself when he says that "no modern reader will find it very attractive."[163] Unfortunately the reason for that unattractiveness is never fully given, since Guyer believes that the implausibility of a teleological supersensible substrate is "too obvious to require any argument."[164] A modern reader will not be persuaded that art is the symbol of morality, and that both are linked to nature by *telos*, Guyer says, partly because of difficulties that Kant himself insists on:

> Why should Kant have been so cautious in going beyond his original interpretation of the link between aesthetic and moral judgment after first suggesting an apparently much stronger result for the thesis of symbolism [of morality by beauty]? A good reason for his caution is the fact that sensitivity to a *symbol* of morality is not itself a state requisite for moral performance, and thus not something which can be demanded as part of a demand for moral action. . . . A final reason for caution in trying to cash in the promise of beauty's symbolism of the morally good is the fact that one of the ways in which beauty may represent the basis of morality—namely, by its representation of a supersensible ground . . .—depends on the thesis that aesthetic judgment does indeed involve such a representation [of a substrate]; this, as we have seen, is a highly questionable thesis.[165]

It should be noted that nothing Guyer says—and he obviously speaks carefully—militates against the Kantian state as the legal realization of some moral ends; all he does say is that those practical ends are not successfully related by Kant to nature's ends or art's ends through a supersensible substrate.[166] But morality and legality, for Kant, are two strands of practice, and Guyer does not question— since he barely treats—Kant's notion that practice *has* ends.

Guyer's doubts about *Judgment* rest mainly on his skepticism about any .possible (strong) connection between morality and art; the doubts of J. D. McFarland, author of *Kant's Concept of Teleology* (1970), relate more to missing spans in a bridge connecting morality and nature. In a 1974 essay, "The Bogus Unity of the Kantian Philosophy," McFarland argues that while "it is indeed widely held that in the *Critique of Judgment*, Kant succeeded in bringing the critical philosophy to a significant degree of systematic, even organic, unity . . . by means of teleological conceptions," this claim is largely "bogus."[167] The reason for that, in McFarland's view, is that Kant could have established a real relation between nature's purposes and human moral purposes only through a God who unifies these purposes:

> It is unquestionable that Kant believes purposes and "orderly adaptations" to be found in nature. But he also believes that there can be no systematic point of attachment for natural purposes unless they are all ultimately synthesized under the conception of creation as a complete purposive whole directed to the fulfilment of man's moral objectives. This would mean that natural purposes would, in *some* way, form a sub-class within the over-all morally purposive unity. . . . We have seen that it is as a moral being that man is entitled to regard himself as the final end of creation, and that he must therefore take it as a matter of faith that his moral end, the *summum bonum*, is also God's final end in the creation of the world, and that the world is, therefore, a systematic, purposive, moral unity.[168]

From this McFarland concludes that "it is faith in a God whose end is also the final end of man that gives the point of systematic attachment between nature and moral action and thereby ensures the synthesis of natural and moral purposes."[169]

He goes on to argue that Kant's radical theological doubts, particularly about proving the real existence of God from the "evidence" of purposiveness or design in nature, kept him from finding a God who could synthesize natural purpose and moral purpose. This must be recognized as a formidable objection; but—without undertaking an excursion into Kant's theology—what is interesting is that in defense of his claim that Kant has failed to find a God-guaranteed synthesis, McFarland quotes this already familiar passage from *Judgment*:

> There is a judgment which even the commonest understanding finds irresistible. . . . It is the verdict that all the manifold forms of life . . . would exist for nothing, if man, or rational beings of some sort, were not to be found in their midst. Without man, in other words, the whole of creation would be a mere wilderness, a thing in vain, and have no final end.[170]

This passage, of course, makes no reference at all to God; it terminates in man. McFarland's argument neglects Kant's notion that man is the final end of creation, and that no end beyond man can be known (strictly speaking). Indeed, the inability to "arrive" at God *qua* final end might even be the condition of man's *being* the final end; otherwise Malebranche might be right about man's being "for" divine purposes.[171] McFarland's view that *Judgment* fails to provide a synthesis is right only if Kant's theological doubts are the decisive thing; but if one stresses reason and reason's ends as the known substrate of morality and as the estimated substrate of nature and art, then a (Godless) synthesis remains possible. As in Guyer's case, nothing McFarland says works against the Kantian republic as legal realizer of a moral *telos;* indeed, McFarland himself says that *Judgment* does establish, negatively, that "the world of nature with its instances of purposes and orderly adaptations . . . is not incompatible with a view of the world as a morally purposive whole."[172] That makes it possible to preserve culture as a mediator between mechanical nature and the kingdom of ends, as "not nature, nor yet freedom."[173]

If Guyer and McFarland have important doubts about Kantian teleology as a bridge—and their work shows, hearteningly, that *Judgment* is as carefully read and warmly contested as when it was new—the judgment of Windelband that the *Third Critique* is the highest synthesis of Kantianism is, in effect, reaffirmed in Hannah Arendt's posthumous essay on "Judging," (grafted by her editors as an Appendix onto *The Life of the Mind: Willing*).[174] Quoting some lines from "Aesthetic Judgment" in which Kant insists that "everyone expects and requires from everyone else this reference to general communication" of disinterested aesthetic delight, as if by "an original contract dictated by mankind itself," Arendt argues persuasively that "at this point the *Critique of Judgment* joins effortlessly Kant's deliberation about a united mankind living in eternal peace."[175] For Arendt, then, the disinterestedness and the generality of aesthetic judgment do make the beautiful the symbol of the moral.

It is this which leads her to say that the *Critique of Judgment* is more closely "connected with the political than with anything in the other Critiques."[176] She also finds—ingeniously—a further bridge between the beautiful and the practical that has remained unsuspected (or at last unstated) by any other commentator: just as aesthetic judgment or appreciation is the (rather passive) activity of a *spectator* who is not a "maker," Arendt says, so too the distinction between *viewing* and *doing* might account for the fact that while in *Conflict of the Faculties* Kant could insist that the French Revolution arouses "in the hearts of all spectators (who are not engaged in this games themselves) a wishful participation that borders closely on enthusiasm," he could still say in other works that "revolution . . . is at all times unjust."[177] In political judgment, as in aesthetic judgment, Arendt insists, there is a "clash between the principle according to which you act and the principle according to which you judge."[178] (Unfortunately, at just this point the editors of "Judging" cut Arendt's manuscript, making it impossible to know whether her detailed *defense* of the distinction between acting and judging might rescue Kant's theory of revolution from the incoherence and vacillation that is often thought to afflict it. But of this more will be said in Chapter 5.)

Of course it is not just "Aesthetic Judgment" that Arendt finds important for Kant's politics; she also gives full weight to "Teleological Judgment," saying that

> In the *Critique of Judgment* you also find the idea of purposiveness: Every object, says Kant, as a particular needing and containing the ground of its actuality in itself, has a purpose. The only objects that seem purposeless are aesthetic objects, on one side, and men, on the other. You cannot ask *quem ad finem*—for what purpose?—since they are good for nothing. But . . . purposeless art objects as well as the seemingly purposeless variety of nature have the 'purpose' of pleasing men, making them feel at home in the world. This can never be proved; but Purposiveness is an idea to regulate your reflections in your reflective judgments.[179]

The phrase "good for nothing" is a little unfortunate, even if one sees what is meant. But what matters is that Arendt has seen that *Judgment* may well be, in Hegel's words, "the most interesting point in the Kantian system."[180] Arendt also sees the political significance of the work, which is rare; she, like Ernst Cassirer before her, awards the palm to culture broadly conceived.

Arendt's reading of *Judgment* is, not surprisingly, not too far from that of Cassirer himself—at least not far from his brilliant 1936 essay, "Critical Idealism as a Philosophy of Culture" (finally published in 1979). Cassirer begins by emphasizing that, for Kant, art has "a sphere of its own . . . an independent meaning and an independent value." But "without being reducible to morality, art is nonetheless in a close relation to morality, a relation which, according to Kant, must be conceived not as a real and, so to speak, physical one, but rather as a symbolic one."[181] And Cassirer goes on to say, in a specially fine paragraph,

> Beauty by no means coincides with morality nor does it depend on it; but it may be called the symbol of morality. For it is by beauty that a new faculty of the human mind is revealed by which it passes beyond the sphere of empirical individuality, by which it strives after a universal ideal of humanity. As Kant expresses his thought, art and morality, without being the same, are nevertheless connected and coherent with each other by their relation to a common basis—to that basis which in the *Critique of Judgment* is called "das übersinnliche Substrat der Menscheit," the "intelli-

gible substratum of humanity." According to Kant, this intelligible substratum is no datum of our empirical world, but it may be and must be conceived as an ideal of reason, an ideal to which all the different energies of the human mind may be referred and in which they find their unity and harmony.[182]

In emphasizing that beauty does not "depend" on morality (nor morality on beauty), Cassirer meets Guyer's main worry about beauty's symbolism of morality. But Cassirer manages to preserve Kant's "intelligible substratum of humanity," which can only be reason and its ends, as an "ideal" to which the different "energies of the human mind" (morality, legality, science, art) can be "referred" and in which "they find their unity and harmony." By speaking of an "ideal," Cassirer avoids turning Kant into Hegel; but by preserving the "intelligible substratum" he shores up Kant's theory of culture as mediator between mechanical nature and the realm of ends. As is characteristic of him, Cassirer finds the true balance; he gives Kant the most favorable reading that is consistent with limitations stressed by Kant himself.[183]

Certainly one may use the very same "energies of the human mind" that Cassirer finds united and harmonized in the "intelligible substratum of humanity" to argue—as does Gerard Lebrun in his cleverly titled *Kant et la Fin de la Métaphysique*—that "whatever [Leon] Brunschvicg may think [in *Le Progrès de la Conscience*], the third *Critique* is not the moment of reconciliation" in Kant. No doubt, Lebrun remarks, *Judgment* is the converging place "of all those shadowy zones where, incomprehensibly, what is sensed seems to communicate with the understanding, nature with art, the fine arts with morality; but these subterranean conciliations attenuate nothing of the practical cleavages in the system."[184] But Lebrun seems to find the relation between culture and morality less problematical; for he says something that, while presenting itself as a "critique" of *Judgment*, in reality simply reaffirms authentic Kantian distinctions:

> In fact, the premonition of morality in culture is never anything but *negative:* it is the manifest inadequacy of reason for [the attainment] of happiness which brought us to believe that reason has a higher function; it is the evils that human egoism inflicts on us which lets us see . . . that an 'aptitude for higher ends is hidden in us.' History indicates just exactly where one should not look for the sense of "the human": among men.[185]

If the slightly cryptic last sentence refers to Kant's own argument, in *Idea for a Universal History*, that history so far has been a "senseless course" of "childish malice and destructiveness,"[186] then Lebrun's entire paragraph—particularly his insistence that Kantian culture is negative, the mere instrument of positive freedom and higher ends—

is a paraphrase and not a critique of Kant. Perhaps the reason that Lebrun *thinks* that he is criticizing *Judgment* by calling Kantian culture a merely negative premonition of morality is that he has confused *Judgment* and the *Idea for a Universal History;* for in the *Idea,* written six years before *Judgment,* Kant had made an argument which he carefully altered in the *Third Critique.* In the *Idea* he had said that in a "law-governed social order," all of man's talents are "gradually developed," and that the "first true steps are taken from barbarism to culture";[187] this much was retained in *Judgment.* But he had gone on to assert that, through culture, "a beginning is made towards establishing a way of thinking which can with time transform the primitive natural capacity for moral discrimination into definite practical principles, and thus a pathologically enforced social union [a law-governed social order] is transformed into a *moral* whole."[188] In *Judgment* this "evolution" of the legal *into* the moral is ruled out, and culture is only negative. Indeed Kant could never have drawn his final distinction between a coercive juridical commonwealth that realizes some moral ends on a legal basis, and an ethical commonwealth operating under noncoercive laws of virtue, had he adhered to the *Idea's* notion that culture and legality can *become* morality.[189] Had Kant stuck to the doctrine of *Idea for a Universal History* in writing *Judgment,* he would certainly have been open to Kelly's already considered charge that "it should be impossible [in Kant] for citizenship of public law-abidingness to make men moral."[190] Lebrun, however, in saying that *Judgment's* culture is *merely* negative, seems to forget that the *Third Critique* abandons a bad argument that Kant ought never to have made. In granting that culture is at least morality's premonition, Lebrun is closer to Arendt and Cassirer than he would wish to be.

Despite the important and carefully stated doubts of Guyer, McFarland and Lebrun, a moderately persuasive case has been made by Windelband, Cassirer and Arendt that holds that the *Critique of Judgment,* by linking the various Kantian realms through reconceived teleology, finds a place for public legal justice and eternal peace *within* culture viewed as a mediator between nature and freedom. It was certainly a bold experiment on Kant's part to link nature and morality by a teleological bridge, then to find culture and the state in the middle of that bridge. In establishing a new *purposive* relation between nature and freedom, Kant dared to "crossbreed the strains whose purity he had developed for two decades" (Leonard Krieger).[191] Evidently he had decided that the "two worlds" are too problematical, if moral purposes are to be realized *in* a nature that mere purposeless mechanism seems (to us) unable to explain. If a reconstructed, critical teleology could link (without ever equating) nature and morality through an intelligible or supersensible substrate that also accommodates art and the civil community, might a bold striking out for systematic unity not be worth a very large risk? If the risk involved in finding the highest systematic unity was worthwhile—and Arendt and Cassirer make it seem a gamble that paid off—then Kantian politics has its "locus" (as Krieger says) "in that crucial realm that connect[s] morality with the temporal world . . . [and converts] freedom into a form not incompatible with the laws of nature."[192]

To be sure, someone could say that Kant's reconceived teleology is a mere reworking of political, moral and scientific elements long familiar in Aristotle. The *Critique of Judgment,* after all, might be viewed as a gigantic meditation on Aristotle's *Metaphysics* 994b:

> The final cause *[telos]* is an end, and that sort of end which is not for the sake of something else, but for whose sake eveything else is; so that if there is to be a last term of this sort, the process will not be infinite; but if there is no such term, there will be no final cause, but those who maintain the infinite series eliminate the Good without knowing it (yet no one would try to do anything if he were not going to come to a limit); nor would there be reason in the world; the reasonable man, at least, always acts for a purpose, and this is a limit; for the end is a limit. [193]

This remarkable passage can be given a perfectly Kantian sense simply by saying that Aristotle's phrase, "for whose sake everything else is," refers to "man considered as a moral agent" (*Judgment,* Section 84).[194] But if Kant could embrace *Metaphysics* 994b, that does not mean that his whole teleology is quasi-Aristotelian; for Kant the only knowable objective ends are moral ones, while nature and art are merely *interpreted* teleologically.[195] In Aristotle, by contrast, one can *know* that both natural things and works of art have their objectively real *telos.* As he says in the *Physics,* "it is both by nature and for an end that the swallow makes its nest and the spider its web, and plants grow leaves for the sake of the fruit and send their roots down (not up) for the sake of nourishment."[196] And he adds that "art partly completes what nature in unable to elaborate, and partly imitates her. If therefore artificial products are for the sake of an end, so clearly also are natural products."[197] For Kant, Aristotle "says" more than he "knows."[198]

But Kant would not quarrel *primarily* with Aristotle's understanding of nature; Aristotle's thought as a whole is heavily colored by biology, and it was precisely biology (the "blade of grass" problem) that partly occasioned *Judgment* itself. What Kant would contest more centrally is Aristotle's occasional effort to assimilate moral ends to natural ones (in the *Politics*), and his usual effort to define the highest human end as contemplation, rather than moral action (in the *Nicoma-*

chean Ethics, for example). The occasional assimilation of politics to biology and biological ends is specially marked in Book I of the *Politics*: "because it is the completion of associations existing by nature, every *polis* exists by nature, having itself the same quality as the earlier associations [such as the household] from which it grew. It is the end or consummation to which these associations move, and the nature of things consists in their end or consummation; for what each thing is when its growth is completed we call the nature of that thing, whether it be a man or a horse or a family" (1252b).[199] From a Kantian perspective, there is simply too much *physis* in this *polis;* one recalls Kant's insistence that culture and the state are "not nature, nor yet freedom."[200] To be sure, Aristotle insists that while the *polis* "grows for the sake of mere life, it exists for the sake of a good life";[201] he is not a primitive advocate of so-called biopolitics. But it is noteworthy that the will and self-determination that Aristotle stresses in the *Ethics* barely appear in the *Politics.*[202]

As for the *Ethics* itself, the *telos* that it recommends is hardly congruent with Kant's insistence on the overriding importance of practice and good will; Aristotle argues (1177b–1178a) that "the contemplative activity of reason seems . . . to aim at no end beyond itself," to be the sole end in itself, while "the life in accordance with moral virtue is happy in a secondary degree."[203] For Kant the whole doctrine is doubly erroneous: *eudaimonia* ought not to be considered as part (or the whole) of morality, and moral virtue cannot be "secondary."[204]

Taking all of Aristotle's teleological notions together, then, Kant could have agreed with the *Metaphysics* that there is indeed something "for whose sake everything else is," and that those who eliminate that final cause "eliminate the Good without knowing it"; but that highest good he would have called practical—not theoretical—respect for persons, not quasi-divine contemplation. And Aristotle's reading of nature he would have called "dogmatic." But if nature cannot be *known* to have objective purposes, then the city cannot be (merely) the highest and most inclusive natural association:[205] it must transcend nature, and legally realize some nonnatural, objective moral ends. For Kant the natural and moral realms can be bridged by a teleological substrate; but bridges, after all, link up things that remain distinct. Kant should be neither pushed backward into Aristotle, nor forward into Hegel; both were surer of *telos*'s appearance in everything, of its universal *formative* power, than Kant was. The notion of purposiveness is crucial to him, but he uses it with boundless cautiousness: it is no accident that *Judgment* speaks of bridging realms, not *fusing* them.

CHAPTER FIVE

The Kantian Republic

I

The place of politics in Kant's critical philosophy is now clear: the *Critique of Judgment*—the final *Critique*—reveals public legal justice as the single most important strand of a culture that also embraces art, science and the development of skill.[1] Culture, and particularly politics (both metropolitan and cosmopolitan) is *"for"* the legal realization of some moral ends (such as peace) which good will would attain were it not for a "pathological" weakness of the flesh.[2] The legal realization of moral ends, coupled with the creation of a legal environment for *motiva moralia*, is the *telos* of politics-as-culture. That makes it wholly appropriate that it should be *Judgment* that shows Kantian politics' place. If public legal justice has as its purpose a paying of homage to morals, to objective ends that ought to be but that are impeded by "anthropology," then public legal justice itself *ought* to be part of a treatise whose end is the illumination of purposiveness. Politics' *telos* crowns a work wholly absorbed in making (nondogmatic)teleology intelligible. The end of politics is uncovered by a work whose end is to (critically) *establish* ends.[3] Given all this it is singularly perverse to say, as did Morris Cohen in his "Critique of Kant's Philosophy of Law," that "Kant's state is what the Germans call a *Polizeistaat*, not a *Kulturstaat*. It is there merely to enforce order."[4] This formulation fails to see that, for Kant, public legal justice—internal and external—is what matters most *for* culture, precisely because that justice legally realizes ends (such as nonviolence) that are *already* moral; while art and science simply curb the dominion of sensibility and, by enhancing "universal communicability," serve as propadeutic to a morality that also involves universality.[5] Cohen's insistence on order would, for once, drive Kant into agreement with Bentham, that is, with the claim of *The Book of Fallacies* that "the worst order is as truly order as the best."[6] For republicanism, after all, rests on more than mere order.

If Kantian politics is "for," or instrumental to, Kantian morality, then there must be a congruence, a fit, between public legal justice and ethics. In a *general* way the congruence is obvious: the Kantian republic respects the liberty ("freedom under law") that is essential to moral activity;[7] enforces some of the ends (though never the incentives) of morality;[8] provides a context of legal security within which acting from good will is not benevolent folly;[9] and, if universalized into a world of republics, brings an end to those practices that are themselves immoral, and that make the state the enemy, rather than the instrument, of morality.[10] But in a few particular respects—such as the rightness or wrongness of disobedience to positive laws that fail to be sufficiently instrumental to (Kant's own) morality, and (more drastically) of revolution—grave problems remain.

II

It is in the *Rechtslehre* that one finds Kant's most complete statement of his republicanism and ideal contractarianism. This statement opens with an argument that is obviously borrowed from Rousseau, and that in some ways does not fully represent Kant's settled convictions: "the legitimate [or sovereign] authority can be attributed only to the united will of the people. Because all right and justice is supposed to proceed from this authority, it can do absolutely no injustice to anyone."[11] Unless Lewis White Beck is correct in his claim that Kantianism is "deepened" Rousseau,[12] this concedes too much to the citizen of Geneva; for it is clear that in Kant "all right and justice" proceed from the natural or moral law as (perhaps) applied by the people's "united will," not just from popular sovereignty. The nature of a citizen in a commonwealth under the united will of the people, Kant goes on to say, involves three "attributes":

> First, the lawful freedom to obey no law other than one to which he has given his consent; second, the civil equality of having among the people no superior over him except another person whom he has just as much of a moral capacity to bind juridically as the other has to bind him; third, the attribute of civil independence that requires that he owe his existence and support, not to the arbitrary will of another person in the society, but rather to his own rights and powers as a member of the commonwealth.[13]

Once again Kant reflects Rousseauean ideas, and again one must qualify his statement that a citizen need obey only those laws to which he has consented. Sometimes, indeed, Kant does insist on (indirect) consent through a "representative system," but often only on the idea that a law must be *worthy* of consent.[14] In any case consent would not be the *ground* of one's obligation to obey the law; if law shares with morality a set of objective ends that we "ought to have," then there is a natural, nonconsensual duty of obedience antecedent to consent (even if politics cannot require anyone to take dutifulness as his incentive).[15] Therefore, one must further qualify Kant's quasi-Rousseaueanism by saying that rational citizens in a Kantian republic might, out of legal self-love, consent to certain ends that are "at the same time" *moral* ends. If this is correct, then Kantian political consent does not generate or produce any new obligation; it is simply an institutional, legal way of realizing some ends that a perfectly efficacious good will would yield automatically. For this reason it is, for once, impossible to agree with Jeffrie G. Murphy when he says, in his excellent *Kant: The Philosophy of Right,* that "we are morally obligated to obey the law, Kant claims, because we have, in the requisite sense, *consented* to it."[16] This statement makes Kant a more orthodox Rousseauean than he really was; for the only way to preserve both Kant's teleological doctrine of objective ends *and* his ideal contractarianism is to say that republican citizens would choose ends that are also the object of good will. Only this reading keeps Kantian politics and Kantian morality in the correct relation, that is, *close* (by sharing ends), but *distinct* (by not sharing motives).[17]

Another borrowing from Rousseau, this time a less visible one, is clear in Kant's distinction between the sovereign, the ruler and the courts. He argues that every state contains three authorities: the sovereign authority "resides in the person of the legislator" (the "united will" of the people); the executive authority resides in the ruler "in conformity to law"; and the judicial authority resides in the judge.[18] Adhering to Rousseau's characteristic magnifying of "generality" and denigrating of "particularity," Kant says that laws are the general determinations of the united popular will, while the determinations of the ruler are mere "ordinances and decrees" because they involve "decisions about particular cases and are considered subject to change."[19] For all the Rousseaueanism in his political thought, however, Kant does not want to adopt Rousseau's radically voluntarist doctrine that "the engagements which bind us to the social body are obligatory only because they are mutual."[20] Kant's idea of natural law, and his belief that morality itself requires public legal justice so that moral ends can be realized even in the absence of *motiva moralia,* would not permit a pure Rousseaueanism.

For Kant, then, there is only one form of sovereignty: the united will of the people under the "Idea" of the social contract. However, there are different forms of states, and on this point Kant shows considerable flexibility. His main concern is with the merits and demerits of autocracy and democracy; aristocracy, which he viewed as a feudal vestige,[22] did not interest him. The merit of autocracy, he argues, is that it is the simplest of political forms. From the point of view of mere administrative convenience this simplicity is good, but insofar as justice and law are concerned it is the most dangerous because it "strongly invites despotism," which would necessarily involve immorality.[23] (On this point Kant spoke not just *a priori* but from "sad experience"—the experience of seeing the comparatively enlightened autocracy of Frederick the Great degenerate into the obscurantist pro-clerical autocracy of Wöllner.)[24] Almost always, then, Kant comes down against autocracy:

> Simplification is indeed a reasonable maxim in the machinery of uniting the people through coercive laws, provided that all the people are passive and obey the one person who is above them; but, under such circumstances, none of the subjects are citizens.[25]

But despotism, Kant thought, might also turn up in democracy, which suffers from the additional disadvantage of great complexity, since it involves three different kinds of willing: first, the will of all to unite themselves into a people; then the will of all citizens to form a commonwealth; finally their will to place a ruler who is "none other than this united will itself" at the head of the commonwealth.[26] Excessive complexity, however, is not democracy's chief flaw; the real problem is that if every political question can be settled (or unsettled) by the immediate lawless whim of the *demos* congregated in the *agora*, then whatever *demos* wants, *demos* gets. And the *demos*, in Kant's view, will not have the moderation of representatives in a republic.[27] (At this point Kant and Hume, for once, join forces; Kant would have agreed perfectly with Hume's assertion in "Idea of a Perfect Commonwealth" that while "democracy is turbulent," a large representative republic that is "modelled with masterly skill" can "refine the democracy.")[28] Kant's strongest thoughts in this vein are to be found in the unpublished *Reflexionen zur Rechtsphilosophie*:

> That government is despotic, in which the sovereign treats the people as its property. Even democracy can be despotic, if its constitution is unintelligent [*ohne Einsicht*]—like the Athenian, for example, which, without rightful cause according to previously ordained laws, permitted anyone to be judged purely by a majority of voices.[29]

Kant had no reason to fear Socrates' fate, but he obviously had not forgotten it.

In Kant's opinion true republicanism, or the ideal state, is far better than either autocracy or democracy. A real republic, he urges, "is and can be nothing else than a representative system of the people if it is to protect the rights of its citizens in the name of the people."[30] Such a system would, he insists, realize "the spirit of the original contract."[31] Given the fact that the contract is only an Idea of reason, however, a people cannot, in the manner of Locke's *Second Treatise*, use the notion of "breach of contract" as a pretext for disestablishing the old political order instantly in order to create the ideal state.[32] On the contrary, Kant argues, it is the duty of "constituted authority"—the established ruler—to "change the government gradually and continually," until a pure republic is finally reached.[33] But during the period of transition to pure republicanism, Kant insists, the old nonrepublican state forms may "continue as long as they are held by ancient, long-standing custom" to be necessary.[34] And that is true even though morality will be better served by a republican than by a nonrepublican legal context, simply because republican citizens and their representatives have an interest in peacefulness and civility that mere subjects weighed down by autocratic oppression are unlikely to have.

Sometimes Kant is more cautious in recommending republicanism, and he occasionally even countenances traditional monarchy, when it seems to be provisionally unavoidable. This he does because it was a fixed dogma in his day that (in Montesquieu's formulation) large countries need monarchy in order to introduce "dispatch" into ruling and to counteract the sheer size of extensive territories. But Kant was also aware that Montesquieu had insisted that "the spirit of monarchy is war and enlargement of dominion," while "peace and moderation are the spirit of a republic."[35] Kant, then, had to find some way to reconcile Montesquieu's *dicta* about the necessity of monarchy and the peacefulness of republicanism; the only possible way out was obviously through the philosophy of history, which (in Kant's version) shows that the political world is slowly and fitfully moving toward republican institutions even if *motiva moralia* never increase in the slightest. On this view, monarchy is something that can wither away through peaceful evolution. And so one must take *cum grano salis* Kant's allowing in *Conflict of the Faculties* that a people which occupies extensive territories "may feel that monarchy is the only kind of constitution which can enable it to preserve its own existence between powerful neighbors."[36] The verb "feel" is a clue to Kant's position, since one recalls his uncharitable remark that "those who cannot think believe that feeling will help them out"; given that, it is no surprise that Kant retracts what he had conceded to Montesquieu, saying that, as the world is republicanized, monarchical states will become "progressively more secure from danger." That means that there need not be eternal monarchy, even in large territories: since the only (temporary) excuse for monarchy lies in fear of external danger, that justification is lost when "representatives" of the sovereign people in republics cease to vote (and pay) for war.[37] (This is treated in a confusing way in Cohen's "Critique of Kant's Philosophy of Law." He asserts that while "as a Prussian, Kant's ultimate conception of government is that of a monarchy," Kant also—apparently briefly liberated from Prussian causality—"supplies the best argument for democracy when he points out that simplicity of government and obedience are not all, that there is a need for developing citizens."[38] In this passage Kant is "determined" as a monarchist, "spontaneous" as a democrat; simultaneously *phenomenal* and *noumenal*. But the fact is that he was neither a monarchist nor a democrat, but a republican.)

While one waits for the full attainment of universal republicanism, which might well preserve constitutional monarchs as executives, autocrats can (in Kant's view) at least govern in "a republican manner":

> It is the duty of monarchs to govern in a republican (not a democratic) manner, even though they may rule autocratically. In other words, they should treat the people in accordance with principles akin in spirit to the laws of freedom which a people of mature rational powers would prescribe for itself.[39]

In works such as *Theory and Practice*, Kant leaves no doubt that it is better to be ruled provisionally by an autocrat—even a somewhat arbitrary one—than to be "devoured by ecclesiastics and aristocrats";[40] if he could not share Hegel's conviction that monarchy is the "constitution of developed reason,"[41] he at least thought it more rational than rule by feudal remnants. For Kant it is conceivable that an enlightened monarch might act "by analogy with laws which a people would give itself in conformity with universal principles of right,"[42] but it is not imaginable that aristocrats and churchmen would be so progressive.

III

The formal requirements of republicanism, however, did not claim Kant's whole political interest. He argued, indeed, that while all legal orders are to some degree instrumental to the realization of some moral ends, a republican legal order is most likely to end political immorality, particularly in the form of war.[43] In *Eternal Peace* he argues that a republican constitution, which springs from the "pure concept of right," is not only "pure in its origin"; it also helps to realize a perpetual peace in which states will require, internally and externally, fewer immoral acts.[44] Kant maintains that in a republic, where men are citizens who would have to undergo personally all the misfortunes of war and violence, there will be "great hesitation in embarking on so dangerous an enterprise." Where people are not citizens, by contrast, "it is the simplest thing in the world to go to war."[45] A monarch unrestricted by even the Idea of what a rational people could agree to is not a fellow-citizen who would have to share the horrors of war with other citizens, Kant insists, but "the owner of a state."[46]

> A war will not force him to make the slightest sacrifice so far as his banquets, hunts, pleasure palaces and court festivals are concerned. He can thus decide on war, without any significant reason, as a kind of amusement.[47]

No doubt this striking passage exaggerates the degree to which Kant actually believed that war is caused mainly by the caprice of monarchs and the wantonness of scheming ministers; after all, he says in other works, which will be examined fully in Chapter Six, that war may even be a "hidden purpose of nature" designed to bring about a new "cosmopolitical" world order through "sad experience" of violence and devastation.[48] Still, he does seem to have thought that even if the morality of the public would not be higher under a republic than in a monarchy, a republic would at least *cause* fewer immoralities simply because rational citizens would not willingly choose to ruin themselves, especially through war.[49] And if war— always for Kant the main form of political immorality—can be made less likely, other good consequences will follow: future generations will not groan under a permanent war debt fastened on them by warlike ancestors, and money reserved for war can be diverted to education.[50]

The notion that intelligently constructed republican institutions can finally lead to the legal realization of moral ends such as peace, even in the total absence of *motiva moralia,* is a notion that escaped some of Kant's would-be followers simply because they failed to grasp his division of morals into *ends* and *incentives.* Wilhelm von Humboldt's *The Limits of State Action,* for example, written only a year or two after the publication of the *Critique of Judgment,* begins by praising Kant as one who "has never been surpassed in profundity," and goes on to insist that "the moral law obliges us to regard every man as an end in himself."[51] Humboldt then asserts that, because it is precisely the "moral man" who feels every "restriction" imposed by the state "most deeply," the state "must wholly refrain from every attempt to operate directly or indirectly on the morals and character of the nation . . . everything calculated to promote such a design . . . lies wholly outside the limits of its legitimate authority."[52] Kant, by contrast, who believes in the indirect realization of moral ends by legal means, does not force himself to embrace so radically minimalist a state; since he insists on separating purpose and motive, he does not fall into Humboldt's hyper-Kantianism.

Kant, then, makes a fairly persuasive case—which one cannot yet call "refuted"—that republicanism (or at least a republican manner of governing) might lead to fewer future immoralities, as well as to the realization of peace and of an improved legal context for good will. This does not mean, however, that he was willing to justify revolution in order to attain republicanism sooner. Some critics of Kant, indeed, insist that he went too far in disallowing revolution, that his insistence on obedience to existing law destroyed his republicanism.[53] And since Kant's republicanism is the most distinctive facet of his political thought—since he thought it both right and peace-producing—one must say something about the charge that antirevolutionary legalism kept Kant from permitting the realization of a *respublica noumenon*.

It certainly seems, at least initially, that Kant's views on revolution, even as a means of hastening republicanism, are not altogether coherent. In his late *Conflict of the Faculties*, which is his most pro-revolutionary work, he says that sympathy for the French Revolution cannot have been "caused by anything but a moral disposition within the human race," and goes on to suggest that

> The moral cause which is at work here [in the French Revolution] is composed of two elements. Firstly, there is the *right* of every people to give itself a civil constitution of the kind that it sees fit. . . . And secondly . . . there is the *aim*, which is also a duty, of submitting to those conditions [of republicanism] by which war, the source of all evils and moral corruption, can be prevented.[54]

But at the other extreme—and this is perhaps more characteristic—Kant in the *Rechtslehre* calls revolution "illegal," a crime deserving of death, and even insists that "it is the people's duty to endure even the most intolerable abuse of supreme authority" because resistance can only be "unlawful."[55] Here, for Kant, the importance of a sovereign last word is decisive; just as, in *Pure Reason*, reason is dissatisfied by the conditionality of everything merely determined in an infinite causal regress, and is finally content only when a spontaneous, undetermined cause is found in rational will,[56] so in Kant's social thought an infinite regress must be cut short by a political spontaneity that is determining but undetermined, i.e., sovereign.[57] But neither kind of spontaneity is willful, since objective ends provide reasons for beings who are free of causes.[58]

Between the extremes of revolution as the effect of a moral cause and revolution as death-deserving, Kant places a rarely stated middle position, which asserts that the principle, " '*Obey the authority which has power over you*' (in everything which is not opposed to morality) is a categorical imperative."[59] This sentence, part of a "Supplementary Explanation" which Kant attached to the *Rechtslehre* in response to criticism, never makes clear what is meant by obedience "in everything which is not opposed to morality"; for illumination one must turn to the *Reflexionen zur Rechtsphilosophie*, where Kant says that

> Force, which does not presuppose a judgment having the validity of law [*rechtskräftig Urtheil*] is against the law, consequently [the people] cannot rebel except in the cases which cannot at all come forward in a civil union, e.g., the enforcement of a religion, compulsion to unnatural crimes, assassination, etc., etc.[60]

One could, for a moment, imagine that Kant was citing the *Summa Theologica*; but even the *Reflexionen* fail to make it clear whether a government's effort to enforce immoral things justifies revolution or only passive disobedience, since the verb *rebel* (wiedersetzen) is not very precise.

If the coherence of Kant's political thought is to be maintained, these apparent contradictions and tensions must be explained in an adequate way. The best way is perhaps the following: even in the *Rechtslehre*, which treats revolution as destructive of all legality, Kant says that the sovereign—that is, the united will of the people—can "take his authority from the ruler, depose him, or reform his administration, but cannot punish him."[61] The removal of some particular ruler—Louis XVI, for example—would not constitute an assault on all legality as such. It would also not be revolution in the most thoroughgoing sense, for the sovereign would remain and would indeed be the agent cutting a defective ruler away from a still living body politic. Kant thus allows that it is "conceivable"—an unenthusiastic term— that the dethronement of a ruler may be "effected through a voluntary abdication," provided that the ruler is not punished, and provided above all that he is not executed.[62] If a people simply strips a ruler of power but lets him live peacefully as a "private citizen," Kant is willing to grant that this may be allowable, though he plainly continues to prefer evolution toward eventual republicanism. It is only the "formal execution" of a former ruler that Kant takes to be an "inexpiable" crime.[63] While his view of revolution is not without its problems, then, it is more coherent than it is often represented as being and at least permits (without enthusiastically endorsing) the removal of a ruler without fear of an anarchy that would destroy the legal structure that is the instrument to moral ends. It is a view that would permit one to draw a reasonable distinction between the cases of, say, Charles I and James II, since the latter abdicated "voluntarily," but the former suffered formal execution.[64]

There is a further reasonable distinction to be drawn, if Hannah Arendt's reading of Kant's theory of revolution, examined in Chapter 4, is right. If, as Arendt says, a Kantian "acts" and "judges" by different principles, then a Kantian spectator may judge that the French Revolution (at least before the Reign of Terror) was advancing the war-diminishing end of republicanism, even if that same Kantian would not, and should not, *will* the illegal overthrow of the ancien régime.[65] This fine-spun distinction is made possible by Kant's own careful separation of moral ends and moral motives, though it seems to involve the assertion, at best paradoxical, that there are good ends that one ought not to will. (Perhaps even this paradox can be partly overcome by relying on Thomas Seebohm's recent ingenious argument, presented at a Hannah Arendt Memorial Symposium: "The [Kantian] principle that a revolution is unjust insofar as it is a return to the [prelegal] state of nature remains unchanged. . . . The moral predisposition [that Kant found in the French Revolution] is revealed by the behavior of the revolutionaries *after* a revolution has occurred as a natural event leading back to the state of nature. . . . There is no just revolution, but there are revolutionaries who are virtuous. Their virtue [is revealed in their postrevolutionary] goal of introducing a constitution that corresponds to a true civil state . . . the goal of their fight is the realization of the *respublica noumenon* in a *respublica phenomenon*."[66] The problem with this ingenious reading, which is part of a careful and responsible paper called "Kant's Theory of Revolution," is that it forces itself to call revolution a "natural event," thereby re-introducing a "state of nature" out of which republicanism can issue *de novo*, while Kant himself calls revolution "illegal." But if an illegality were a natural event, then responsibility would be swept away by causality; and that Kant would never countenance.)[67]

IV

It is at least arguable, then, that Kant makes a moderately persuasive case that republicanism will lead to less immoral conduct (if not to better motives) in the future, and that his theory of revolution is more coherent than it is sometimes taken to be. But problems remain in his theory of public legal justice as something supportive of, but not identical to, morality. The most obvious difficulty appears in his justification of legal punishment: Kant is clear that what matters in morality is good will, or the incentive of one's actions, while all that counts in politics and law is that one's external behavior (however motivated) be consistent with everyone's freedom under a universal law.[68] In his treatment of crime and punishment in the *Rechtslehre*, however, it at least seems that his distinctions collapse. The reason one punishes a criminal, Kant urges, is that he *deserves* it; his actions must receive "what they are worth."[69] Legal penalties must be "equivalent" to crimes because all other standards (such as reform and deterrence) are arbitrary; therefore murderers must be executed, so that their "inner viciousness" may be "expiated," and what Kant calls "blood-guilt" will not be on the hands of a society that treats murderers too tenderly out of "sympathetic sentimentality" or an "affectation of humanity."[70] The sneer at "humanity" is all the more striking, coming from Kant; but the central question is whether the idea of what people deserve because of the malevolence of their will should be taken into account by public legal justice. Might it not be better— or at least more Kantian—to say that murder, from a political-legal viewpoint, is not consistent with the external freedom of all under a universal law, and that one correctly punishes murder by negating the negation (crime) and thus affirming the positive value of liberty-preserving law?

Kant himself, of course, provides for exactly that view of punishment in another part of the *Rechtslehre*:

> Any resistance which counteracts the hindrance of an effect helps to promote this effect and is consonant with it. Now everything that is contrary to right is a hindrance to freedom based on universal laws, while coercion is a hindrance or resistance to freedom. Consequently, if a certain use to which freedom is put is itself a hindrance to freedom in accordance with universal laws . . . any coercion which is used against it will be a hindrance to the hindrance of freedom, and will thus be . . . right.[71]

In some ways, at least, this is a better theory of coercion and punishment for Kant to use than any argument turning on the idea of inner viciousness or what actions are worth, because it keeps punishment, like the law itself, external. But if a proto-Hegelian "negation of negation" is better than expiation of inner viciousness, it does not make Kant's theory of punishment wholly satisfactory; to see why that is so a slightly fuller view of the reasons that led Kant to his reflections on punishment may be of use.

Kant often wants to be able to say that punishment must be deserved or merited; if it were not deserved, and deserved because of bad will, then one might punish people—even the innocent and the good-willing *(bene-volent)*—in order to maximize utility or to appease divinities.[72] So deserving punishment matters; one cannot just think of the good (or allegedly good) end that punishment may effect. But thanks to the very rigorousness of Kant's own distinction between ends and motives, that he is debarred from considering desert seriously in his legal theory. He cannot let desert matter and still keep the law wholly external.

The main problem with punishment as a negation of negation is that it is *designed* not to take motives (such as deserving) into account; its strength is its weakness. It must treat all murder (for example) simply as the negation of life and punishment as negation negated; it does not seem to be able to accommodate ordinary distinctions between, say, first-degree murder and manslaughter, for those distinctions turn on questions of intentionality.[73] Kant not only tries to keep law external, at least when he is not thinking of inner viciousness; he even insists that real motives cannot be known, so that it would be impossible to take them into account even if a purely external law permitted that. (The only absolute knowledge in Kant, of course, is knowledge of the moral law—not of causality, not of God, not even of *one's own* motives.) On this the *Critique of Pure Reason* is quite clear:

> The real morality of actions, their merit or guilt, even that of our own conduct, thus remains entirely hidden from us. Our imputations can refer only to the empirical character. How much of this character is ascribable to the pure effect of freedom, how much to mere nature, that is, to faults of temperament for which there is no responsibility, or to its happy constitution *(merito fortunae)*, can never be determined, and upon it therefore no perfectly just judgments can be passed.[74]

This fine passage, as humane as it is "critical," is Kant's best thinking on the subject of legal accountability. That being so, it is shocking that he should speak so confidently of the expiation, through execution, of a "blood-guilt," *knowledge* of which, according to his own doctrines, is "transcendent" for any but a "searcher of hearts."[75] This same passage from *Pure Reason* also overturns his notion that punishments must be equivalent to crimes, or at least symbolically equivalent, as in the castration of rapists;[76] if "no perfectly just judgments can be passed," then the search for "equivalence" is vain. What Kant probably ought to have said about the punishment of murderers is that since murder is the negation of an objective end, it ought to be arrested; but that, since motives cannot be known, murderers should be restrained by confinement unless there is reason to think that "faults of temperament for which there is no responsibility" can be overcome by an autonomy-preserving treatment.[77]

There is a passage in Kant's very late *Anthropology* (1798) that throws further light on his difficulties with "desert" as the foundation of legal punishment, and that then relates "deserved punishment" both to his theory of revolution, and to his notion that suicide is the most striking instance of failure to treat *oneself* as an objective end.[78] In a remarkable paragraph in which these three strands—desert, revolution and suicide—converge, Kant argues that

> It is not always just depraved, worthless souls who decide to rid themselves of the burden of life by suicide. . . . Although suicide is always terrible, and man makes himself a monstrosity by it, still it is noteworthy that in revolutionary periods, when public injustice is established and declared lawful (as, for example, under the Committee of Public Safety in the French Republic), honor-loving men (such as Roland) have sought to anticipate by suicide their execution under the law, although in a constitutional situation they themselves would have declared this reprehensible. The reason is this: there is something ignominious in any execution under a *law*, because it is *punishment*; and when the execution is unjust, the man who falls a victim to the law cannot recognize the punishment as one he *deserves*. And he proves it in this way: that, having been doomed to death, he now prefers to choose death as a free man, and he himself inflicts it. . . . But I do not claim to justify the morality of this.[79]

Everything in this remarkable paragraph, down to the exquisitely equivocal last sentence, must have cost Kant a great effort. For it reveals the deepest tensions in his practical thought. Roland could not *know* (in Kant's sense of knowing) that he deserved no punishment, since for Kant motives are as clouded as imperatives are clear, and therefore "no perfectly just judgments can be passed";[80] but at the same time Kant would not want to give Robespierre a license to negate whatever struck the Committee of Public Safety as a negation of the Committee's justice. That leads straightway to a problem in Kant's doctrine of sovereignty: he maintains that subjects of a *new* order—even one illegally established—have a duty of obedience as good citizens;[81] but in the *Anthropology* he complains of "public injustice" that is "declared lawful," and treats Roland's suicide as a justice-loving protest against a new sovereign. By viewing Roland as motivated by love of justice, though that motive must be *assumed*, since it cannot be known, Kant grants that some suicides are not "depraved" and "worthless" (contrary to his general condemnation of self-destruction in the *Tugendlehre*).[82] All of the strains in Kant's practical thought—moral, political, legal—emerge in this passage from the *Anthropology;* it is no wonder that he ends on a less than clarion note.

V

Kant's theory of public legal justice as the realizer of moral ends, then, has its difficulties; and these difficulties are most visible when Kant treats, not always with sufficient consistency, the ideas of revolution and of legal punishment. Often, however, if one looks at everything he has to say, even on these matters, a fairly consistent view can be uncovered. This is, perhaps, even true of what is plainly the least satisfactory thing in the whole of Kant's social thought: his view of the relation between legal equality and economic inequality. In *Theory and Practice* Kant had insisted that

> [the] uniform equality of human beings as subjects of a state is, however, perfectly consistent with the utmost inequality of the mass in the degree of its possessions, whether these take the form of physical or mental superiority over others, or of fortuitous external property and of particular rights (of which there may be many) with respect to others. Thus the welfare of the one depends very much on the will of the other (the poor depending on the rich), the one must obey the other (as the child its parents or the wife her husband), the one serves (the laborer) while the other pays, etc. Nevertheless, they are all equal as subjects *before the law,* which, as the pronouncement of the general will, can only be single in form, and which concerns the form of right and not the material or object in relation to which I possess rights. For no one can coerce anyone else other than through the public law. [83]

The last sentence could at best read, "no one *should* coerce anyone else other than through the public law," for some of the social institutions that Kant describes *are* coercive; to see that, one need not even recall Anatole France's witticism that modern society allows the rich and the poor "equally" to sleep under bridges. [84] To be sure, Kant modifies his theory at once by insisting that "the idea of the equality of men as subjects in a commonwealth" leads to the "formula" that "every member of the commonwealth must be entitled to reach any degree of rank which a subject can earn through his talent, his industry and his good fortune. And his fellow subjects may not stand in his way by hereditary prerogatives or privileges of rank and thereby hold him and his descendants back indefinitely." [85] Even this comparatively liberal notion of a "career open to talents," which defends equality of opportunity if not equality of outcome, [86] seems to forget Rousseau's argument that where there is radical economic inequality the law "only gives new power to him who already has too much."[87] That fact is not wholly offset even by the argument of *Judgment*, Section 83, that skill, which helps to produce a culture that legally realizes some moral ends, itself unavoidably generates inequality, simply because skills themselves are unequal.[88]

But the gravest problem is that Kant, after insisting that civil equality is consistent with economic inequality, then modifies even *civil* equality by saying that a citizen—the person who has a right to vote on "the basic law"—must "of course" be an "adult male," and that he must "be his own master *(sui juris)*, and must have some property (which can include any skill, trade, fine art or science) to support himself."[89] In cases where a person "must earn his living from others," Kant adds, "he must earn it only by selling that which is his, and not by allowing others to make use of him; for he must in the true sense of the word *serve* no one but the commonwealth."[90] This last phrase, reminiscent of Rousseau's insistence that citizens should be "completely independent of all the rest" but "very dependent on the city,"[91] puts the doctrine in a better light; Kant is anxious to avoid giving a citizen's vote to mere creatures of feudal landowners and proprietors of large estates. That is why he says that "the number of those entitled to vote on matters of legislation must be calculated purely from the number of property-owners, not from the size of their estates."[92] Of course, he does add, in the *Rechtslehre*, that everyone should be at liberty to "work up" from a "passive" condition to "active" citizenship.[93]

Even if, however, one represents these remarks as an effort to extend citizenship as far as possible given certain historical limitations prevailing in Kant's day, it is still arguable that they concede too much to the mere de facto institutions of the eighteenth century. (As Manfred Riedel has skillfully shown, Kant's would-be liberal principle that citizens must be independent may, ironically, restrict citizenship if that independence is actually possessed by only a few, and if Kant permits the radical inequality that makes dependence hard to overcome. Thus Kant's insistence on independence—the third attribute of a citizen—may struggle against the first attribute, namely civil equality.)[94]

This makes it doubly important to recall that while Kant restricts civil equality in some works—at least while the many are working up from a passive to an active status—he expands it in some others. For a balanced view one must recall this fine passage (characteristically both ringing and cautious) from *Religion within the Limits*:

> I grant that I cannot reconcile myself to the following expressions made use of even by clever men: 'A certain people (engaged in a struggle for civil

freedom) is not yet ripe for freedom'; 'The bondsmen of a landed proprietor are not yet ready for freedom'; and hence, likewise, 'Mankind in general is not yet ripe for freedom of belief.' For according to such a presupposition, freedom will never arrive, since we cannot *ripen* to this freedom if we are not first of all placed therein (we must be free in order to make purposive use of our powers in freedom). . . . I raise no protest when those who hold power in their hands, being constrained by the circumstances of the times, postpone far, very far, into the future the sundering of these three bonds. But to proceed on the principle that those who are once subjected to these bonds are essentially unfit for freedom and that one is justified in continually removing them farther from it is to usurp the prerogatives of Divinity itself, which created men for freedom. It is certainly more convenient to rule in a state, household and church if one is able to carry out such a principle. But is it also more just?[95]

This passage, to be sure, does not negate less attractive passages in other works, but it does balance them. It also serves to remind that it is Kant's *own doctrine* that only with the advent of universal republicanism, in which all are citizens, can one reasonably hope that eternal peace will be legally realized.[96] If Kant was not a pure enough Rousseauean to agree that social institutions are worth having only if "everyone has something and no one has too much,"[97] he at least looked forward to a day in which the expansion of citizenship would yield a sufficient number of persons unwilling to vote for war. But the largest number of possible citizens—and hence the best legal guarantee of peace—is *all adults:* Kant's better thoughts drive his worse ones out.

CHAPTER SIX

Eternal Peace Through Federalism in Kant's Political Philosophy

I

Kant argues in *Eternal Peace* that without a universal *foedus pacificum* (pacific federation) of republics there is no security anywhere for public legal justice;[1] and in the *Rechtslehre* he adds, in a now familiar passage, that "if public legal justice perishes then it is no longer worthwhile for men to remain alive on this earth."[2] This seems, then, to be a strong argument for some sort of federalism—at least in the international forum, between sovereign republics, if not necessarily within the domestic structure of each of those republics. (One might think that any federalist would want to break down indivisible sovereignty by creating federal structures both below and above the national-state level, and to be a partisan of both domestic and international federalism; but Kant's federalism moves mainly in one direction—*above* the national state. Whether this limiting of federalism to the international sphere is a defect in Kant is arguable; Carl Friedrich insists that Kant failed to "carry his idea of federal union back to the lower levels of government,"[3] but one cannot say whether this limiting is a failure until one looks at Kant's whole theory of republicanism and eternal peace.) A kind of international federalism, in any case, is more important to the political theory of Kant than to that of any other thinker, since for him the possibility of a public legal order at *any* level is jeopardized by the absence of such an order at the highest level, the relations of independent states. Only an international peace (roughly) comparable to the peace that ought to be enjoyed by individual men in a particular state can guarantee state law.[4]

II

Even if a *potestas executoria* is well established within some particular state, in Kant's view it is insecure so long as states themselves remain in a condition of "lawless" freedom.[5] "The problem of the establishment of a perfect civic constitution depends on the problem of a lawful external relationship of the states and cannot be solved without the latter," Kant writes in the *Idea for a Universal History*. "One commonwealth must expect from the others the very same evils which oppress individual human beings [in a state of nature] and which compelled them to enter into a lawful civic state."[6] If states continue to exist in lawless freedom, he said, they will constantly violate their citizens' rights in their expansionist efforts; they will wrongly enslave future generations with war debts; they will corrupt morality rather than provide a framework of security for it.[7] The possibility of a fully lawful state at the national level is therefore dependent on some sort of world order, an order that he commonly calls the *foedus pacificum*. For Kant, the realization of such an order is a duty insofar as a Hobbesian "state of nature" is not "right."[8] But it is also an historical inevitability, if only at the end of political time, inasmuch as (for Kant) the antagonism of men and societies will finally develop reason to the point that it can effectively prohibit war. (This, of course, it could have done originally, by pointing out what ought to be, if the gap between man's reason and his actions were not so great, and did not need the whole of human history to narrow).[9] Kant, then, has two distinct grounds of hope for a federal eternal peace: first, it is a duty to attain it, as the condition of stable public legal justice at all levels; and second, nature (or human history) will gradually force men into a "cosmopolitical" order.[10]

Both reason and "universal violence and the necessity arising therefrom" suggest that men "subject themselves to national law and . . . set up a political constitution," Kant argues in *Theory and Practice*. Similarly, he goes on, "the evils arising from constant wars by which the states seek to reduce or subdue each other bring them at last, even against their will, to enter into a universal cosmopolitical constitution."[11] (Here Hobbes's argument about the *reasonability* of peace is carried to its logical limit: the shores of England give way to a "cosmopolis.")[12]

But is this Kantian cosmopolis a true world city? Not quite, for before recommending a true world state of coercive universal law as a solution to this problem, Kant reflects that "such a condition of universal peace [through a world state] . . . as has often been the case with overgrown states," might be "even more dangerous to liberty on another side than war, by introducing the most terrible despotism."[13] Given this, Kant feels constrained to recommend nothing stronger than a world federation: "The evils from which deliverance is sought will compel the introduction of a condition among the nations which does not assume the form of a universal commonwealth or empire under one sovereign, but a federation regulated by law, according to the law of nations as concerted in common."[14] As Siegfried Brie, author of one of the first important books on federalism (*Der Bundesstaat*, Leipzig, 1874) put it, Kant substitutes the notion of a "Föderalism freyer Staaten" for the idea of "die ganze Menschheit umfassenden Einheitsstaat."[15]

In *Eternal Peace* Kant enlarges slightly on the problems of a true world state. A proper international order would be a "Union of Nations which would not necessarily have to be a state of nations," since "a state of nations contains a contradiction." Many nations, he argues, "would, in a single state, constitute only one nation, which is contradictory since what we are here considering are the rights of the nations towards each other as long as they constitute different states and are not joined together into one."[16] Each state, indeed, Kant observes, "insists upon seeing the essence of its sovereignty in this, that it is not subject to any external coercion."[17] If occasionally Kant seems a bit ambivalent about the desirability of state sovereignty—he says at one point that the idea of world government is valid in theory but that state vanity rejects it—most of the time he seems to say that a world organization must be worked out in terms of sovereignty, in terms of a free federation of *corporate* bodies voluntarily obeying international law, and not a world law for individuals.[18] Kant's *foedus pacificum* is to be, in Montesquieu's words, a *société de sociétés*, not a society of individual persons.[19] (As Carl Friedrich has correctly observed in his fine *Inevitable Peace*, Kant's fear that "a united government for the world" might well lead to "the specter of a world-wide despotism" led him to the conclusion that it would be "wiser to stick to . . . federalism.")[20]

Moreover, Kant did not believe that states are in quite the same position as men in a state of nature, that they are under the same obligation to leave that condition as "natural" men. "For states," Kant argues, "have internally a legal constitution conceived in terms of their own legal norms and hence have outgrown the coercion of others who might desire to put them under a broadened legal constitution conceived in terms of their own legal norms."[21] (This might seem, indeed, to concede too much to the mere de facto sovereignty of the states of Kant's day; after all, if a juridical state of affairs is *universally* necessary, then it is not merely coercive people who might desire to establish a broadened legal constitution in the form of a strong *foedus pacificum*. It is arguable that Kant accepts too much sovereignty for one who is arguing against Hobbes.) In any event, Kant argues that states do not have a strict duty to abandon their sovereignty, and goes on to claim that "the positive idea of a world-republic must be replaced by the negative substitute of a union of nations which maintains itself, prevents wars and steadily expands." Peace under this system, according to Kant, will be less certain than in a world republic, but liberty will also be safer from possible universal despotism.[22]

The "preliminary articles" of Kant's *Eternal Peace*, far from undercutting the notion of state sovereignty, actually reinforce it. They stipulate that,

1. No treaty of peace shall be held to be such, which is made with the secret reservation of the material for a future war.
2. No state having an independent existence, whether it be small or great, may be acquired by another state, through inheritance, exchange, purchase or gift.
3. Standing armies shall gradually disappear.
4. No debts shall be contracted in connection with the foreign affairs of the state.
5. No state shall interfere by force in the constitution and government of another state.
6. No state at war with another shall permit such acts of warfare as must make mutual confidence impossible in time of future peace: such as the employment of assassins. . . . the instigation of treason [and so forth].[23]

In his remarks on the preliminary articles, Kant amplifies some of these stipulations. "A state," he says concerning Article 2, "is not a possession like the soil. . . . It is a society which no one but themselves is called upon to command or dispose of. Since, like a tree, such a state has its own roots, to incorporate it as a graft into another state is to take away its existence as a moral person and to make of it a thing."[24] This would contradict, according to Kant, "the idea of the original contract, without which no right over a people can even be conceived."[25] It would also contradict, still more centrally, the duty to respect persons as ends and never to use them as mere means to an arbitrary purpose, such as the acquisition of *Lebensraum*. Kant even insisted that, in principle, states which had lost their freedom (e.g., Poland) should have it restored, though he did not insist on instantaneous restoration for fear of creating anarchy.[26] (It is precisely the fear of anarchy, the loss of a political-legal context for morality, that leads Kant to say harsher things than expected about revolution and reform: "Any legal constitution, even if it is only in small measure lawful, is better than none at all, and the fate of a premature reform would be anarchy."[27])

Even more remarkable for its emphasis on the independence of the sovereign state is an article in which Kant introduces—or rather resuscitates, following mainly Vitoria's *De Indis*[28]—the notion of the "cosmopolitan" or world law, which (in Kant's words) "shall be limited to conditions of a universal hospitality." Hospitality, in its turn, means for Kant "the right of the foreigner not to be treated with hostility when he arrives on the soil of another [state] . . . it is not the right of becoming a permanent inhabitant."[29] This extreme limitation on world law indicates very plainly that Kant meant to preserve substantial state sovereignty.

F. H. Hinsley, the fine Cambridge historian of international relations theory, has argued persuasively that a Kantian *foedus pacificum* could not be a super-government of universal coercive law modelled on something like the Abbé de St. Pierre's *Projet de Paix Perpétuelle* (1712). What Kant "envisaged," Hinsley claims, "was the replacement of the existing imperfect, customary international law by a structure of international society based on a treaty between independent states."[30] In support of this view—which begins with the obvious merit of rendering *foedus* correctly as "treaty"—Hinsley quotes a key but neglected passage from the *Idea for a Universal History*, the essay that argues that civilization and even reason itself develop out of conflict. Since Kant had defined a "lawful international constitution" as one "where every state, even the smallest, may expect its security and its right not from its own powers . . . but alone from this great union of nations *(Foedus Amphictyonum)*, from a united power and from decisions according to the will of them all"; and since he had declared that the very antagonism of states (even the horrors of war) were part of a hidden "design of nature" to hasten new and better international arrangements, Kant asserted that what was needed was not a universal sovereign but "a counterbalance to the intrinsically healthy resistance of many states against each other, resulting from their freedom . . . a united power which will give support to this balance."[31]

This solution—resting eternal peace on something more than an ordinary treaty, but something less than government—would not be "without all danger," in Kant's view; for "we must see to it that neither the vitality of mankind goes to sleep" (in "universal despotism") not "those states destroy each other as they might without a principle of balance and equality in their mutual effects and counter-effects." This is why Kant repeatedly argues that "reason must necessarily connect such a federation with the concept of the law of nations," that is, with a *ius gentium* between states, not a universal *ius civile* over states. "There must exist," Kant insists, "a union of a particular kind which we may call the pacific union *(foedus pacificum)* which would be distinguished from a peace treaty *(pactum pacis)* by the fact that the latter tries to end merely one war while the former tries to end all wars forever. This union is not directed towards securing some additional power of the state, but merely towards maintaining and making secure the freedom of each state by and for itself and at the same time of the other states thus allied with each other."[32] Within the *foedus pacificum*, Kant goes on, "these states will not subject themselves (as do men in the state of nature) to laws and the enforcement of such laws."[33] The new Kantian international order must then turn, not on a world state, but on voluntary acceptance of good international conduct.

Kant, as has been indicated, bases his hope for the states' acceptance of the *foedus pacificum* on two grounds: first, the development of republican government in all states; and second, the historical conflict of states leading to a closer union through "sad experience" and developed reason. For Kant a republican constitution, as was seen in Chapter 5, is based on three principles:

> First, the principle of the freedom of all the members of a society as men; second, the principle of the dependence of all upon a single legislation as subjects; and third, the principle of the equality of all as citizens. This is the only constitution which is derived from the idea of an original contract upon which all rightful legislation must be based.[34]

Kantian republicanism also requires (very much like Montesquieu) the separation of legislative and executive powers and a representative system. Asking, in a passage fully treated in Chapter 5, whether a republican constitution is "the only one which can lead to perpetual peace," Kant replies that "a republican constitution does offer the prospect of the desired purpose" because "if the consent of the citizens is required in order to decide whether there should be war or not, nothing is more natural than that those who would have to decide to undergo all the deprivations will very much hesitate to start such an evil game." On the other hand, Kant argues, where men are not legally equal citizens and there are no republican institutions, "it is the easiest thing in the world to go to war," through the unrestricted caprice of a monarch or the schemes of an irresponsible minister.[35]

But Kant did not rest all of his hopes for a pacific federation on the goodness of republicanism, nor on the prospect of republican states' acceding to such a *foedus*. In part, at least, he relied on his historical view that nature's purpose for man was the extension of reason and reasonable conduct in the species as a whole through conflict, and that a series of clashes would ultimately (though very late) bring states into new and more rational relations in which international good conduct would be voluntarily accepted.[36]

Before proceeding with this second ground of Kantian hope, however, a word needs to be said about Kant's use of the idea of *nature* in his philosophy of history. As George Kelly has pointed out in *Idealism, Politics and History*, "a fair amount of nonsense has been written about Kant's 'ruse of nature,' according to which nature wills, urges or grants this or that, leading men in ways they do not suspect and toward goals which, ultimately, will prove to be compatible with a voluntary moral destiny."[37] Compounding this difficulty, as Kelly suggests, is the fact that "nature" for Kant frequently means simply the external world, something wholly explicable through mechanical causality—in short, something that could not conceivably have "purposes," for men or anything else. The solution, to which Kelly direct us, is this:

> Nature means, in effect, two things for Kant. It means first the external or sensible world, insofar as this is scientifically explicable . . . At the same time, nature retains its classical meaning of the full development or actualization of a thing according to its *telos*. Thus, regarding man as a creature of liberty, Kant can write: "Whatever good man is able to do through his own efforts, under laws of freedom, in contrast to what he can do only with supernatural assistance, can be called *nature*, as distinguished from *grace*."[38]

For Kant man, as naturally free, ought to respect others as ends; but this is facilitated by public legal justice; and that, in turn, is facilitated by a federal eternal peace. Men, then, have a natural duty in Kant to bring about a *foedus pacificum* as the keystone of the legal order that sustains the categorical imperative. When Kant speaks of nature's purpose for man, he is thinking of what men ought naturally to become—moral, law-abiding, peace-loving. All this is reinforced by a passage from the third pillar of Kant's philosophy, the *Critique of Judgment*:

> The production in a rational being of an aptitude for any ends whatever of his own choosing, consequently the aptitude of a being in his freedom, is *culture*. Hence it is only culture that can be the ultimate and which we have cause to attribute to nature in respect of the human race.[39]

Kant goes on to make it clear that the pinnacle of this culture would be—possibly will be—"a rule of law governing the freedom of states" which will replace the "terrible calamities" of war with "a system established on a moral basis."[40] This law, this system, would be precisely the *foedus pacificum.*

This, then, is what Kant means by "nature's purpose" with respect to human beings. It is this notion of nature that leads him to assert in *Idea for a Universal History* that "all natural faculties of a creature are destined to unfold themselves completely and according to an end."[41] In man as "the only rational creature on earth," Kant goes on, "those natural faculties which aim at the use of reason shall be full developed in the species, not in the individual." Reason, however, does not develop unassisted, and so, nature has put men in a state of opposition, "the antagonism of men in society." The "asocial sociability" of men—their "propensity to enter into a society, which propensity is, however, linked with a constant mutual resistance which threatens to dissolve the society"—forces the development of reason in defense of individual vanities and pretensions. Nature should be thanked, Kant says with grim irony, for man's quarrelsomeness, vanity, and "insatiable desire to possess or to rule," for "without them all the excellent faculties of mankind would forever remain undeveloped." Man wants repose, he says, but nature wants discord to advance reason.[42]

In the international forum, according to Kant, "nature has again used quarrelsomeness [of states] . . . as a means of discovering a condition of quiet and security through the very antagonism inevitably among them":

> Wars, the excessive and never-ending preparation for wars . . . are means by which nature instigates attempts . . . which, after many devastations . . . may accomplish what reason could have suggested to them without so much sad experience, namely: to leave the lawless state of savages and to enter into a union of states. . . . All wars are . . . so many attempts (not in the intention of men, but in the intention of nature) to bring about new relations between the states and to form new bodies by the break-up of the old states to the point where they cannot maintain themselves alongside each other and must therefore suffer revolutions until finally . . . there is created a state which, like a civic constitution, can maintain itself automatically.[43]

The history of mankind, for Kant, "could be viewed on the whole as the realization of a hidden plan of nature to bring about an internally—and for this purpose also externally—perfect constitution."[44] In *Eternal Peace* he enlarges on these ideas, saying that a single world state would do more harm than good, that nature, through different languages and religions, had kept states apart; and that, with the development of reason through conflict, "as culture increases and men gradually come closer together towards a greater agreement of principles for peace and understanding," the latter goals will come about by "balancing these forces in a lively competition," not by bringing about a weakening of states, which would produce only the "graveyard of freedom."[45] (It is, of course, with an image of the graveyard that Kant *begins Eternal Peace:* "Whether the above satirical inscription ['to eternal peace'], once put by a certain Dutch innkeeper on his signboard on which a graveyard was painted, holds of men in general, or particularly of the heads of states who are never sated with war, or perhaps only of those philosophers who are dreaming that sweet dream of peace, may remain undecided."[46] Here Kant is obviously borrowing from his great predecessor Leibniz, whose 1712 letter concerning the Abbé de St. Pierre's *Project for Perpetual Peace* had been published in the fine 1768 edition of Leibniz' *Opera Omnia:* "I have seen something of the project of M. de St. Pierre, for maintaining a perpetual peace in Europe. I am reminded of a device in a cemetery, with the words: *Pax perpetua;* for the dead do not fight any longer: but the living are of another humor; and the most powerful do not respect tribunals at all."[47] Kant may also have known a passage from Leibniz' *Codex Iuris Gentium* (1693), which says that "a fashionable joker in Holland, after he had attached to the facade of his house, according to the local custom, a sign which read 'perpetual peace,' had placed under this fine slogan a picture of a cemetery—since there death does bring about peace."[43] Kant's point in borrowing from Leibniz is that one must have the right *kind* of eternal peace—not the peace of exhaustion and desperation under universal despotism, but a peace constantly renewed by the citizens of a universe of republics.)

Until most of the world is ready for republicanism and a *foedus pacificum*, Kant adds in "Conjectural Beginning of Human History," "lively competition" and even "conflict" itself may be provisionally necessary to freedom; without the threat of war, Kant asks rhetorically, "would there be as much freedom" as there is in Europe "albeit under laws which greatly restrict it?" For, Kant goes on, "it is surely the fear of war," which necessitates the cooperation of subjects, "that extorts from the heads of state at least this much respect for humanity." This becomes clearer, Kant adds, if one looks at China, "which, because of its geographical situation, has to fear at most the odd, unforeseen small attack, but no powerful enemy; and where for that reason every trace of freedom is extinct."[49] Here, for once, Kant skirts the margin of Hegel's argument that war preserves the "ethical health" of nations.

The hope, finally, for eternal peace through a new kind of world federalism—not a universal "republic" to replace the defunct *Respublica Christiana* (as in a writer like the Abbé de St. Pierre), but an agreement of all states to observe lawfulness (if not law) out of "sad experience" and developed reason—had two bases in Kant: first, that to found peace through a *foedus pacificum* was a duty to the extent that state law makes positive freedom (morality) possible for individuals by creating "negative freedom" (security) for all; and second, that there was a hidden plan of nature—where nature means culture produced by free human actions—to bring about world lawfulness through the final sublimation of conflict.

III

The *distinctiveness* of Kant's version of *Eternal Peace*—its uniqueness, though it borrows some elements from St. Pierre and Leibniz—can best be seen by first examining in detail the Abbé de St. Pierre's *Project for Perpetual Peace*, which was the most celebrated peace plan of Kant's own century, and which was treated seriously not just by Kant and Leibniz, but by Rousseau and Voltaire as well.[51] Even a bare comparison of titles is instructive: the Abbé, with characteristic optimism, speaks of peace as a realizable "project"; Kant, with characteristic evolutionary gradualism, speaks in his later political works of moving "toward" eternal peace. (In his pre-critical *Lectures on Ethics*, c. 1780–82, Kant had been closer to the Abbé: he had thought that if St. Pierre's "senate of the nations" were established, that would constitute a "great step forward" toward "the highest moral perfection" as the "universal end of mankind." Later, of course, in *Religion*, Kant was to draw a firm line between "juridical" and "ethical" commonwealths; and in the late writings peace is to be realized without benefit of *motiva moralia*. At the end Kant was no longer urging the doctrine of the *Lectures* that "the authority, not of governments, but of conscience within us, will . . . rule the world."[52] But he never ceased to praise the good intentions of the Abbé de St. Pierre.)

The Abbé de St. Pierre was an inveterate creator of projects of reform and correction of abuses, ranging from the maleducation of women to the extermination of corsairs and Barbary pirates; his *Project for Perpetual Peace* was only the most ambitious of an inexhaustible store of political plans.[53] First published in 1712, it went through several revised and enlarged editions, and finally became quite famous, if sometimes as the object of Voltaire's and Frederick the Great's jokes.[54] While the earnest desire of the Abbé for peace was undoubted and his condemnation of war quite eloquent, it is often thought that his plan vacillated between a true federation of independent sovereignties and a modified medieval *Respublica Christiana;*[55]

and, what is more serious, that the Abbé based his hopes for the success of his scheme on an utterly erroneous analysis of the nature of the seventeenth-century German Empire as a federal system (which, he thought, could serve as the model for a European Diet), and on a most inaccurate view of the Duc de Sully's quasi-federal *The Great Design of Henry IV* (c. 1635).⁵⁶ This left the Abbé with only the rationality and the utility of peace as a defense; hence the jokes at his expense.

"My design," said the Abbé, "is to propose means for settling an everlasting peace amongst all the Christian states." Enlarging on the disadvantages of war—cruelty, the ruin of commerce, constant instability, and fear—the Abbé insisted that without a European federal congress "the Christian princes must never expect anything but an almost continual war, which can never be interrupted but by some treaties of peace, or rather by truces, which are necessary productions of the equality of force."⁵⁷ The existing means of preserving peace— unenforceable treaties and the balance of power—he found unsatisfactory. "There will never be any sufficient security for the execution of treaties of peace and commerce in Europe," St. Pierre said, "so long as the refuser cannot be constrained by a sufficient force to execute them." Such a permanent force, he maintained, could "never be found until some permanent society be established among all the Christian states."⁵⁸ A balance of power (mainly between France and Austria) he rejected as well; it was not a "sure preservative" against war, it could not prevent civil war (a great object of the Abbé), it could not create security for a state nor for commerce, and it was "difficult and expensive" to establish and maintain. At best such an equilibrium had a transient value—it was better than nothing. If the Abbé did not want an equilibrium of existing European forces, neither did he want to enfeeble large powers in order to preserve the weaker; it was "either impossible to ruinous" to carve up large states to achieve a "chimerical equilibrium." Rather he thought that a European federal union "might give to the weaker a new augmentation of very strong allies . . . not to deprive the stronger of anything he possesses, but to take from him the power of ever disturbing the others, either in their possessions at home, or in their commerce abroad."⁵⁹

Since neither the "present constitution of Europe" (unenforceable truces and treaties) nor an equilibrium of power was desirable, the Abbé argued that

> if the eighteen principal sovereignties of Europe . . . would make a treaty of union, and a perpetual congress much after the model, either of the seven sovereignties of Holland [sic], or the thirteen sovereignties of the Swiss, or the sovereignties of Germany, and form a European union from

what is best in those unions . . . the weakest [states] would have a sufficient security, that the great power of the strongest could not hurt them; that everyone would exactly keep their reciprocal promises; that commerce would never be interrupted, and that all future differences would be terminated without war. [60]

The Abbé based much of his hope for the success of his scheme on its likeness (as he thought) to the Holy Roman Empire, and on its similarity (as he believed) to the *Great Design of Henry IV*. On the first point, he observed that "in examining the government of the sovereigns of Germany, I did not find that there would be more difficulty in forming the European body now than formerly there was in forming the Germanic body." One need only "penetrate" the "motives and means" by which the Empire (and Switzerland and the Netherlands) was formed to see that "those same motives, and those same means, are sufficient to form a society . . . which might continue to increase till it take in all of Christendom." [61] Here St. Pierre's case was dependent on a wholly inaccurate account of the course of German history since the time of Charlemagne (Kant of course knew better). He believed that the German princes had become literally sovereign, in the full sense, by the Middle Ages, and that the Empire as it existed in his time was the product of an actual treaty signed by the princes and cities. He referred constantly to "those sovereigns of Germany who first signed the treaty of the Germanic Union"; and (never recognizing that the Empire had become quasi-federal out of the degeneration of a feudal monarchy, not out of explicit federal treaties) he even argued that it had been a mistake to "give" the Emperor any power at all. Characteristically, he thought of the founding of the federal Empire as a project: "the wise German who proposed the project of the Germanic union," was to be excused for giving the Emperor power, because "he was obliged . . . to imitate the plan of the Empire, and to build a sort of republic upon some of the foundations of an ancient monarchy." [62]

It is obvious why St. Pierre saw German history in this historically wholly inaccurate way; he wanted to discover in the motives of the German princes in founding the German republic a parallel to the motives that *ought* to impel European sovereigns to join a European Diet. (Kant, obviously, would never have tried to derive "ought" from history.) [63] "Since the Germanic society was founded notwithstanding the predictions of the ancient mockers, the European society may yet more easily be formed, notwithstanding the predictions of the modern mockers." [64] This was pure fantasy; the Abbé ascribed to the German princes of old, at great length, all the motives that he thought ought to bring modern states into a federal union. Had he rested his case on the analogy of the Swiss and Netherlandish governments—which were products of treaties, if more than simple alliances—he might have had a point; but his inaccurate history of federal Germany (which took up a great many pages) cast doubt on his judgment.[65] The Abbé did not even reach the point of asking whether a valid analogy could be drawn between a federation like the United Provinces (which was, after all, a geographically restricted and fairly homogeneous grouping) and a federation of all Europe; nor did he consider whether a federation of monarchies was as viable as a federation of small republics.[66]

The Abbé relied for support not only on the German analogy, but on a hoped-for similarity between his project and the *Great Design of Henry IV.* "The approbation which most of the sovereigns of Europe gave to the project for an European society, which Henry the Great proposed to them," remarked the Abbé, "proves that it may be hoped such a project will be approved of by their successors." He even claimed that his project was not new, but only revived "the finest and most glorious project that ever could enter the mind of the best of princes."[67] Because of his ardent desire to see in the *Great Design* a prop for his plan, the Abbé could not believe that Sully and/or Henry IV really intended to divest the House of Austria of its possessions— though the *Great Design* discussed quite openly the intention to weaken the Hapsburgs and to strengthen France. He was unable to believe this simply because he himself wanted peace on the basis of the status quo, and read his desire back into the *Great Design.* "I am persuaded," he persuaded himself, "that he [Henry IV] would not have pitched upon such a remedy had he reflected that the European society would easily remedy that inequality of power without taking anything from anybody."[68] This is a complete misunderstanding, if not a willful distortion, of Sully's clear intentions; the Abbé inflicted his own dislike of mere equilibrium on Sully, who had wanted just such an equilibrium—with France *primus inter pares.* He inflicted even more of his personal beliefs on the *Great Design* when he asserted that Henry IV "found that to maintain the peace it was necessary for everyone to confine all his pretensions to what he actually possessed"; whereas, in fact, the motive of Henry's allies in the divesting of the Hapsburgs was the territory each would get from a morcellated Austria. St. Pierre concluded with an analysis of the *Great Design* that makes one suspect that he did not really know whether he wanted a federation of true sovereigns or a quasi-medieval hegemonical organization. The *Design,* he said, "was to make one single republic of all the Christian states"; Henry IV "desired so perfectly to unite all Christendom, that it might be but one body, and might actually be in its nature, as well as name, the CHRISTIAN REPUBLIC." How little this was Sully's intention, anyone who knows the *Great Design* may judge.[69]

Having sketched his two main grounds of hope for the success of his own plan—both of them not very relevant to his views, and obviously far inferior to Kant's two grounds of hope for eternal peace—the Abbé discussed at some length the arguments for doing away with war: force was not a good way to obtain right, national progress was arrested, the arts and sciences were left backward, sovereigns became cruel and unjust, troops were too expensive, and sovereign houses became insecure. Because all of these disadvantages of war seemed so clear, and because peace seemed rational and useful to the Abbé, he assumed that if a European union could be established all sovereigns would join it—first two would join, then a third, then a fourth, and so on.[70]

His actual federal plan was contained in twelve "fundamental" articles and in other "important" and "useful" articles. Article I stipulated that "there shall be . . . a society, a permanent and perpetual union, between the sovereigns subscribed."[71] Even in the first article, St. Pierre's lack of clarity on the nature of the union is evident; it was to be "between sovereigns," and yet it was to be a European supergovernment. Similarly, there was some contradiction between his claim that reason and utility would lead sovereigns to union and his claim that force would be needed to make them adhere to the rational and useful decisions of a European Diet. Almost immediately, however, a defect even more serious than these arose in the project: the constant emphasis on the status quo as the basis of peace. The union, said the Abbé, will "assist" a sovereign member "to subdue rebellious spirits . . . so that the union will never concern itself about the conduct of the sovereign, but only to support his will."[72] It was because of this provision—a well-intentioned but misguided lure for sovereigns—that Rousseau and St. Simon rejected the Abbé's solution.[73] Even stranger was his argument that republics should support the status quo because, if kings ruled badly, exiles would flee to the republics "together with their riches and talents."[74] This kind of argument may have brought down the criticism on the Abbé's head; this was certainly not the way that Kant proposed to strengthen republicanism.

The Abbé continued his insistence on the status quo in Article II. "The European society shall not at all concern itself about the government of a state, unless it be to preserve the fundamental form of it, and give speedy and sufficient assistance to the princes in monarchies, and to the magistrates in republics, against any that are seditious and rebellious." Hereditary kingdoms were to remain hereditary forever, elective ones elective forever. All of this was not mere reaction on the Abbé's part; he had a genuine horror, the product of studying the French and English civil wars of the sixteenth and seventeenth centuries, of internal violence. Civil war was "of all evils in a state, the most terrible and fatal."[75] The problem was that the Abbé went rather too far to suit Rousseau and even Kant, for whom he endangered legitimate opposition and necessary change in his effort to prevent civil war. The Abbe's insistence in Article III that the union would protect the sovereigns' rights and prerogatives by armed force against their own subjects did not help matters.[76]

By Article IV, each sovereign was to "be contented, he and his successors, with the territory he actually possesses." No new territories were to be added to old kingdoms; no changes were to be allowed by succession, agreement, election, donation, cession, sale, conquest, or voluntary submission of subjects. This was simply because, for the Abbé, hopes of aggrandizement and claims to old rights led to war.[77] Article V provided that no one should henceforth possess two sovereignties;[78] Article VI that Spain was to remain Bourbon; Article VII that the European congress was to "digest all the articles of commerce," with a view to the establishment of universal and equal commercial laws for all of Europe. By this article, as well, chambers of commerce were to be set up in the principal European cities to settle commercial claims between citizens of different states; and the commercial laws were to be voted provisionally by a simple majority of the Diet, definitively by a three-fourths majority.[79]

Article VIII was the heart of the plan. According to its terms, "no sovereign shall take up arms or commit any hostility but against him who shall be declared an enemy to the European society." Complaints between member states were to be mediated; any sovereign who without authorization took up arms was to be placed under a "Ban of Europe," and the union was to make war on him and disposses him of his territories.[80]

St. Pierre's *Project* was clearly a plan for the creation of lasting peace in Europe; it had no side motives of attacking "infidels," going on a crusade, or creating a universal hegemony. It tried to overcome the central defect of the independence of states—war—by means of sovereignty, of contract and agreement.[81] But the precedents on which the Abbé built his hope of success were all wrongly analyzed; he put too much emphasis on repression and the status quo and relied on the rationality of peace even while he contradictorily asserted that sovereigns would have to be forced to comply with rational European laws. His insistence, moreover, on bolstering the stability of the very sovereigns whose wills brought about war was inconsistent; "that sovereignty which he had assured princes they would not lose was nevertheless in his opinion the cause of war" (Hinsley).[82] What one cannot gainsay, however, is the Abbé's earnestness and, despite his confusions, his systematic effort to sketch the most comprehensive pre-Kantian international federal system of the eighteenth century. His plan has never lacked philosophical critics of real stature: Leibniz, Voltaire, Rousseau, Kant, and St. Simon all took him seriously enough to write about his theories of peace. (What his plan lacked in terms of actual implementation, as Frederick the Great observed, was "the consent of Europe and a few similar trifles.")[83]

Among St. Pierre's abler critics it is arguably Voltaire who formulated the most thoroughgoing objections; Leibniz and Kant found much to praise in the *Project*, or at least in the Abbé's good intentions; and even Rousseau began his *Jugement* of the plan by calling it "the most worthy to fascinate a man of high principle," though he ended by rejecting it.[84] But Voltaire clearly thought the *Project* wrong, both in principle and in detail. He wrote commentaries, most of them acid, on some of the principal political works of his time, including Montesquieu's *Esprit des Lois* (which, on the whole, he approved),[85] Rousseau's *Social Contract* (which he found incorrect and arrogant),[86] and the Abbé de St. Pierre's *Project for Perpetual Peace* (which he found naive). In his *De la Paix Perpetuelle* (1769), which he wrote under the name of Dr. Goodheart, Voltaire used his criticism of the Abbé's work as an introduction to an attack on intolerance, particularly the intolerance of Christianity. Most of Voltaire's essay is a long history of Christian outrages practiced in the name of truth; and his central position is that only tolerance, not any league of sovereigns, can bring about perpetual peace. "The only perpetual peace which can be established among men is tolerance," he wrote. "The peace imagined by a Frenchman named the Abbé de St. Pierre is a chimera which will never subsist between princes any more than between elephants and rhinoceroses, between wolves and dogs. Carnivorous animals always tear each other apart at the first occasion."[87]

Voltaire thought the project of peace through a European supergovernment "absurd," and counted on growing enlightenment, rather than on international institutions, to end war. War will end only when "men shall know that there is nothing to gain in the happiest wars, except for a small number of generals and ministers"; when those who advocate war are considered "the enemy of all nations"; when "peoples are convinced that the interest of each is that commerce be absolutely free," so that commercial wars will end; and when "men agree that if the inheritance of a prince is contested, it is for the inhabitants of his state to judge the contest of the competitors [for the crown]" and that outsiders have no influence. When all of these conditions come about, said Voltaire, then perpetual peace can arise.[88] One must place his hope on enlightenment, not on international federal leagues.

Voltaire admitted that "the establishment of a European Diet could be very useful" in extraditing criminals, in settling commercial questions, in resolving conflicts between different national laws in international dealings; he even granted that princes could be persuaded to allow arbitration of disputes by such a Diet, since it is possible to convince a ruler that "it is not in his interest to defend his rights or his pretensions by force."[89] But arbitration and persuasion are not federal government; indeed, they assume perfect external sovereignty that schemes like St. Pierre's were designed to overcome. On this point Voltaire was clear: it is absurd to propose to princes that they renounce their rights and pretensions. All one can hope for is a general change in public opinion that will obviate war without international federalism. "The sole means of rendering peace perpetual among men is then to destroy all the dogmas that divide them, and to reestablish the truth which unites them; that is what perpetual peace really is." Although dogmatic "imbeciles" still outnumber the enlightened, Voltaire feared, "the small number which thinks, will lead the great number in time." When "the idol falls," and "universal tolerance rises every day from the debris," then perpetual peace will be possible.[90]

Voltaire's criticism of St. Pierre is interesting not only it itself, but for its anticipation of Kant's dependence on the development of rationality through state conflict. Both thought that conflict would lead states to peace, not through true government, but through enlightened recognition, brought about through hard experience, of the *need* of observing international laws. But Voltaire, though first to conceive the idea of "universal history" as the development of human reason in and through history,[91] never showed explicitly how or why intolerance would be overcome and perpetual peace established. That more comprehensive project was left to Kant's *Eternal Peace* and *Idea for a Universal History*—writings that describe a quasi-federal equilibrium of republican (constitutional) states voluntarily adhering to international laws whose value has gradually been learned through "sad experience."[92] Kant's notion of a pacific federation of republics, then, draws together some of St. Pierre's reliance on international *institutions*—though in much weakened form—and some of Voltaire's notion that it is only enlightenment that will put men and states in a position to see the value of a pacific federation. If St. Pierre's *Project* expresses the greatest faith in international institutions as the foundation of lasting peace, and if Voltaire's *De la Paix Perpetuelle* represents the conviction that only increased rationality over time can end international violence, the works of Kant arguably involve the most intelligent drawing together of what is most plausible in both of these extreme positions. But this did not stop Kant himself from saying, in agreement with the Abbé de St. Pierre, that "a permanent universal peace by means of a so-called *European balance of power* is a pure illusion," nor from remarking that, however much the Abbé's *Project* might have "always been ridiculed by great statesmen, and even more by heads of state, as pedantic, childish and academic," it was still "valid in theory" and therefore "valid in practice"—at least in so far as it paralleled Kant's own *Eternal Peace*.[93]

IV

While international federalism is, for Kant, essential to the stability of states and their laws, it is extremely doubtful that he would or could have advocated federalism in the interior structure of any particular state. The principal reason that some of Kant's near-contemporaries (above all Montesquieu and Rousseau) advocate internal federalism is their conviction that true republics (such as Sparta or Geneva) have to be small and that a federal government alone can preserve "small republicanism" in a dangerous world of large, powerful monarchies. "It is . . . very probable." Montesquieu urges in Book IX of *De l'Esprit des Lois*, "that mankind would have been obliged, at length, to live constantly under the government of a single person, had they not contrived a kind of constitution which has all the internal advantages of a republican, together with all the external force of a monarchical, government. I mean a confederate republic."[94] For Kant, who cares comparatively little about the size of governments (except for rejecting universal despotisms), republicanism has to do solely with the liberty and equality of citizens under general public laws, and with the prevention of (domestic) despotism through separation of legislative and executive power. When republicanism is at issue, Kant is closer to Locke than to Montesquieu and Rousseau.[95] For Kant, a republic is not a small, popular state (or city) in which all the citizens can actually assemble in person to consent to fundamental laws, as in Rousseau;[96] just laws for Kant need only correspond to the Idea of an original contract—that is, be such that reasonable men could consent to them.[97]

Moreover, since for Kant both morality and religion are private and individual concerns, the state does not need to be as small as

Rousseau's ideal city-state. The re-creation of an inward-looking morality of the common good (general will) produced by intense patriotism, strict education, and civic religion is not one of Kant's objects; Kant, despite his reverence for Rousseau, could not have admired the nationalism and isolationism of which Rousseau made use in the defense of small republics, as in *Project for Corsica*.[98] Finally, since direct democracy is for Kant a form of despotism in that those who make the laws (everybody) also execute them, a Greek or Genevan or Dutch smallness is not an advantage, and a federation of small Rousseauean or Montesquieuean republics would not preserve a single thing that he valued. Kant favors only a functional division of power at the central level—that of separated executive and legislative powers—not a territorial division.[99]

Beyond this, Kant believed strongly enough in the sovereignty of the modern national state, both as guarantor of public legal justice and as stifler of private coercion, that he would never have set up or countenanced a system of divided sovereignty in which local units could be supreme even within limited spheres. His insistence on an ultimate power to protect legal justice is too strong to allow government by a *foedus* of sovereign units.[100] (This is not to say that Kant was obsessed with wholly unitary rule; as he makes clear in the *Reflexionen zur Rechtsphilosophie*, it is only in a despotic "art of governing" that the *collegia* (corporate bodies) within a state do not have "the right of remonstrating," the right of "representing" to the ruler their notion of the state's "welfare."[101] But this is still a functional, not a territorial, power division.)

It is conceivable that Kant never advocates anything more federal than the right of the *collegia* to "remonstrate" because, in addition to the reasons just given, he believes internal federalism to be too closely connected with the medieval and feudal politics that he so strongly condemns. All of Kant's political works, like those of Turgot, his great French contemporary,[102] radiate a hatred of that medieval corporative federalism (as one can call it by a kind of courtesy) which allowed private privilege to trench on public law. Here Kant is very strict, very much a "Jacobin." Asking whether it is "consistent with the rights of the people to have a class of persons above them who are, by reason of their birth, commanders in relation to them, or, at least, have certain privileges," and repeating his dictum that "what the people . . . cannot decide with regard to themselves or their fellows also cannot be decided by the sovereign regarding them," he argues that rulers cannot justly create a class of nobles "who acquire their rank before they merit it." Under the feudal system, Kant insists, an "anomoly such as subjects who want to be more than just citizens" may have sprung up; but hereditary privileges are unjust, and must be gradually eliminated, "either by agreement or by allowing the positions to become vacant." When public opinion finally realizes the injustice of hereditary prerogative, Kant asserts, the "threefold division into sovereign, nobility and people" will give way to "the only natural division, namely, sovereign and people."[103] Like many French theorists during the Revolution, Kant seems to have suspected that a federal divided sovereignty was simply a mask behind which unjust feudal prerogatives would be sustained.[104]

This attack on noble privileges—which might involve, of course, the territorial autonomy of, say, a count in his county—is part of Kant's general assault on the (unjust) advantages gained from perpetual and heritable land ownership. In this vein he argues that no "corporation, class or order in the state . . . can under certain statutes transmit land to succeeding generations for their sole and exclusive use (for all time)." If compensation is made, confiscation is allowable because such property ownership depends on the suffrage of public opinion. Even churches, according to Kant, are not exempt; they can be, he says with some sarcasm, "deprived of their estates if public opinion does not want to sue them to save the people of the state from eternal fire by means of masses for departed souls, prayer, and a multitude of clergy."[105]

Not only, however, are the property of the nobility and churches, which had sustained that form of corporatism that one might call medieval federalism, subject to compensated confiscation; the Kantian state also has a right to "inspect" the influence of great corporate bodies. "No association that can have any influence on the public welfare of the society," Kant argues in the *Rechtslehre*, "may remain concealed." Moreover, though Kant's state has no right to meddle in religious doctrines or enforce any particular belief, it does "have a negative right to prevent any activities of the public teachers that might prejudice the public peace," and could intervene in internal affairs "to prevent any danger to civil harmony."[106] Kant, in brief, does not propose to tolerate any trespassing on public legal justice by traditional noble, ecclesiastical, or city prerogatives. In this he represents a departure from earlier German political thought, such as Althusius's and Leibniz's, which had defended a federalized state with large degrees of corporative autonomy. Leibniz, indeed, argues in his essay called "On Natural Law" that the state is only the fifth degree of a quasi-federal hierarchy that has substantially autonomous corporations, provinces and cities below the state and a universal *Respublica Christiana* as the sixth degree above it;[107] but Kant has no interest in rationalizing the peculiar structure of the Holy Roman Empire of his day. As a political thinker, in fact, he is not distinctively German at all.

It is, perhaps, partly because of the medieval German tradition of noble and ecclesiastical territorial superiority—a form of private sovereignty that is brilliantly explained by Oakeshott in his "The Character of a Modern European State"[108]—that Kant rejects federalism in the interior structure of the state. Since local democracy in the form of regional autonomy is not of interest to him, it is natural for him to fear that a federal government, which restricts central authority, will merely shore up ancient territorial privileges. Kant certainly does not want to permit mere territorial property rights to permit and perpetuate private coercion—for example, the coercion of a serf by the lord of a manor. "No one has a right to compel or coerce anyone whomsoever in the state," Kant concludes, "otherwise than by the public law and through the sovereign or ruler executing it."[109] The key term here is *public*; for Kant, a modern, national government that makes and enforces general laws is instrumental to the freedom that makes good will more nearly possible, while the private law of German medieval federalism simply perpetuates coercion and prerogative. Some see federalism as advancing freedom (or at least autonomy); but, as Franz Neumann effectively pointed out, the connection between federalism and freedom is not irresistible.[110] It depends on what one takes freedom to be.

V

Kant, then, rejects internal or domestic federalism within particular states; but in the end the most striking thing about his international federalism, his *foedus pacificum*, is that the stability of national states depends on it. Kant's national states, indeed, without being federal, need federalism. The uniqueness of his system is the interlocking character of law and public order at all levels, the mutual need of republican constitutionalism and international federalism for each other, and the dependence of constitutionalism itself on peace through international lawfulness. Kant, then, is a "federalist," as he is often taken to be, if only in the special sense that has been suggested here. In another sense, however, he took federalism more seriously than any other great political theorist ever took it, insofar as the possibility of morality, of respect for persons as "ends in themselves," turns on a context of public legal justice that is secured and stabilized by a universal *foedus pacificum*. If, then, as Kant urges, the good will that constitutes morality is a "jewel which shines by its own light,"[111] and if national law is the "setting" that supports it, then a federal eternal peace is literally and figuratively the crown of Kant's political philosophy.

CHAPTER SEVEN

Some Recent Interpretations of Kant's Political Thought

I

The present "instrumental" understanding of the relation between Kant's political theory and his moral philosophy—which treats republicanism and eternal peace as supportive of Kantian moral "ends" through "legal" incentives, and sees "civility" as the core of a Kantian "culture" that also embraces art and science—can be thrown into higher relief by contrasting it with six other recent efforts to illuminate Kant's social thought: Alexandre Kojève's *Kant* (1973),[1] Lucien Goldmann's *Immanuel Kant* (English translation 1971),[2] Robert Paul Wolff's *In Defense of Anarchism* (1970),[3] Susan Shell's *The Rights of Reason: A Study of Kant's Philosophy and Politics* (1980),[4] Hans Saner's *Kant's Political Thought* (1973),[5] and John Charvet's *A Critique of Freedom and Equality* (1981).[6] Since, however, Kojève's *Kant*, which will be treated first, offers a Kant refracted through a Marxianized Hegelian lens, one can judge the justice of his account of the relation between politics and morality only by examining that lens.

In his brilliant and influential *Introduction to the Reading of Hegel*, which constitutes the glass through which Kant is ultimately filtered, Kojève makes his treatment of Hegel's *Phenomenology* revolve around Hegel's great set-piece, "Master and Servant," rendered by Kojève as "Master and Slave". And in this treatment Kojève argues that for Hegel human society and human "discourse" began when men were first willing to risk their animal and biological existence in a "fight to the death" for "pure prestige," for "recognition" by the "other."[7] The man who became the Master was he who was "willing to go all the way" in this fight; the potential Master "preferred, to his real,

135

natural, biological life, something ideal, spiritual, nonbiological—the fact of being recognized in and through [another] consciousness, of bearing the name 'Master,' of being called 'Master.' "[8] The (potential) Slave, on the other hand, was the one who saw and feared his own "nothingness" should he die in the struggle, and who recognized the Master rather than die.[9] The Master, for his part, finds that he is not satisfied with mastery, since he has risked his life for recognition by a mere Slave whom he uses as a thing; the Master has the "pleasure" of not having to work, but this pleasure is not a true *satisfaction*. "To get oneself recognized by a Slave is not to get oneself recognized by a *man*"; hence the Master never attains his end, the end for which he has risked his very life." (For this reason, according to Kojève, mastery is ultimately "tragic" and "an existential impasse.")[10] The Slave, who submits to and works in the service of the Master, can ultimately find satisfaction in his work, by which he transforms the natural world of "given being," and himself as well: through work, which negates "given being, the Slave overcomes the world. "The man who works transforms given being . . . where there is work there is necessarily change, progress, historical evolution." Although this progress and evolution involves alterations in the "means of production," the essential change is in the Slave himself: "thanks to his work, the Slave *can* change and become other than he is, that is— in the end—cease to be a Slave."[11] For work, according to Kojève, is *Bildung* or education "in a double sense of the word: on the one hand it forms and transforms the world, humanizes it, by making it more adapted to man; on the other hand, it transforms, forms, educates man, humanizes him in bringing him closer to the idea which he makes for himself"—the "idea" of being "free" and "recognized".[12]

Since the Slave's "overcoming"—of the natural world of "given being," of his fear of the Master and of death, of slavery itself—is not historically complete until men choose their own work and become citizens of a "universal and homogeneous" Hegelian state,[13] history is, *inter alia*, a history of "slave ideologies" by which Slaves conceal their slavery for themselves. "The transformation of the Slave, which will permit him to surmount his terror, his fear of the Master . . . is long and dolorous."[14] At first, Kojève in his reading of Hegel asserts the Slave "raises himself" through his work to the "abstract idea" of liberty—an abstract idea that he does not realize because "he does not yet dare to *act* in view of this realization, that is to struggle against the Master and risk his life in a struggle for liberty."[15] Before realizing liberty, the Slave "imagines a series of ideologies, by which he seeks to justify himself, to justify his servitude, to reconcile the *ideal* of liberty with the fact of slavery."[16] For Stoicism, the first of the "slave ideologies," Epictetus in his chains and Marcus Aurelius on his throne are "equal" as "wise men"; hence for the Stoic ideology the chains do not "matter."[17] In Christian ideology equality is of a different sort: all men are equal "before God," whatever their earthly stations; but this is simply another escape to a "beyond" (beyond the historical world of work and struggle). Moreover, in this beyond, though there are no earthly masters, there is one universal Master (God) to whom everyone is enslaved. Christianity, according to Kojève, "does not take account of social distinctions, but leaves them intact. Equality is transposed into the beyond (men are brothers 'in Jesus Christ'; that is, all slaves of an absolute Master)."[18] A modern bourgeois may, by contrast, appear to be "his own master," but bourgeois ideology is simply a new slavery: one is now enslaved to property and to capital. "The bourgeois does not work for another. But neither does he work for himself, taken as a biological entity. He works for himself taken as a 'juridical person,' as a private proprietor . . . he works for Capital."[19]

As long as there is slavery—whether to a Master, to God, or to Capital—man will never be truly satisfied or truly free, since true satisfaction and freedom come from being recognized as an equal by an equal, which is possible only in the Hegelian state. "Man can only be truly 'satisfied,' history can only end, in and through the forma-tion of a Society, of a State, in which the strictly particular, personal, individual value of each is recognized as such . . . *by all*." Such a state, *selon* Kojève, "is only possible after the 'suppression' of the opposition between Master and Slave."[20]

This "suppression," to be sure, is brought about mainly through the Slave's work. "Only the Slave," Kojève urges, "'suppresses' his 'nature' and finally becomes a Citizen. The Master does not change: he would rather die than cease to be Master. The final struggle, which transforms the Slave into a Citizen, suppresses Mastery in a non-dialectical fashion: the Master is simply killed, and he dies as a Master."[21] But by this point, the end of history, the Slave is ready for the reality of freedom, not its mere "imagination," as in Stoicism or Christianity. "The complete, absolutely free man," Kojève insists, "will be the Slave who had 'overcome' his slavery. If idle Mastery is an impasse, laborious Slavery, in contrast, is the source of all human, social, historical progress. History is the history of the working Slave." In the "raw, natural, given world," he adds, "the Slave is the slave of the Master. In the technical world transformed by his work, he rules—or, at least, will one day rule—as absolute Master. And this Mastery that arises from work . . . will be an entirely different thing from the 'immediate' mastery of the Master. The future and history hence belong not to the warlike Master . . . but to the working Slave."[22] In another passage of his *Introduction*, Kojève enlarges and refines this view. "History will end when man no longer acts in the strong sense of the term, that is, no longer negates, no longer transforms given being and social being through bloody struggle and creative work. And man no longer does this when what is Real *[le Réel donné]* gives him full satisfaction, by realizing fully his Desire (which in man is a desire for universal recognition of his personality, which is unique in the world)."[23] As Kojève puts it in his essay entitled "Hegel, Marx and Christianity," history will end "necessarily" when "man is perfectly satisfied by the fact of being a recognized citizen of a universal and homogeneous State, or, if one prefers, of a society without classes encompassing the whole of humanity." If man is fully satisfied *"by what he is,"* the only desire left—on the part of a *philosopher*—is that of "understanding what he is . . . and revealing it through discourse."[24] This "understanding" and "revealing" are provided by Hegel, standing at the end of time, who offers an "adequate description of the Real in its totality." Hegel, in short, provides a satisfying account of a Reality which has (finally) become satisfactory.[25]

No one has doubted the ingenuity of this reading of the *Phenomenology;* if it is not an irresistible or a "natural" reading—since, to use George Kelly's language, it treats the Master and Servant "tableau" as "the synoptic clue to a whole philosophy"[26]—it is one that works for substantial and important sections of Hegel's greatest work. The notions of "work," "struggle," "recognition," "satisfaction" and "freedom" are really *there;* if, strictly speaking, the notion of "ideology" is a Marxian importation, it is arguably prefigured in Hegel's remark about philosophy as the "thought of the world" arriving to paint its "grey in grey" after reality is "cut and dried."[27]

However far these concepts may go in illuminating (parts of) Hegel's *Phenomenology,* nonetheless, they are arguably *not* the notions that cast the strongest or the fairest light on philosophers who are not Hegelians. This emerges clearly in Kojève's treatment of Kant. It is no accident that in his *Kant* Kojève argues that if one suppresses Kant's idea of the "thing-in-itself" ("beyond" the empirical world, in a realm of "transcendence") and treats freedom and purposiveness as "real" rather than as "necessary hypotheses" (as Kant treated them), one can "transform" Kantianism "quasi-automatically" into the Hegelian "system of knowledge"[28]—as if such a transformation would necessarily be advantageous. (Kojève, to be fair, grants that this would be a "violent interpretation.")[29]

Now Kant *did* treat freedom as a "necessary hypothesis" whose reality could neither be demonstrated nor denied; in his *Fundamental Principles of the Metaphysic of Morals*, indeed, he argues that "freedom is only an idea of reason, and its objective reality in itself is doubtful." Nonetheless, Kant urges that if the idea of a free will as a "noumenal" or intelligent "causality" is given up, all morality will become merely "empirical," and concludes that every being that "cannot act except under the 'idea' of freedom" is "from a practical point of view" really free; that while freedom cannot be proved to be "actually a property of ourselves or of human nature," it must be presupposed "if we would conceive a being as rational and conscious of its causality in respect of its actions, that is, as endowed with a will."[30] Unless men *take themselves to be free*, that is, they cannot make intelligible to themselves their own notions of duty, responsibility, blame, and so forth. And this hypothetical freedom has a very immediate bearing on Kant's politics, since he argues in a now familiar passage from *Eternal Peace* that if there exists "no freedom and no moral law based upon it, and if everything which happens . . . is simply part of the mechanism of nature," then it is appropriate to manipulate men as natural objects in order to govern them; but that if "right" is to be the "limiting condition of politics," morality and politics must be conceded to be "compatible," and politics must be capable of treating men as they ought to be treated—as "ends in themselves."[31]

What distresses Kojève is that the Kantian "categorical imperative" of treating men as "ends," as free beings who ought to be "respected," is based on freedom which is only *hypothetical:* one builds categorical moral requirements, which also serve as the "limiting condition" of politics, on "as if" foundations. Or, as Kojève himself puts it, "one cannot effectively speak of 'morality' without speaking of 'freedom', and good sense would be scandalized by a 'commandment' addressed to someone who would be materially incapable of following it."[32] Kant, he goes on, succeeds only in talking about "what one ought to do, IF the will is free";[33] but this reduces the categorical to the hypothetical (with a devastating effect on the limiting condition of politics). Since, according to Kojève, Kant failed to treat freedom as something real, he could not account for efficacious free action: "he never wanted to admit the *efficacity* of free or conscientious human activity in the world and as a result refused to identify (discursive) truth with history"—a history characterized by work and struggle.[34] For this reason, Kojève argues in *Introduction to the Reading of Hegel*, Kant accepts the result of the French Revolution, but rejects the means, which include "bloody struggle and work by all."[35]

Since at least a part of this criticism is a serious one, and since, at the same time, one cannot reopen the question of Kantian freedom at this juncture, it will have to suffice (for present purposes) to say that (1) even if freedom could be shown to be something more than a necessary "idea of reason," Kant would have had no reason to "identify truth with history," since he needed freedom to account for the conceivability of common moral concepts (duty, responsibility, etc.), not to explain historical work and struggle;[36] and (2) it is by no means clear that it is legitimate to reduce the Kantian notions of "necessary hypothesis" and "idea of reason" to a mere "as if": Kant does not say that it is as if men were free (but really not), but that men must "necessarily" conceive themselves as free if their ordinary moral ideas are to be intelligible.[37] (The philosophy of "as if" is not strictly Kantian and is, in fact, an invention of the "neo-Kantian" Hans Vaihinger.)[38] Kant, after all, may have been perfectly right in thinking that freedom can be neither more nor less than a necessary hypothesis; if one makes it more one may go beyond what can legitimately be claimed, and if one makes it less common moral concepts may vanish.

The strengths and weakness of Kojève's insistence on the "as ifness" of Kant's philosophy emerge with particular clarity in his handling of the *Critique of Judgment*, which (as was seen in Chapter 4) is Kant's greatest treatment of teleology or "purposiveness." Kojève begins by observing, correctly enough, that Kant undertook the *Critique of Judgment* "with a view to looking for a connecting-point between the *given* natural world and man as possessor of a free will";[39] that the connecting point was to be "purposiveness," since the natural world has a purposive structure and man *qua* free agent has purposes. But Kant failed, according to Kojève, to talk about "struggle and work," which are the most "striking" instances of a purposive freedom operating on a purposively organized nature; and this failure can be traced to the fact that in *Judgment* Kant treated purposiveness "in the 'as-if' mode."[40] Now there *is* something in this: Kojève is correct when he says that Kant accounts better for (say) artistic *judgments* than for artistic *production;* hence Kant judges that a work of art involves "purposiveness without purpose" (what a brilliant definition of the "argument" of a sonata movement!) but is hard pressed to account for the work and struggle of *producing* that sonata movement. In complaining that Kant failed to see work as the most "striking" instance of purposive freedom, Kojève is almost certainly under the influence of the passage in Volume I of *Kapital*, where Marx says:

> We suppose labor in a form that stamps it as exclusively *human*. A spider conducts operations that resemble those of a weaver, and a bee puts to

shame many an architect in the construction of her cells. But what distinguishes the worst architect from the best of bees is this, that the architect raises his structure in imagination before he erects it in reality. At the end of every labor-process, we get a result that already existed *in the imagination of the laborer* at its commencement. He not only *effects* a change of form in the material on which he works but he also *realizes a purpose* of his own that gives the law to his *modus operandi,* and to which he must subordinate his will.[47]

Of course Marx's notion of "giving the law" through a "purpose" of "one's own" is not far from Kant's own account of artistic production in "Aesthetic Judgment";[42] indeed Marx's theory of labor is closer to the "Aesthetic" half than to the "Teleological" half of *Judgment.* Still, Kojève has something of a point; Kant talks *much* more of aesthetic "judgment" than of artist's "struggles."

Even if what Kojève says in this connection is partly true, one can still complain that finding this truth has cost him another: namely, the fact that in *Judgment* Kant was trying to link up nature, human freedom, and art through the notion of purposiveness (plants have purposes that men impute to them, men both *have* purposes and *are* the final purpose or end of creation, and art is purposiveness without purpose).[43] But Kojève misses Kant's effort to achieve this tripartite linking up when he says that Kant limits "his teleology to natural and artistic beauty and to organic life," that he excludes purposiveness from "the domain of human action, of struggle and work."[44] This not only contradicts what Kojève himself earlier called Kant's effort to find a connecting point between nature and human freedom, but leaves wholly out of account the very section of *Judgment* that is most important for Kant's moral and political philosophy. In Section 84, as was argued in Chapter 4, Kant says that while the purposes of things in the natural world are imputed by us to those things, man is the ultimate purpose of creation on earth because "he is the only being upon it who can form a concept of purposes, and who can by his reason make out of an aggregate of purposively formed things a system of purposes"; that one cannot ask "for what end" man exists, since "his existence inherently involves the highest end."[45] Since the argument that only man can *conceive* purposes—let alone conceive of himself as the "ultimate" purpose—constitutes Kant's most effective defense of the notion that men are "ends in themselves" who ought never to be used merely as means to arbitrary purposes; and since that argument supports the "limiting condition" of rightful politics in *Eternal Peace;* it is difficult to understand why Kojève argues that Kant excludes purposiveness from "the domain or human action." Even though Kant treats purposiveness, like freedom, as a necessary hypothesis, this involves no exclusion; indeed Kant argues that teleology is the *one* concept that draws together nature, human freedom, and art.[46]

If Kojève's "Hegelian" emphasis on work and struggle permits him to see some parts of Kant clearly at the cost of slighting others, his insistence on "satisfaction" leads to a further difficulty. Now Kant is famous for the asceticism of his moral philosophy, and is rightly celebrated as the enemy of eudaemonism and utilitarianism (hence of Aristotle and Bentham); "the majesty of duty," he once observed, "has nothing to do with the enjoyment of life."[47] But Kojève interprets Kantian morality as turning on "satisfaction" in a "beyond." To be sure, Kant sometimes argued that the "supreme good"—happiness connected with *worthiness* to be happy—does not exist on earth, that there ought to be immortality in which God provides this connection;[48] then, *selon* Kojève, those who have been *good* are "satisfied".[49] But this interpretation, to which Kojève gives an enormous weight, is (to use a good Hegelianism) "one-sided"; it leaves out of account the fact that Kant increasingly doubted this "moral proof" of God and immortality, as evidenced in his *Opus Posthumous*,[50] and it seems to make "satisfaction" the *precondition* of morality. But if there was ever a philosopher who separated moral philosophy from psychology, it was Kant; for him, if one's motive in "acting well" involves a hope for happiness ("satisfaction"), one does not have a "good will" at all.[51] Kant's idea of the "supreme good" is problematical enough without trying, a la Kojève, to make "satisfaction" the pivot of Kantian morality—which is not, after all, just a Benthamism in which "satisfaction" is maximized in a "beyond" rather than on earth.

But Kojève's occasional reading of Kant as a transcendentalized Bentham is not the final oddity; the final oddity is also the final irony. That irony is apparent in this way: while Kojève reads Kant as standing in need of transformation into the "Hegelian system of knowledge," the Hegel that emerges from Kojève's reading may "preserve" more of Kant, and "cancel" more of Hegel,[52] than he imagines. For the goal of history in Kant is assuredly a state of affairs in which there will (finally) be universal respect for all persons as ends in themselves; and this Kantian aim seems to be realized more nearly in Kojève's "universal and homogeneous state" in which every man is "recognized in his reality and in his human dignity by *all* the others"[53] than in the state "understood" by Hegel in the *Philosophy of Right*. After all, the state offered in the *Philosophy of Right* is not "universal" but national, not "homogeneous" but class-stratified.[54] One could, perhaps, call this irony "Kant's revenge," were it not for the fact that revenge is so very un-Kantian a notion. But Kojève's reading of Hegel, particularly when it ignores the *Philosophy of Right*, seems to involve some "quasi-automatic" transforming of Hegel into Kant. Kojève's refurbished Owl of Minerva "recognizes" Königsberg, even if it goes on to land in Berlin.

II

If it is Kojève's wish to transform Kant into a (Marxianized) Hegel, it is Lucien Goldmann's more modest aim in *Immanuel Kant* to move Kant a *little* closer to his greatest German successors. For this reason Goldmann's study is the most persuasive version of left-Kantianism that has been produced.

Beginning with a rejection of the charge that Kantian morality is a contentless formalism, Goldmann insists that the content of Kant's ethics is to be found in the concept of objective ends: "What, then, is the *content* . . . of the maxims which should direct man's actions? Clearly, it can only be a categorical rejection of individualist man as he is today. Indeed, Kant succeeds in concentrating into a few words the most radical condemnation of bourgeois society and in formulating the foundations for any future humanism: *Act in such a way that you always treat humanity, whether in your own person or in the person of any other, never simply as a means, but always at the same time as an end.'* "[55]

In this reading of the teleological strand of Kant's moral thought, which Goldmann is quite right in emphasizing, there is undoubtedly a certain amount of well-meaning wishful thinking; Kant's condemnation of feudal land ownership and hereditary aristocracy is, after all, characteristically *bürgerlich*, as is his insistence on careers "open to talent" and on the compatibility of civil equality with (perhaps radical) economic inequality.[56] Here Goldmann ignores much of what Kant says in the *Rechtslehre*, and tries to spin a kind of pre-Marxism out of Kant's notions of "humanity" and "ends." Perhaps Kant *ought* to have said what Goldmann wishes he had said; the fact remains that he didn't. But among Hegelo-Marxist "readings," Goldmann's Kant as antibourgeois at least represents something that Kant could (without logical contradiction) have been; whereas Georg Lukács in *The Young Hegel*, in treating Kant as an incipient *bourgeois* whose distinction between "mind" and "the senses" is merely an ideological "reflection" of "the capitalist division of labor," as a proto-*Bürger* who "unconsciously equates" the "as yet non-existent bourgeois society with the 'kingdom of reason,' "[57] simply reduces Kantianism to an epiphenomenon of the mode of production. Goldmann preserves Kant, in a left-leaning form; Lukács simply cancels him. If the choice is between an antibourgeois Kant who upholds humanity and objective ends (as in Goldmann), and a bourgeois Kant whose whole philosophy is a reflection of capitalism (as in Lukács),[58] the first alternative is plainly preferable, since it stresses *telos* and declines to view Kantianism as merely superstructural. But the truth is probably to be found in a *bürgerlich* Kant who also upholds humanity and objective ends.

In fleshing out his understanding of Kant as a sort of pre-Marxian humanist, Goldmann goes on to insist that

> Once we realize that this formula [of treating persons as ends] condemns any society based on production for the market, in which other men are treated as means with a view to creating profits, we see the extent to which Kant's ethic is an ethic of content and constitutes a radical rejection of existing society. Moreover, and no less radically, it lays the foundations for any true humanism in establishing the only supreme value upon which all our judgments must be based. That supreme value is humanity in the person of each individual man—not just the individual, as in rationalism, not just the totality in its different forms (God, state, nation, class), as in all the romantic and intuitionist doctrines, but the *human* totality, *the community embracing the whole of humanity* and its expression in *the human person* . . . The totality would be the realization of a 'kingdom of ends', that is to say, the very reverse of present-day society where, with the exception of a few rare and partial communities, man is never more than a means.[59]

This eloquent and heartfelt paragraph is, obviously, a mixture of permissible interpretation at the left-hand margin of Kant's thought and quasi-Marxian transformation. The opening sentence has Kant condemning a market that he never even discussed; doubtlessly the categorical imperative *can* condemn the extraction of surplus value, but that is an extrapolation from anything that Kant actually says. The next sentence, in insisting that Kant "lays the foundations for any true humanism," is much more acceptable; even Cassirer or Arendt could agree with it.[60] But in the last half of the paragraph Goldmann's own generous instincts ("the totality would be . . . the community embracing the whole of humanity") lead him to forget that Kant, in *Religion within the Limits*, falls back on juridical republicanism and eternal peace out of fear that a universal ethical commonwealth will probably not be realized.[61] This in turn leads Goldmann to denigrate states and nations more than Kant himself ever did.

A closer look at Goldmann's eloquent paragraph reveals that he is not just *interpreting* the "kingdom of ends," but bringing about a *union* of two kingdoms: Kant's *Reich der Zwecke* and Marx's *Reich der Freiheit* (from *Kapital*, Book III, Chapter 48.)[62] For the animadversions against production for profit or the market that Goldmann *thinks* to find in Kant have their full existence only in Marx; and it is in Book III of

Kapital that Marx describes a "realm of freedom," of nonalienated production, in language that is sometimes not so far from Kant's.

> The realm of freedom [*Reich der Freiheit*] actually begins only where labor which is determined by necessity and mundane considerations ceases . . . Freedom in this field can only consist in socialized men, the associated producers, rationally regulating their interchange with Nature, bringing it under their common control . . . and achieving this with the least expenditure of energy and under conditions most favorable to, and worthy of, their human nature. But it nonetheless still remains a realm of necessity. Beyond it begins that development of human energy which is an end in itself, the true realm of freedom, which, however, can blossom forth only with this realm of necessity at its basis. The shortening of the working day is its basic prerequisite.[63]

Evidently, Goldmann has fused a *Reich* in which production will be free and satisfying with another *Reich* (Kant's "kingdom of ends"), by relying on the very passage in which Marx's kingdom is closest to Kant's (thanks to Marx's use of Kantian phrases such as "end in itself" and "worthy of human nature"). In that composite, Kanto-Marxist realm, the kingdom of ends will be attained when labor has a "rational," satisfying relation to nature.

It is only because Goldmann has carefully moved Kant to the left that he can finally say, at the end of *Immanuel Kant*, that Kant's attitude toward the French Revolution was "unambiguous" and "unequivocal";[64] in fact it was both ambiguous *and* equivocal. Goldmann has Kant greeting the revolution with "the last salute of the imprisoned giant to his brothers who have broken the bars of their prison and begin now to live in freedom"—a salute that refutes the claim that "in his old age Kant allowed himself to be yoked to the wagon of German nationalism and of Prussian reaction."[65] But this, though edifying, is a false antithesis; the choice for Kant is not either the Revolution or "Prussian reaction." The real choice is evolutionary approximation to republicanism and eternal peace.

Actually, the passage from *Conflict of the Faculties* that Goldmann cites to establish his unequivocally revolutionary Kant indicates instead Kant's hesitations and careful qualifications. What Kant actually says is this:

> The revolution which we have seen taking place in our own times in a nation of gifted people may succeed, or it may fail. It may be so filled with misery and atrocities that no right-thinking man would ever decide to make the same experiment again at such a price. . . . But I maintain that this revolution has aroused in the hearts and desires of all spectators who are not themselves caught up in it a *sympathy* which borders almost on enthusiasm. . . . We are here concerned only with the attitude of onlook-

ers as it reveals itself *in public* while the drama of great political changes is taking place: for they openly express universal yet disinterested sympathy for one set of protagonists against their adversaries, even at the risk that their partiality could be of great disadvantage to themselves.[66]

This carefully nuanced passage, in which Kant separates the sympathy of spectators from the action of protagonists and uses the aesthetic terminology of the *Critique of Judgment* ("drama," "universal yet disinterested," "onlookers"), supports Goldmann's Jacobin Kant rather less well than it upholds Hannah Arendt's Kant: a Kant for whom principles of political "action" and principles of aesthetic "judgment" *differ*.[67] But Goldmann, with his usual honesty, quotes every word of the passage which fails fully to support his own reading.

Whatever may be the weaknesses of Goldmann's interpretation, he preserves the crucial teleological dimension of Kant's practical thought, and vindicates (even exaggerates) his liberalism. The Kant he offers is a very attractive one, even if it sometimes fails to correspond to the whole of what Kant actually said. Unlike Kojève, Goldmann gives full weight to *telos*, to persons as ends.

III

If it is Kojève's view that Kant's "as-if" morality makes true politics impossible, it is Robert Paul Wolff's thesis that Kant's morality makes politics unnecessary (and even leads to "anarchism").[68] In his *In Defense of Anarchism* what Robert Paul Wolff has done, while borrowing the "cloak" of Kant's "legitimacy,"[69] is to argue that only a "unanimous direct democracy" in which everyone actually consents to everything is "legitimate" because only in such a scheme is everyone truly "autonomous"—autonomy not being preserved, on this view, by tacit consent, representative government, and rule by majority: in short, by Lockean politics.[70] Wolff's practical thought depends on the notion that autonomy is "the primary obligation of man"; that such autonomy can be politically protected only in a unanimous direct democracy in which everyone "gives laws to himself"; and that, in the absence of such a democracy, one must pronounce in favor of philosophical anarchism.[71] Such a political theory might, Wolff says—"if I may steal a title from Kant (and thus perhaps wrap myself in the cloak of his legitimacy)"—be called *Groundwork of the Metaphysics of the State*.[72]

The striking thing here, of course, is that Robert Paul Wolff has turned "autonomy" into a substantive moral duty, into "the primary obligation of man." But Kant's argument, whose authority Wolff would like to "steal," is that unless one considers man, from a hypothetical point of view, as an autonomous being, as spontaneous, then none of his substantive moral duties is *conceivable*. Kant maintains, that is, that while the objective reality of autonomy cannot be proven, it must nevertheless be presupposed as the necessary condition of conceiving oneself as responsible, good, or just; that a being that is unable to conceive itself as an autonomous "moral cause" can never imagine itself responsible or good or just.[73] Autonomy, then, for Kant is a necessary point of view, or a necessary hypothesis, in explaining the possibility of the common moral concepts that we actually use (not a mere Kojèvian "as if"); but autonomy is not *itself* a substantive moral duty. Since Kant did not say that we have a duty to *be* autonomous, he would not support Wolff's politics either. While Kant preferred republicanism, indeed, he supported any legal order that creates a context for self-moralization by removing impediments to that process.[74]

It is problematical enough to borrow the "cloak" of Kant's legitimacy, only to use it in a questionable way; even more serious is the difficulty of relating the common moral duties, such as refraining from murder, to Wolff's "primary obligation" of autonomy. Would one say, for example, that one acted autonomously by refraining from murder, such that refraining from murder becomes an instance of autonomous action? Is the obligation, then, one of not murdering (*simpliciter*), or is it one of not violating one's own autonomy *by* murdering? In short: if the primary obligation of man is autonomy, "the refusal to be ruled," are all obligations *ultimately* "obligations to oneself"? Along what lines, then, does one view "secondary" obligations to others? If one says that everyone's autonomy is to be respected, that takes care of both self-regarding and other-regarding obligations; but this is not what Wolff argues—though Kant of course does.[75] Moreover, if one's primary obligation were to respect everyone's autonomy, the anarchism that Wolff recommends when "unanimous direct democracy" cannot be attained would not necessarily follow. After all, one could say that respect for the autonomy of everyone necessitates a legal order insofar as "respect" is only an imperative rather than a fact; but if one's primary obligation is autonomy, or the refusal to be ruled, then anarchism seems to be more nearly inevitable, and perhaps more natural than unanimous direct democracy itself.[76] Wolff apparently believes that having a primary obligation to be autonomous is equivalent to having an obligation to respect the autonomy of everyone, but that of course is not correct. And so he has not only mis-used Kant, whose authority has been illegitimately borrowed; he has provided too convenient a foundation for his anarchism.

It can be reasonably argued, then, that Wolff's treatment of autonomy as the "Kantian" primary obligation of man has the following consequences: (1) it leads to treating autonomy as a substantive duty, contrary both to Kant and to common moral reasoning; (2) this error leads to neglect of Kant's notion that the primary substantive moral duty of men is to treat other men as ends in themselves whose dignity ought to be respected (i.e., to respect others' autonomy, not just one's own); and (3) this initial error leads to the further misfortune of suggesting (or at least implying) that anarchism is a Kantian doctrine necessitated by autonomy *qua* the refusal to be ruled—whereas in fact Kant argues that government is absolutely necessary to realize moral ends legally and to provide a context or environment within which one can pursue a good will.[77] Properly understood, Kantianism neither argues for autonomy as a substantive moral duty (still less as the primary obligation of man), nor urges that anarchism is necessitated by the refusal to be ruled. It does indeed insist on *moral* autonomy (as the ground of the possibility of conceiving and having duties), but not just on *one's own* autonomy; nor does it ever argue that moral autonomy and government are incongruent. One cannot wrap the cloak of Kant's legitimacy around an anarchist argument that he would have thought illegitimate.

It is *only* by conceiving autonomy as a substantive duty, as a "primary obligation" that requires that one "refuse to be ruled," that one could possibly represent a theory of anarchism based on autonomy as Kantian. But this Kantianism vanishes when one unwraps the cloak of Kant's legitimacy from *In Defense of Anarchism* and sees that this conception is a misconception. Thus it is heartening to see that much of this misconception is either abandoned or moderated in Wolff's new and very instructive commentary on Kant's *Fundamental Principles*, which he has entitled *The Autonomy of Reason*. With a refreshing and admirable candor that seems to be missing in the more dogmatic *In Defense of Anarchism*, Wolff says, "I find Kant's treatment of the principle of autonomy perplexing . . . my real problem is that . . . despite some very strong contrary indications, Kant turns out not to be saying what I personally want him to say."[78] Now what Wolff wants Kant to do is to stick to a particular definition of autonomy that he put forward in the *Fundamental Principles*— a definition that Wolff takes to be "the classic explication of the concept of autonomy." Wolff begins by citing Kant himself: "The will is therefore not merely subject to the law, but is so subject that it must be considered as also *making the law* for itself and *precisely on this account* as first of all subject to the law (of which it can regard itself as the author)."[79] In his gloss on this passage Wolff urges that "the words which I have italicized in this passage are the heart of the concept of autonomy. From them, I believe, flow the most far-reaching consequences for politics as well as for ethics"—consequences that he thinks the reader will find in *In Defense of Anarchism*, which he cites in a footnote.[80] In representing the Kantian autonomous man as "making the law for himself"—a quasi-existentialist representation that leaves out of account the fact that Kant simply treated autonomy as a hypothetical property of a free will, and that ignores the fact that one cannot "make" moral law if it is already "there" (in the form of a duty to respect the dignity of others as ends in themselves)—Wolff acknowledges that he is insisting on what (he thinks) Kant *ought* to have said, rather than on what Kant actually did say. For if one looks at the next part of "the classic explication" of autonomy, Wolff says, "it becomes clear that acting only on laws that one has given to oneself and being bound by them only because one has so given them is not at all what Kant has in mind!" Instead, he grants, the notion of autonomy, far from meaning simply "giving laws to oneself," seems to mean "legislating disinterestedly, that is to say, legislating independently of or in abstraction from the particular interests of the agent."[81] Wolff finds this "unsettling"—which indeed it is, if one thinks of autonomy as a primary obligation and as a capacity to make law; but which it is not if autonomy is simply a hypothetical property of the will and involves nothing more than recognizing (and applying to oneself and others) the single "objective end" that is "also a duty."[82]

Since he finds it "unsettling" that Kant fails to define autonomy in the way that he "wants," and since he conceives of autonomy in the way that he does, Wolff professes to find "two incompatible doctrines" at the heart of Kant's moral philosophy:

> On the one hand, he believes that there are objective, substantive, categorical moral principles which all rational agents . . . acknowledge and obey. If this is true, then the notion of self-legislation seems vacuous. On the other hand, he believes (I think correctly) that rational agents are bound to substantive policies only insofar as they have freely chosen those policies. But if this is true, then one must give up the belief in objective substantive principles and recognize that the substance or content of moral principles derives from collective agreements to freely chosen ends.[83]

Now this extreme contractarian interpretation of Kant's ethics— though it does reveal a real tension examined earlier—is difficult to support. Even if Kant is sometimes a quasi-contractarian in his political theory, he is not in his moral philosophy (unless Beck's reading of Kant as "deepened" Rousseau is more persuasive than it seemed to be in Chapter 3).[84] Kant never says, with Rousseau, that "the engagements which bind us to the social body are obligatory only because they are mutual";[85] on the contrary his notion that the "objective end" of respect for the dignity of persons as ends constitutes everyone's duty is aptly summarized in his claim that among laws "those to which an obligation can be recognized *a priori* by reason are *natural laws*"[86]—that is, not laws made by collective agreements. Wolff might have avoided these difficulties had Robert Nozick's *Philosophical Explanations* been published earlier than 1981. For Nozick is entirely right when he says, à propos of Kant, that "between not wanting to devote oneself to pursuing anything that one created oneself"—even a practical law—"and viewing anything given externally as a constraint upon autonomy and dignity, there is not much room for maneuver."[87] But if natural law is simply "there," a priori, then it is neither created by oneself *nor* given externally (like a mere command). On the contrary, if natural or moral law is derived, as in the *Fundamental Principles,* from the general concept of a rational being, then it is precisely "internal" or (in the language of *Religion within the Limits*) "within."[88]

Wolff could not think that autonomy and "objective moral principles" constitute "two incompatible doctrines" in Kant unless he first defined autonomy in terms of *making* law and of *refusing* to be ruled; but that of course is what he has done. And as a result he has represented as an inconsistency *in Kant* a "problem" which arises mainly out of the fact that Kant fails to say (by Wolff's own admission) what he "wants" Kant to say. Hence the representation of Kant as a contractarian in moral philosophy who believed that "men are bound by substantive policies only insofar as and only because they have legislated those policies themselves."[89] (This is not only a questionable account of Kant's ethics; it is even a questionable account of his quasi-contractarian politics, which does *sometimes* rely on the "Idea of the original contract." It is an account which turns Kant into Rousseau.)

It is no accident that Wolff is reduced to offering such a contractarian account of Kant's ethics; it is an inevitability, given Wolff's view of the (non)viability of the notion of "ends" in Kant's philosophy. "How," Wolff asks, "might Kant go about demonstrating the existence of an end in itself?" The answer is that "strictly speaking, he offers no argument at all."[90] After citing Kant's injunction to "act in such a way that you always treat humanity, whether in your own person or in the person of any other, never simply as a means, but always at the same time as an end," Wolff observes that while Kant has "touched the very heart of morality," it is nonetheless "very difficult to tell what Kant means by the injunction to treat humanity as an end in itself."[91] Now there is no doubt that this is problematical, and that one must look outside the *Fundamental Principles*—particularly to the *Critique of Judgment*—in trying to decide what Kant means by an "end in itself"; nonetheless in *The Autonomy of Reason* Wolff succeeds in making persons as ends not merely a difficult notion, but a virtually unintelligible one. At one point he says the following:

> Presumably, what Kant means by treating humanity as an end-in-itself is that I must never fail to take account of the fact that I am dealing with rational moral agents rather than things. In short, I must keep in mind that *they* have purposes too. This in turn involves respecting their purposes, rather than ignoring them.
>
> Now, however true this injunction may be—and I believe it is the very bedrock of morality—we are still without the substantive criterion that Kant seeks. For consider: either respecting the purposes of other moral agents means making their purposes my own, in which case I am implicated in their pursuit of immoral ends; or it means making their *moral* purposes my own, and I am left to discover a criterion for distinguishing good from bad purposes.[92]

But Kant does not suggest that we take others' purposes as our own; he argues that we should respect others *as ends*. That involves not treating them as mere means to some arbitrary purpose: i.e., not killing, or robbing, or deceiving others with a view to pleasure or convenience. It is not only not difficult to make this intelligible, it is one of the more straightforward tasks in interpreting Kant. If, for example, on entering one's box at the theater, one slaps the attendant across the face with a view to demonstrating one's social superiority, one is treating him as a means to a relative end; but if one simply permits him to perform his normal functions, one treats him at the same time as an end.[93] Admittedly the notion of treating others as ends is often negative in Kant: it involves not killing, not robbing, not deceiving, and so forth.[94] Even so, this is an intelligible moral content, and one that is not so difficult that one needs to fall back on a contractarian interpretation of Kant, or to suggest that in Kantianism one might have to take others' immoral purposes as one's own.

Despite this difficulty, *The Autonomy of Reason* is at least a wholly candid exposition of what Kant actually said, coupled with suggestions about what he "ought" to have said. It constitutes an advance on *In Defense of Anarchism* because it separates the real Kant from a reconstructed and improved Kant. If one fixes his attention on what Kant *actually* said, it turns out that autonomy is a hypothetical property of a free will, not a substantive moral duty; that there is thus—at least on Kantian grounds—no "primary obligation" to be autonomous, to "refuse to be ruled"; that since there is no obligation to refuse to be ruled—to be an anarchist, when unanimous direct democracy is impossible—there is in fact an obligation to recognize government and law as legal realizers of a moral *telos* and as providers of a "context" within which a good will is more nearly possible;[95] that for Kant the substantive moral duty which is *not* constituted by autonomy *is* constituted by the duty to respect others as ends-in-themselves; that in view of this all duties *cannot* be "duties to oneself." If, in short, one removes the cloak of Kant's legitimacy from Wolff's groundwork, one finds that that cloak does not profit from being draped around something else—even a something else constructed by one who grants that Kant "correctly identified the principal problems of moral philosophy and . . . had some genuine insight into their solution."[96]

IV

It is always reasonable to ask whether an interpretation is as sound as it is merely conceivable, whether an interpreter has endowed bare possibility with probability, or probability with irresistible necessity. Now Susan Shell, in her effective and ingeniously argued book, *The Rights of Reason*, as well as in her earlier article, "Kant's Theory of Property,"[97] has certainly avoided claiming necessity for her quasi-Hegelian view of Kant: the critical philosophy "can" be understood, she urges, and was understood by Hegel, as "an explanation and defense of man's appropriation of the world." This "appropriation," she goes on, takes two forms: "one, theoretical and epistemological, concerns objects of knowledge; the other, practical and political, concerns objects of the will."[98] Looked at "from this perspective," she claims, Kant's thought "can" be construed as "a study in human alienation," and his epistemology and politics can be viewed as "means of partially overcoming this alienation."[99] She concludes by suggesting that "the central problem uniting Kant's speculative philosophy and his politics is his perception of the human subject as a 'stranger' who must appropriate and so transform the world if it is to be his own."[100] (This crucial last sentence is identical in the book and the article.)

Obviously, then, Shell claims no necessity for her interpretation;

she speaks of a "perspective" that "can" be employed, and that she thinks Hegel employed. Still, a reading can have some plausibility, and even a certain limited force, without being a "natural" reading. It is therefore fair to ask, would a reader of the *Critique of Pure Reason*, upon reaching the "Transcendental Deduction" (whose importance Shell stresses),[101] *naturally* come up with the notion that (for Kant) thinking involves the "appropriation" of an "alien" world by a "stranger" who "transforms" that world by conceiving it? Or would one use this language only if one were trying (perhaps even straining) to find a parallel between Kant's theoretical and practical philosophy, trying to persuade oneself that "the justification of property is, for Kant, not merely the concern of jurisprudence, but . . . *the* task of critical philosophy"?[102] Even if one were searching for such a parallel, should one abandon Kantian language—which does, after all, speak in quasi-juridical fashion of our "right" to "use" certain concepts[103]— and employ the Hegelian-cum-Kojève-cum-early-Marx vocabulary of "alienation," "transformation," "appropriation" and "negation?" Is not this "alienation" something alien to a philosopher as *angstfrei* as Kant—Kant *an sich*, as it were, seen without benefit of an Hegelian "perspective" that "can" be deployed?

This is not to say that a notion such as "alienation" never appears anywhere in Kant. Indeed, in an important letter to Moses Mendelssohn dealing precisely with the *Critique* Kant says that he regrets that Mendelssohn feels "alienated from metaphysics";[104] and the terms "appropriation" and "negation" are to be found occasionally in Kant as well, though not perhaps in the sense in which Shell employs them.[105] But the point to be made here is that when the notions of "alienation," "appropriation," "transformation" and "negation" are used as an ensemble, as a family of related concepts, then they constitute not a mere stringing together of terms occasionally to be found in Kant, but a quasi-Hegelian ensemble that refracts Kant through a post-Kantian lens. This lens is not even purely Hegelian, since the Hegel of these terms is a Hegel partly reconstructed by interpreters such as Kojève who read the Master and Servant "tableau" in the *Phenomenology* as if it were (to recall George Kelly's telling phrase) "a synoptic clue to a whole philosophy."[106] So in viewing the entire Kantian critical enterprise as being concerned with the "justification of property," property that is "appropriated" by an "alienated stranger" and "transformed" by his activity, Shell is looking at Kant through a prism that is partly genuine Hegel, partly Hegel as reconstructed by Kojève and partisans of early Marx. It is not to be expected therefore that Kant should filter through this prism in a wholly recognizable shape. (One should be the more careful, actually, in supplying Kant with a transformed form that is alien to him, in view of his clear strictures on this point in his "Open Letter on Fichte's *Wissenschaftslehre*": "Since some reviewers maintain that the *Critique* is not to be taken literally . . . and that anyone who wants to understand the *Critique* must first master the requisite 'standpoint,' . . . because Kant's precise words, like Aristotle's, will kill the mind, I therefore declare again that the *Critique* is to be understood by considering exactly what it says.")[107]

Nor is the superimposition of this alien, transforming, quasi-Hegelian vocabulary merely a question of the wrong tone or color: it runs the risk of saying things that Kant explicitly ruled out. If for example one views Kant's theory of knowledge as "an epistemology which ascribes the unity and order of things to the informing activity of human reason"—to quote Shell's summary of the *Critique*[108]—is the notion of "transformation" an adequate shorthand way of summing up this epistemology? Does not the notion of *trans*forming (as distinguished from *in*forming) involve what Kant complained of in Fichte—namely leaving "things in themselves" (even as "transcendental object = X") wholly out of account and treating "ego" as all-creative, all-formative?[109] Only if "the informing activity of human reason" can be expressed in a kind of nondistorting shorthand by the notions of "transformation" and "appropriation" is it an *advantage* to treat Kant in non-Kantian language; but one can reasonably doubt this advantageousness. Similarly, one can doubt whether the Kantian notion that self-knowledge has limits is best expressed in this language: "The mind's transcendental synthesis is, paradoxically, expressed in the grounding concept of something utterly alien. Self-awareness, and critical philosophy, cannot penetrate beyond this seeming negation. In a world whose affinities the mind has itself conferred, reason remains a partial stranger to itself."[110] Each of these sentences is subtly transformed by the use of a single non-Kantian term: the first by "alien," the second by "negation," the third by "stranger." But these three small transformations simply shore up the great transformation of Shell's perspective. "Transformation," then, is indeed an appropriate word: but only insofar as Kant is being transformed by this interpretation, not insofar as his epistemology can reasonably be styled "transformative."

One cannot exactly claim, for that matter, that the notions of "appropriation" and "mental property" are much more helpful. Indeed, so anxious is Shell to find a parallel between ownership and epistemology ("having" in general) that she actually falls into claiming (though only in the article) that in the "Transcendental Deduction" Kant calls "mental property" *das Meine*.[111] If he had used that phrase in that connection, it might well support the existence of a strong parallel; for *das Meine* (together with *das Deine*) is indeed a juridical term, a term descriptive of property; it is nothing more than the German form of the old Roman-law notion of *meum* (and the corresponding *tuum*).[112] A mere *meine* (as contrasted with *das Meine*) would not have served Shell's interpretive purpose. For in all of Kant's epistemological arguments that use the term "mine" it is clear that "ours" or even "one's" would serve equally well; and indeed *unser[e]* appears more frequently in the text than *mein[e]*.[113] Besides, to extract a notion of "mental property" from a mere *meine* would have been too evidently presumptuous; it would have involved squeezing a substantive doctrine out of a mere possessive pronoun, hacking a political theory out of bare grammar. Hence the need for *das Meine*, a genuinely juridical term; but the fact is that the phrase *das Meine* does not appear, at all, in the "Transcendental Deduction"—not in the original version of 1781 ("A") or in the revised version of 1787 ("B").[114] Nor, incidentally, does the phrase appear anywhere else in the *Critique of Pure Reason*, or in the *Prolegomena* written to popularize the *Critique*, or in Kant's philosophical correspondence dealing with the *Critique*.[115] Again one asks, even if the phrase *das Meine* were actually in the "Transcendental Deduction," would it naturally and accurately express Kant's clearly stated aim of showing *by what right* (*quid juris*) we use the concepts that we do use? Does "rightful use of concepts" naturally translate into "appropriation" or *"das Meine"*? Or is it simply that Kant "can" be viewed in the light of those notions? But if that light has no necessity, and if it is a transforming rather than an illuminating light and gets Kant to seem to say things that are, indeed, not impossible for him, but that fail to flow naturally from his actual words, then what is the advantage of this "can"?

There is, after all, some advantage to this perspective; but Shell, in appealing to a nonexistent *das Meine* and in superimposing a quasi-Hegelian vocabulary, has obscured what is perfectly valid in her argument, and that sometimes emerges in a natural and illuminating way. Indeed, when she sticks to Kantian language and leaves aside what he "can" be seen as, she is often very penetrating: "The 'Transcendental Deduction' of the *Critique of Pure Reason* would establish the 'rights of reason' to the use of its concepts; the juridical deduction in the *Doctrine of Right* would establish the rights of rational beings to their use of objects in the world."[116] That is economically, elegantly, and very justly expressed; it points out a genuine if limited parallel between Kant's theoretical and practical philosophy, and it refrains from all transforming. There are other substantial passages amounting to more than half of Shell's book and article that sustain this just expression and make exactly the right claims.

Nonetheless, the search for parallels that unite Kant's theoretical and practical philosophies leads Shell to make an extraordinary claim about the place of politics in Kant's thought, a claim introduced by a parallel between thought and money:

> As universal medium of . . . exchange, money is, for Kant, the man-made, material expression of an *a priori*, rational form. Likening it to books (which similarly facilitate the circulation of ideas), Kant describes money as matter mined from the earth—to which man himself gives form. As the product of both nature and universal human consent, money is a proto-type of and substitute for the world government which would, if only it could be achieved, embody the general will on earth. In the absence of such perfect government, Kant asserts a duty to obey the powers that be, softening the rigors of this command with the hope of a political improve-ment brought on by intellectual and economic progress, i.e., the so-called "spirit" of enlightenment and commerce. Money and thought, for Kant, almost supplant politics as the means by which men are to obtain justice. [117]

Since this striking passage brings down the curtain on part II of Shell's article, and is preserved almost verbatim (with some reorder-ing of sentences) in her book;[118] and since, at the same time, it is hard to recognize in Shell's characterization the Kant who could argue that "if public legal justice perishes then it is no longer worthwhile for men to remain alive on this earth,"[119] it is reasonable to ask whether the search for parallels (surely money must be *das Meine*, if thought is!) has not permitted Shell to let Kantian politics wither away a little prematurely. To be sure, Kant hoped that enlightenment and eco-nomic interdependence would help to further eternal peace;[120] but this never led him to "supplant" politics with "money and thought." That being so, it may be useful to recall briefly the place of politics in Kant's complete practical philosophy.

Politics and law, as Chapters 1, 4, and 5 established, serve a high purpose in Kant's practical philosophy; they are the guarantors of those (negative) conditions that make respect for the dignity of men as "ends in themselves" more nearly possible. They make the exer-cise of a good will less difficult by removing impediments (such as fear of violence or domination) that could incline, though never determine, the will to act on maxims that cannot be universalized in a way that is congruent with the rights of man. They also legally realize some moral ends through republicanism and eternal peace.[121] So in the end there are two fundamental questions to be asked about Kant's politics: (1) How well does Kantian public legal justice *succeed* in being instrumental to morality? and (2) How adequate is the Kantian morality to which politics is supposed to be instrumental? No reason-able answer to either question would involve the "supplanting" of politics by "thought and money."

In any case, the search for parallels that "unite" Kant's philosophy—a search which turns up thought as mental property, concepts as *das Meine*, and enlightenment coupled with money as a substitute for politics—leads to an interesting but odd consequence. That consequence is that while Kantian politics tends to wither away in Shell's perspective, what she calls "epistemology" is correspondingly *politicized*, so that everything that is drained away from true politics is used to fatten epistemological notions (thus thought is transformed into property, into something "appropriated").[122] There is, on this view, a kind of conservation of (political) force; the total quantity of politics in the Kantian system remains constant, but most of it turns up in epistemology, while true politics is something that no one "has."

At least the notion of "having" holds a real place in Kant's thought, even if Shell places more weight on it than it can bear; but in *The Rights of Reason* (though not in the earlier article) she adds a wholly new line of thought that is certainly novel but probably not possible. Given Kant's radical distinction between morality and "pathology" it is a mistake to reconstruct Kantian morality (and then politics) as a reflection or epiphenomenon of pathology. But this is exactly what Shell does in *The Rights of Reason*. She insists that for Kant "man first expresses his sense of right in anger and resentment against the resistance which his will naturally encounters . . . man's primal indignation represents his unhappy and almost unsupportable awareness of his condition. Morality fortifies and rechannels this indignation while dissipating its initial cause. Morality turns anger inwards against the self, then outward against other selves . . . right, properly understood, is rational indignation, anger objectified." By "universalizing anger," she maintains, Kantian "right" transforms "a physically destructive self-forgetting into a morally constructive one. The rational alternative to self-destruction is the adoption as one's end of a universal legislation which serves all."[123] For Shell, who relies principally on her reading of Kant's *Anthropology* and "Conjectural Beginning of Human History," the moral law (as well as "right") is a constructive reconstruction of destructive pathology. But, whatever might be said for this view of morality as the rationalization of the irrational, it cannot be reconciled with Kant's insistence that the moral law is—*already*—a "fact of reason,"[124] and, more strikingly, with what Kant says about separating morality and "pathology" in the *Critique of Judgment*: "The fear that, if we divest . . . our representations of the moral law and of our native capacity for morality . . . of everything that can commend it to the senses, it will thereupon be attended only with a cold and lifeless approbation and not with any moving force or emotion, is wholly unwarranted."[125] Kant goes on to say that "the moral law . . . is a sufficient and *original* source of determination within us; so it does not for a moment permit us to cast about for a ground of determination external to itself. If enthusiasm is comparable to delirium, fanaticism may be compared to mania."[126] Moreover, everything Kant goes on to say about "unbridled" imagination and "brooding" passion make it clear that the moral law (in its "pure" state) is above and beyond "delusion" and "rational raving."[127] It is absolutely inadmissable, then, to view the categorical imperative as an epiphenomenon of "pathology" in Kant; the moral law is not simply "anger" given a constructive turn. It seems, then, that Shell's insistence that for *both* Kant and Nietzsche "the concept of *Rache* [revenge] stands with *Recht* [right] at the crux of moral evolution;[128] is simply perverse; Nietzsche himself knew better when he called Kant a "calamitous spider" and an "under-handed Christian."[129] All of Shell's remarks in this vein are grounded in the *Anthropology* and in "Conjectural Beginning"; had the *Critiques* been given their central place, such a reading would not seem possible. The valuable part of her study does not lie here; it lies in her discovery of limited but genuine parallels between Kant's theories of knowledge and of property. There her novelty is not just new, but (sometimes) true.

V

The better part of Shell's work is built on a (sometimes strained) parallel between "having" ideas and "having" property; similarly, in his *Kant's Road from War to Peace: Conflict and Unity*, Hans Saner builds on a parallel between peace in politics and peace in philosophy. But the translator-imposed title under which Saner's work appeared in English—*Kant's Political Thought*—conveys the real import of *Kants Weg vom Krieg zum Frieden: Widersteit und Einheit* about as well as *The Rebel* provides a clue to Camus's *L'Homme Revolté*: that is to say, scarcely at all.[130] For Saner's book is not the systematic critical exposition of Kant's political thought that its English title suggests, but a special argument about the relation of Kant's philosophy as a whole, and above all about the way in which he philosophized, to a few of his political ideas. Roughly speaking, the idea of *Kants Weg vom Krieg zum Frieden* is that Kant characteristically looked for and admired the same things in philosophy and in politics: unity arrived at through free discussion and debate rather than unity imposed externally by "violence," reliance on reason rather than on authority, freedom from "tutelage" (freedom that, however, does not degenerate into mere "license").[131] Saner treats Kant as one who wanted to bring "eternal peace" to philosophy as much as to political life; it can be shown, he urges, that for Kant "war has no more place in the idea of a perfect world than controversy has a place in the idea of scientific metaphysics." It is not surprising, then, that Saner claims that "in a sense Kant's politics is the most lucid sample of his philosophizing," since in his politics the "secret basic structure of his metaphysics—the conquest of antagonism—has become the theme itself." Kant's politics is thus "the concrete model of his metaphysics."[132]

Now this is novel and ingenious, and in its according "central significance" to Kant's political philosophy it is certainly preferable to those interpretations of Kant that treat his politics as late and minor efforts. The question remains whether the thesis is as sound and illuminating as it is novel and ingenious, whether the "burden of our theme" (to use Saner's phrase) does not sometimes lead to a strained effort, as with Shell, to see too many political elements in Kant's speculative philosophy and too many parallels and analogies between "thought forms" and "contents of a political nature." In the end, Saner's work is a kind of prescription for eliciting Kant's politics, obliquely, from his methods as a philosopher and particularly as a polemicist; perhaps an appropriate English title for it would be *The Politics of Kant's Philosophy*.

Sometimes, however, an even more appropriate title would seem to be *Kant as a Political Strategist in Philosophical Debates*. A great deal of space, perhaps too much, is given over to shoring up the "burden" of the notion that "philosophy begins in conflict but wants peace," that philosophy, like politics, evolves in an "infinite way" toward greater adequacy;[133] hence the huge weight—pages 69 through 214 in a text of 313 pages—placed by Saner on polemics in Kant's writing. Indeed, the author claims flatly that "all of Kant's creative activity can be understood as polemicizing—against the great thinkers of the past, against his contemporaries, and against himself."[134] Though this claim permits Saner to deliver himself of what is certainly the most effective part of the book—a quite lucid and sometimes brilliant account of Kant's disputes with Eberhard, Feder, Garve, Fichte et al., mostly in connection with the *Critique of Pure Reason*—one might ask whether Saner has not made the argument a bit too grateful to his own theme by speaking of a "typology of combat forms" in polemicizing (debate, dispute, quarrel) that is all too evidently parallel to political ideas; and whether the emphasis on Kant's polemical writings, however well brought off, can be justified if it involves giving ten times more space to the conflict with Eberhard than to the *Critique of Practical Reason* or to the *Metaphysical Elements of Justice*.[135]

This is not to say that some of the parallels and analogies are not true ones; Saner has great success in showing, for example, that Kant appealed to the principle of publicity in unmasking anonymous philosophical opponents, just as he insisted on publicity in unmasking secret diplomacy in *Eternal Peace*: "The exposure of . . . the secret intentions and impulses of his opponents helps Kant to force them to use methods that can stand up before the forum of public reason. At the same time, he creates the conditions for a fight '*inter pares*,' a struggle in which there is no 'incognito,' no guarantee by great names, and no security in 'political' alliances."[136] Despite successes such as this one, the heavy emphasis on polemics leads to some strange transvaluations. The important treatise *Theory and Practice*, for instance, is treated not so much as one of the best statements of Kant's distinction between morality and happiness or as a trenchant criticism of Hobbes, as it is as a polemical reply to Christian Garve. Now *Theory and Practice is* a reply to Christian Garve. But to consider it mainly *qua* polemic of a certain kind (as a "debate," rather than as a "quarrel" or a "dispute") is not so much false as perverse; the quality or content of the argument takes second place to the fact of its being formally a certain kind of polemic.[137]

Sometimes, moreover, in his effort to show that "in looking at Kant the polemicist we get to know Kant the politician,"[138] Saner not only fails to show that Kant has consistently parallel goals in philosophy and in politics, but actually treats Kant as a politician à la Machiavelli, rather than as the "moral politician" praised by Kant in *Eternal Peace*. "It is amazing to see . . . with how much political acumen Kant was fighting. . . . He sought to drive a wedge between Eberhard and the most dangerous foe . . . to isolate Eberhard and to crush him alone, by the demise of his journals."[139] Here Saner's picture of Kant as one who sought peace and unity through freedom and reason, in philosophy as much as in politics, is rather broken down, such that his own distinction between "unity in freedom" and "unity in violence" tends to disappear.

One might, of course, want to question in the first instance whether "unity" was really as important to Kant as Saner makes it. He claims early on that for Kant "the cardinal problem of all politics is the establishment of civic unity, whether among many individuals or many states"; but this, as he later grants, fails to take the quality of unity into account, since the "universal despotism" that Kant feared clearly provided unity of a certain kind.[140] And it is not at all self-evident that in his practical philosophy Kant was trying to establish what Saner calls "the unity of the will";[141] what is certain, though Saner does not mention it, is that Kant treated the will as a "necessary hypothesis," as a faculty of determining oneself to action in accordance with the concept of a law, as a moral capacity without which common moral concepts such as responsibility, inputability, desert, and so on, would not even be conceivable. Since, however, Saner concentrates on the "unity of the will" rather than on what Kant most characteristically says about volition, he speaks at one point of the noumenal and phenomenal realms being "united in the same determination by laws,"[142] whereas Kant's essential point is that phenomenal beings act according to laws (laws of gravity and the like) but that noumenal beings act according to the *conception* of laws (laws of duty and the like).[143] This is crucial in Kant, but gets very short *schrift* from Saner.

The emphasis on "unity" as the "parallel" between "eternal peace" in metaphysics and in politics is at its clearest, and most problematical, in Saner's treatment of the *Critique of Judgment*. Confining himself entirely to Part I of that work, the half that deals with aesthetic principles, Saner urges that for Kant artistic activity involves "the unity of imagination and the intellect, of spirit and taste"; that "in the field of beauty we were inquiring about the relations of conflict and unity . . . the forms and premises of unity, and the road that leads to unity."[144] Despite the almost obsessive use of the word "unity," Saner succeeds in providing a good brief account of Kantian aesthetics. But in a work which purports to be a treatment of Kant's politics it is surely odd that in his desire to talk about the principle of unity in Part I, Saner does not mention at all Part II, which contains Kant's most persuasive account of the idea that men are ends in themselves who ought never to be used merely as means to some arbitrary purpose.[145] Nor is this a mere detail: since there is little or no systematic treatment in Saner of the Kantian notion of men as "ends," neither is there any treatment of Kant's "public legal justice" as a context or framework of security in which one can have a good will. Since the notion that man is the only being "who can form a concept of purposes" and thus conceive himself as the ultimate end or purpose of creation,[146] is left almost completely out of account by Saner, he falls back on the idea that Kant's moral philosophy has no ends in view, that it involves simply an "aprioristic, formal, universal, categorical law of reason."[147] This is to concede, however inadvertently, everything that Hegel and Mill said about the "formalism" and "contentlessness" of Kantian ethics; but anyone who wants to do justice to the whole of Kant's political philosophy must say *something* about the doctrine of men as final ends, about the connection between the theory of men as ends and natural rights, about legality as a context within which the dignity of men as ends will be respected, and so on. Much of this comes through only fleetingly in Saner's book.

However much one may think that the notions of "unity" and

"peace" are strained in the effort to see Kant's politics as the "concrete model" of his metaphysics; that it is not the unity of Kant's good will that matters as much as its being both necessary and hypothetical; that for Kant's politics it is the concept of an end or purpose that matters more in the *Critique of Judgment* than does "the unity of spirit and taste"; or that minor polemical writings should not be given greater emphasis than the *Critique of Practical Reason* simply because they show Kant as a "strategist"—however much one wants to stress these things, it should also be said that Saner's study is conceived on an admirably large scale, that it is worked out with impressive consistency, that it is stimulating and often forces one to look into one's own copies of Kant's works. It is even possible that since *Kants Weg vom Krieg zum Frieden* is marked "Volume I" in the German edition,[148] a fuller treatment of Kant's politics is forthcoming from Saner and that this book will then appear in a more appropriate light, as a kind of "prolegomena" to Kantian politics rather than as an account of it. In its present form, it is *not* such an account.

VI

Saner's study deals almost exclusively with Kant; the Kant chapter in John Charvet's *A Critique of Freedom and Equality*, by contrast, is only a single *strand* in a wide-ranging book that aims to show that modern political thought has fallen into the polar errors of granting too much to men in their *particularity* (as in Hobbes's effort to build morality on self-interest) *or* as mere members of a *collectivity*, so that persons are "generalized" into "citizens" at best (as in Rousseau and Hegel) and "species-beings" at worst (as in Marx).[149] This means that treating Charvet's Kant chapter *in isolation* must fail to do him perfect justice; but since he is, with Quentin Skinner and John Dunn, [150] one of the three ablest younger English political philosophers, imperfect justice may be better than total neglect.

Charvet begins with a sound claim about Kant's moral philosophy: "The central conviction of Kant's ethical view is that the only thing that is good in itself is the good will, and the good will is that will which aims at realizing the morally good for its own sake, not as a means to anything else." (The very next sentence, however—"duty must be done for duty's sake"—leans on Bradley's hostile reading of Kant.) The problem of Kant's ethics, for Charvet, is to show "how this good will is possible."[151]

If good will is to be efficacious, or if "pure reason is to be practical," Charvet goes on, "then the [Kantian] individual must be capable of being determined to action by the idea of a universal law alone," since "a categorical imperative must command independently of its content, and that means in respect of its form only." [152] (This, of course, is a loose paraphrase of the nonteleological part of *Practical Reason*, which does indeed stress "legislative form.")[153] But if, Charvet insists, the categorical imperative is purely "formal" (or "empty," as he says elsewhere), one is left embarrassed, because "the categorical imperative has in itself no content, and some substantive content is necessary if men are to be guided by law to action."[154] Charvet apparently does not accept Kant's claim that all the "formulae" of the categorical imperative are "the same"—which would mean that the formal version of the imperative to will universal law is "at bottom" *equivalent* to the injunction to treat persons as "ends in themselves." This equivalence would provide the categorical imperative with a teleological content: namely, respecting a "rational nature" as an "objective end."[155] The only opening left to him, therefore, is to assert that since "substantive" moral content cannot be "derived" from "pure empty form," "Kant's idea is that it can be derived through bringing subjective or empirically determined maxims [such as the desire to profit from promise-breaking] to the bar of the categorical imperative, and those [maxims] that pass the test of universalization are thereby demonstrated to be universally valid and substantive moral laws."[156]

At this point, not surprisingly, Charvet's argument turns into Hegel's, the notion that one can will the "universalization" of anything, if one is willing to endure the consequences. Here, indeed, Charvet all but paraphrases *Glauben und Wissen*: "Where would be the self-contradiction in willing the [universal] disappearance of promising? There is only self-contradiction if one both wills the practice of promising and at the same time the lying-promise maxim."[159] This is simply a recasting of Hegel's insistence that "a contradiction must be a contradiction of something."[158] But of course Charvet has driven Kant into this position by insisting that since the categorical imperative is "pure empty form," it can have no "content" save the "subjective" or "empirical" maxims that it then tries to "universalize." On this view Kant can scarcely fail to fail, since Hegel was right to insist that *mere* universalizing can never yield a substantive ethics. Had Charvet given any weight—or indeed any consideration—to Kant's claim that "formal universality" is "at bottom" *the same* as "respect for persons" as "objective ends,"[159] he could not have said that "it is not pure reason that tells one to will the practice of promising."[160] If one takes seriously (at least provisionally) the claim of *Religion Within the Limits* that reason proposes to us objective ends that we ought to have,[161] then reason does indeed tell one to will promising—or at least *not* to will promise-breaking. By not treating the crucial, though admittedly problematical, strand in Kant that views reason as the spontaneous giver of objective ends, Charvet forces himself finally to see Kant through the eyes of Hegel and Bradley. (This may account for Charvet's terse and cryptic passage on the doctrine of persons-as-ends; after quickly paraphrasing Kant, Charvet argues that "Kant is simply wrong in holding that man *necessarily* conceives his existence as an end in itself. For he can conceive it, and must initially do so, simply as an end for himself, an end of purely subjective worth, from which universalizing fails to produce a moral conclusion."[162] But this is too convenient; if mere universalizing has *so far* failed to yield substantive morality, it cannot suddenly do better. If "universalizing" is the whole of Kantian morality, then Hegel is right; but there is reason to believe, as we have seen in Chapters 3 and 4, that Hegel failed to give serious weight to Kant's notion of "objective ends." Charvet's argument, insofar as it follows Hegel's, cannot be more effective than Hegel's.)

But if Charvet is unwilling to find a content for the categorical imperative in the shape of respectable objective ends, and must therefore represent Kant as vainly struggling to universalize subjective maxims, he *is* willing to treat teleology when it appears in Kant's doctrines of nature and history. In this connection he offers a précis of the *Critique of Judgment* which, if not exactly sympathetic, is at least reasonably fair:

> Kant's way out [of the tension between freedom and determinism] is to produce as another idea of reason a teleological conception of nature and history, according to which the necessary union of free will and natural determination is built into the structure of the world to be approached in the course of history. . . . Hence we must think of the system of nature as an overall self-unfolding teleological process, a process that is developing itself towards a final goal. This final goal can only be the full development of man's capacities as a rational being. For the only goal of absolute worth . . is rational being. Man is the only rational being in nature, hence nature must have men in his rational aspect as its final end. Otherwise nature has no end, but is a thing in vain.[163]

So far (mainly), so good: for this account of *Judgment* is acceptable if by the "union" of "free will" and "natural determination" in the "course of history" Charvet means that free will and natural determination may yield the same ends through different incentives; that citizens in a republic, for example, who are "naturally" determined by the desire not to ruin themselves, may consent to an eternal peace that good will would *freely* elect.[164] Here "union" would mean that an objective end can be attained either "naturally" (from self-love) or morally.

But Charvet's further formulations make one wonder whether he adheres to an acceptable reading of *Judgment*. He goes on to say that, for Kant, "man as *a natural being* will be acting in accordance with his nature in such a way as to bring about in the course of history the conditions for the realization of the pure moral will."[165] It scarcely seems possible that a Kantian "pure moral will" could depend on "conditions" for its "realization"; one can, negatively, remove *impediments* to good will, get rid of "occasions of sin", but that does not positively "realize" good will. Charvet has failed to draw Kant's essential distinction between moral "ends," which *can* be historically realized, as when self-loving peace-lovers want the peace that they ought to will, and moral "incentives," which *cannot* be realized.[166] (For "realized" means *caused*, and the notion of a "caused will" is the fatal error of Hobbes, as was seen in Chapter 2.)[167]

Had Charvet seen this more clearly, he would not have tried to incorporate in his account of *Judgment* a passage from *Idea for a Universal History* that Kant took care not to repeat in the *Third Critique*: "antagonism within society leads to the development of men's talents, which in the end can transform 'a pathologically enforced social union into a moral whole.' "[168] In *Judgment*, as was seen in treating Lebrun in Chapter 4, Kant avoids speaking of "culture" being "transformed" into a "moral whole," and speaks more carefully of culture as the merely "legal" realizer of certain moral ends (above all peace), even if *motiva moralia* are absent and "devils" abound.[169]

If this is right, then Charvet's final complaint against Kant is not a real complaint at all:

> In so far as his argument purports to show how through the operation of man's unsocial sociability a social arrangement is produced which coincides with the commands of pure reason, he has not shown that a moral will is actual in man.[170]

Just so: but then Kant never claimed to be able to show that a moral will is "actual" in man. He claimed to show that one ought to have a moral will; but he also maintained that knowledge of motives is impossible.[171] One can know that one ought to have a good will, and that if everyone had such a will mere "unsocial sociability" would yield to an "ethical commonwealth";[172] but one cannot know whether anyone has ever (actually) acted simply from good will. On this point, what Charvet sees as a criticism is really just a restatement of the limitations on our knowledge stressed by Kant himself.

To be sure, there are striking things in Charvet's Kant chapter: his insistence, for example, that Kant's claim that we can only "comprehend the incomprehensibility" of pure reason's capacity to serve as our necessary and sufficient motive "must be admitted to be a defeat."[173] But this is perhaps more striking than persuasive, for Charvet himself insists that it is "absurd" to try to justify morality, which is one of Kant's *own* reasons for refusing to go beyond reason in search of a motive that will bring us to act *from* reason.[174]

Finally, then, Charvet seems to combine an Hegelian or Bradleyan view of Kant as an empty formalist with a limited recognition of Kantian technology—*seriously* limited, since if Charvet had granted that rational natures serve as objective ends in one of Kant's main formulations of the categorical imperative, then he could have connected the determinant objective ends of the *Fundamental Principles* with the reflective ends of *Judgment*, and thus found a unity in Kant that one cannot find if Kant is treated as an ethical formalist who (suddenly, inexplicably) turns into a teleologist.[175] It is better to start with Kant's general notion of "purposive unity" as the "highest unity"[176] that holds all of Kant's realms together.

VII

The Kant-studies of Kojève, Goldmann, Wolff, Shell, Saner and Charvet are valuable, not just to highlight the teleological reading offered here, but because the very effort to give *telos* sufficient weight leads to an almost unavoidable neglect of strands that are really present in Kant's practical thought, and that other studies make more visible. Thus Kojève, Goldmann, and Shell bring out (but also exaggerate) Kant's affinities with his greatest immediate successors, Hegel and Marx; while Wolff bring outs (and again exaggerates) Kant's affinities with his greatest immediate predecessor, Rousseau. Saner brings out (but also overstresses) the forms (debate, quarrel, polemic) of Kant's political writings; while Charvet brings out (and again overstresses) the form of the categorical imperative at the expense of objective ends, and is therefore unable to see all Kantian ends bridged in *Judgment*. But exaggeration is not falsehood or misrepresentation: Kojève, Goldmann, Wolff, Shell, Saner and Charvet provide a partial truth that may be—if the teleological reading is wrong—the whole truth.

CHAPTER EIGHT

Conclusion: Estimate of Kant's Political Philosophy

I

This study began with a paradox of Kant's own devising: that true politics must pay homage to morals, but without being able to count on the moral incentive (good will) that, if completely efficacious, would transcend (mere) politics altogether and produce an ethical commonwealth under laws of virtue.[1] In order to make sense of a paradox that makes politics both cling to and shun morals, it was necessary to draw (or rather point to) Kant's distinction between *ends* and *incentives*, and to say that republicanism and eternal peace might well be moral ends that are legally attainable (or at least approachable) through the self-love of citizens of a republic, even if those citizens should be devils divested of all good will. That stress on *ends* as the link or bridge between Kantian politics and Kantian morality turned out to have the additional large advantage of tying into (and then supporting) a teleological reading of the whole of Kant, governed by the *Critique of Judgment*, in which all "ends"—"objective" and "relative," moral, natural and aesthetic—find their place in a general theory of ends.[2] A general teleological reading, which seems to work in all of Kant's realms, provides a sufficient reason to settle the tension between morality as "respect for persons as objective ends" and morality as "giving the law to oneself" in favor of the former—in favor of a Kant who finds the moral law in "the general concept of a rational being" as the "final end," sooner than in quasi-Rousseauean "legislation."

Thus the only fully intelligible reading of Kant's insistence that "true politics cannot take a single step without first paying homage to morals"—the reading which insists that morals and politics share a realm of overlapping ends or purposes, but differ *wholly* over motives—coheres with the only fully comprehensive reading of Kant's theoretical, practical and aesthetic philosophy taken as a totality.[3] Kantian politics, then, can most reasonably be understood as something that legally realizes certain moral ends—generally characterizable as peacefulness and civility—in a way that is indeed inferior to a (probably unattainable) universal ethical commonwealth, but that (admittedly by relying on nonmoral motives) keep persons, the "final ends of creation," from being used as mere "means" to arbitrary purposes (above all war).

Such a reading not only makes sense of Kant's initially paradoxical view of politics, by appealing to a *telos* that—either "determinantly" or "reflectively"—bridges all of the Kantian realms; it also preserves, and even enhances, the stature of Kant's political thought. For in linking republicanism and eternal peace to Kant's moral doctrine of "objective ends" that we "ought to have," the teleological reading shows that the (fairly common) view that Kant's moral philosophy is perhaps the most important modern one but that his politics (in sharp contrast) is at best a mélange of Hobbes, Montesquieu and Rousseau,[4] and at worst a mere reflection of "Prussia,"[5] will not hold up as a general view (though it may be right in points of detail). If the teleological reading is right, then Charles Taylor (to take an example) must be at least partly wrong when he insists that while "Kant starts with a radically new conception of morality, his political theory is disappointingly familiar. It does not take us very far beyond utilitarianism."[6] It is not simply that this statement fails to notice that Kant declined to count utilitarianism as a moral theory at all; it is that it fails to take seriously Kant's efforts to "limit" and "condition" politics through the concept of "right," so that universal republicanism might yield a legal approximation to the "kingdom of ends."

Kant is clear, after all, as Chapters 5 and 6 established, that citizens (not mere subjects) in a republic would *dissent* from war, out of the legal motive of self-love. Therefore republicanism (internally) and eternal peace (externally) are interlocked, absolutely inseparable. This is why Kant says that in "a constitution where the subject is not a citizen, and which is therefore not republican, it is the simplest thing in the world to go to war"—despite the fact that "reason, as the highest legislative moral power, absolutely condemns war as a test of rights."[7] Therefore republican citizenship is instrumental to an essential moral end that good will alone may never realize, thanks to "pathology". For this reason, W. B. Gallie's strict division between Kant's internal politics as a stale academic rehash of Hobbes and

Rousseau, and Kant's external politics as imaginative and revelatory, while an advance on Taylor's general denigration of Kant's politics, will not bear scrutiny; it is *only* republicanism that (for Kant) tends naturally to produce *ewige Frieden*.[8] For Kant the outside is shaped by the inside; it is that which leads him to say that the "first definitive article" of eternal peace is that "the civil constitution of every state shall be republican."[9]

All of this is brought out by Kant himself in the splendid last pages of the *Rechtslehre:*

> Moral-practical reason within us pronounces the following irresistible veto: *There shall be no war,* either between individual human beings in the state of nature, or between separate states, which, although internally law-governed, still live in a lawless condition in their external relationships with one another. For war is not the way in which anyone should pursue his rights. Thus it is no longer a question of whether eternal peace is really possible or not, or whether we are not perhaps mistaken in our theoretical judgment if we assume that it is. On the contrary, we must simply act as if it could really come about (which is perhaps impossible), and turn our efforts towards realizing it and towards establishing that constitution which seems most suitable for this purpose (perhaps that of republicanism in all states, individually and collectively). By working towards this end, we may hope to terminate the disastrous practice of war, which up till now has been the main object to which all states, without exception, have accommodated their internal institutions. And even if the fulfillment of this pacific intention were forever to remain a pious hope, we should still not be deceiving ourselves if we made it our maxim to work unceasingly towards it, for it is our duty to do so. To assume, on the other hand, that the moral law within us might be misleading, would give rise to the execrable wish to dispense with all reason and to regard ourselves, along with out principles, as subject to the same mechanism of nature as the other animal species. It can indeed be said that this task of establishing a universal and lasting peace is not just a part of the theory of right within the limits of pure reason, but its entire ultimate purpose *[Endzweck.]*[10]

This simply confirms, and ties together, what has been said in various parts of this study: that it is morality itself that "vetoes" war (doubtless because war treats "ends" as mere "means," persons as mere things); that peace as a moral end can be legally approached by "establishing that constitution" (namely "republicanism in all states, individually and collectively") that brings self-loving rational citizens to "veto" war; that to think that the moral law that forbids war might be "misleading" is to renounce reason (the "fact of reason") and to fall back on the "mechanism of nature" (in the manner of Hume's "feelings" or Rousseau's *sentiments*); that "right," which legally realizes some moral ends (even without good will), has "universal and

lasting peace" as its "entire ultimate purpose" *[Endzweck]*. It is doubtful whether there is any other passage, anywhere in Kant, that so
vividly and movingly fills out his notion of a politics that pays
homage to the ends of morals. It is a passage whose visionary but
sane breadth redeems the drier parts of the *Rechtslehre*. And it is a
passage that confirms what should never have been doubted: that
Kant is a political philosopher of the very first rank whose "evolutionary" political goals would, if realized, constitute the first wholly
valuable revolution in history.

II

If the valuable part of Kant's politics is not this or that detail borrowed
from Rousseau or Montesquieu, but the notion that republican civility
and peacefulness (internal and external) are instrumental to some of
morality's ends even in the absence of *motiva moralia*, then everything
finally turns on the adequacy of the case that Kant makes for the
"objective ends" that we "ought to have" and to which public legal
justice could pay homage. For peace, obviously, cannot be an end
whose attainment is a duty unless there are ends that we "ought to
have." Unless moral ends are *real*, there is no reason to hope that self-
loving citizens of a republic will choose the right thing for the wrong
reasons.

It is doubtful, however, whether much additional light can be shed
on this question. As was seen in Chapter 3, the teleological reading of
Kant's morality—arguably the strongest one—insists on a "rational
nature" as an "end in itself" and as the "final end of creation" that
one must "never act against";[11] but the contractarian reading, not
given preference here, holds that a person *is* an end, and a member of
the kingdom of ends, only insofar as he "gives the law to himself."[12]
The strength of the teleological reading is that it supports important
claims that Kant makes in several moral works: it supports his notion
in the *Fundamental Principles* that there are "objective" ends,[13] his
claim in the *Tugendlehre* that morality would be "destroyed" without
objective ends,[14] his insistence in *Religion within the Limits* that reason
proposes objective ends that we "ought to have."[15] But this strength is,
from another perspective, a limitation, or rather a limit; if, as *Judgment*
asserts, one cannot ask "for what end" rational beings exist (since
there are no higher ends),[16] one has obviously arrived at what the
Fundamental Principles call the "extreme limit of all moral inquiry."[17] Of
course one wants to be sure that one has arrived at the *real* limit,
beyond which there is no "beyond." One will want to be certain that
one's "apodictic certainty" is certain. Thus the hardest, though also

the most important question, in Kant's practical thought, is: how can Kant (or indeed anyone) *know* that there are "objective ends" that ought to limit our willing of merely relative ends?

On this point perfect satisfaction is probably not to be hoped for; Kant himself, as will be recalled, can do no more than show that moral ideas cannot conceivably be derived from nature (external or human), and that they therefore—by exclusion—must be given or proposed by reason, as "facts" of reason.[18] (He stood by this view to the end, saying in the *Opus Posthumous* that "the concept of freedom is based on a fact *[ein Factum]*: the categorical imperative.")[19] Kant is certain of nothing so much as that some things "ought" to be; but he makes a powerful case that mere understanding will never find that "ought" in nature—not in the external nature of stones and butterflies, nor in the internal nature of passions and desires. This seems to make him a rational intuitionist not wholly unlike Plato, even if Rawls is quite right to say that Kant, in glorifying *personality*, must be distinguished from a more orthodox neo-Platonist such as Leibniz, who makes ethics the immediate analogon of reason's "other" manifestations, mathematics and logic.[20] Every reading of Kant, as was argued in Chapter 3, must terminate somewhere. Kant seems to find morality's limit in a reason-given "objective end"—the person, the "rational nature"—that is both indubitable and (necessarily) beyond validation. For a validation would have to appeal to a "higher" authority (the real sovereign) which would then *become* the practical law; the whole point of a limit is to avoid an infinite regress, or even (in Kant's case) a regress to God. To be sure, it is Kant himself who insists—in the beautiful closing passage of the *Fundamental Principles* that Judith Shklar once called "the most moving in all philosophy"[21]— that we shall never comprehend *how* the moral law can serve as our complete and sufficient incentive, that we can only "comprehend its incomprehensibility."[22] For Kant, however, one does not supply real comprehension if one says, with Bentham, that the moral law's validation is found in maximized satisfaction. That simply destroys the nonnatural *distinctiveness* of moral ideas; and their distinctiveness, their nonderivability is, for Kant, precisely what we *do* comprehend. Alternatively, reflection on Benthamism forces one to ask *why* maximized satisfaction ought to be, and that immediately restores "ought's" conceptual autonomy. If Ernst Cassirer is right, as he so often is, then Kant really did find the limit of moral inquiry: "freedom and the moral—which are put forward [by Kant] in the categorical imperative—indeed do have to be recognized as inscrutable in Kant's sense. They signify for us the ultimate 'Why' of all being and becoming, since they relate becoming to its ultimate end and anchor it one supreme value, but no further 'why' can be demanded of them themselves."[23]

Should one say, then, that the "critical" Kant turns into a "dogmatist" *at the point that matters most?* Some assure us that this is so; in a forcefully argued new article (1981), Karl Ameriks insists that in declining to give a "justification" of the moral law in *Practical Reason* Kant "frankly acknowledged that his practical philosophy was 'dogmatic' and that only his theoretical philosophy was to be called critical."[24]

It is difficult to see, however, how Kant could conceivably have justified the moral law; he could, and did, justify the theoretical distinction between *phenomena* and *noumena* in the name of "saving" freedom—a freedom without which moral notions such as "justification" cannot be used;[25] but to justify *ultimate* practical principles—to justify justifying—one would have to appeal to an "end" that is *(per impossibile)* "beyond" the "final end of creation." This would involve arriving at the "extreme limit of moral inquiry," beyond which nothing is comprehensible, and then marching on into a total darkness where (in Kant's words) reason can only "impotently flap its wings without being able to move in the . . . empty space of transcendent concepts."[26]

Absolute skepticism is a contradiction in terms—one must at least be certain of skepticism's truth—and there is no conceivable system of thought that fails to rest on *one* certainty. Kant's whole imposing edifice rests, like a pyramid on its point, on the apodictic certainty of "ought"—a moral necessity that indicates objective ends that soon find teleological relatives in nature and culture. But if Kant is right about the underived *ultimacy* of "ought," and if ought's "ends" blossom into a general teleology that holds all of Kantianism together, then who has ever balanced a better-proportioned pyramid on a stronger point? If absolute skepticism is impossible, and if Kant has built everything around the sole notion (morality) that tells us what everything is worth, then he has "teleologically subordinated"[27] everything known to the single (underived, irreducible) principle that shows us why there should be "something rather than nothing." And *that* is something.

III

That Kant himself took persons, viewed as the final ends of a teleologically subordinated creation, to be the bridge between morality and true politics, is clear from an inspection of parallels that he deliberately draws, in works published back-to-back in 1797 and 1798, which rules out fortuitous parallels. The 1797 work, the *Tugendlehre*, argues that

> Man in the system of nature . . . is a being of little significance and, along with the other animals, considered as products of the earth, has an ordinary value. . . . But man as a person, i.e., as the subject of a morally practical reason, is exalted above all price. For as such a one (*homo noumenon*) he is not to be valued merely as a means to the ends of other people, or even to his own ends, but is to be prized as an end in himself.[28]

In his remarkable work from 1798, the *Conflict of the Faculties*, Kant "translated" this very passage—or so it almost seems—into the language of politics:

> In the face of the omnipotence of nature, or rather its supreme first cause which is inaccessible to us, the human being is, in his turn, but a trifle. But for the sovereigns of his own species also to consider and treat him as such, whether by burdening him as an animal, regarding him as a mere tool of their designs, or exposing him in their conflicts with one another in order to have him massacred—this is no trifle, but a subversion of the ultimate purpose of creation itself.[29]

On this teleological view, sovereigns deny the rights of man (or perhaps more properly the rights of persons) by treating men as mere means to a relative purpose (e.g., territorial aggrandizement); in Kant's view war, which necessarily treats men as mere means to an immoral purpose, causes the state to attack and subvert morality, when in fact the state and the legal order ought (as qualified goods) to provide a stable context of peace and security within which men can safely exercise the sole unqualified good, a good will.[30] So the notion that persons are ends who ought never to be used merely as means to arbitrary purposes provides good will with an objective end that is the source of the categorical imperative, and it sets a limiting condition to what politics can legitimately do. To be sure, though persons as ends both provide a content for the categorical imperative and limit politics, there will (in Kant's view) always be an unbridgeable difference between moral and legal (political) motives. In morality men are to be respected simply and solely because this ought to be done (and hence is a duty), whereas politics can tolerate any motive (interest, fear) that will produce the desired external conduct.[31] (It is precisely the failure to see that, for Kant, politics and morals share ends but not incentives, that leads the excellent Hobbes scholar Howard Warrender to say that "the greatest stumbling block for the significant application of ethical theory to politics has been the widespread adoption . . . of Kantian terminology" and that while "politics are essentially concerned with an *external* social environment," Kant by contrast was a "motivational" theorist.[32] Warrender seems to think that Kantian politics requires the right kind of *willing;* but if that were so eternal peace could not be attained by "devils.")

Despite this distinction between moral and legal incentives, however, it remains true that willing maxims that, if universalized, respect persons as ends *constitutes* Kantian morality and *limits* Kantian politics, and therefore true that, *pace* Hegel, Kantianism is not merely a "formal" doctrine in which (to quote Hegel's language) "chill duty is the final undigested lump left within the stomach."[33] The main disadvantage of a teleological interpretation of Kantian ethics is that it seems to reduce drastically the importance of universalizing maxims of action: if the end of a moral maxim matters at least as much as its formal universality, then universalizing proposed principles of action simply permits one to see more clearly what a maxim (originally peculiar to oneself) would look like if it were conceived as a universal law generally valid for all moral agents. But this reduces universalizing to a kind of technical operation and deprives universality of its (authentically) Kantian character as "the objective principle of all practical legislation."[34] So stressing ends and downplaying universality does have its costs, and part of that cost is borne by Kant himself. This may, however, be an acceptable price to pay if it is the case that *without* objective ends Kantianism really would be formalistic and contentless. Use of critical teleology enables one to meet charges against Kant with other authentically Kantian doctrines that may be a little hard to reconcile with each other but that can be given a coherent reading (although in providing this coherent reading one will necessarily undervalue something—e.g., "universality"—that other Kant interpreters, on perfectly good grounds, will want to stress).

Whatever general (and quite reasonable) doubts one could have about Kant's special version of *telos*,[35] it is certain that the teleological standpoint helps to make intelligible Kant's insistence that "true politics cannot take a single step without first paying homage to morals." For someone might, after all, plausibly say that Kantian politics could not *conceivably* "pay homage" to Kantian morality: that since the core of Kantian morality is a purely internal good will, and the core of Kantian politics a purely external freedom under general laws, there is no *mediating* element linking these branches of "practice." (Something like this objection may be what Michael Oakeshott has in mind when he says, in his remarkable *On Human Conduct*, that no "civil prescription" or "civil rule" can be "deduced" from "the Kantian categorical imperative.")[36] But if good will means (or could mean) willing to act from respect for a categorical imperative whose source is the sole knowable objective end—that is, the person, or rational nature that is an end in itself; and if public legal justice can (on the basis of purely legal incentives) realize some moral ends (above all the preservation of persons), then *telos* is both the mediating element that throws bridges across the Kantian system and the one thing that brings the Kantian republic as close as it will ever be to unqualified moral good.

IV

Both the *necessity* of a politics that must (sometimes) be coercive, and the *possibility* of a politics that must (always) be more than merely coercive, is revealed by a page in Kant's *Opus Posthumous*, where fate or chance or editorial discretion has juxtaposed the "extreme limits" between which the Kantian political realm must be founded. Those limits are the following antipodal claims:

> *Philosophie ist die Liebe des Vernünftigen wesens zu*
> *den höchsten Zwecken der Menschlichen Vernunft.*
> *Homo homini lupus.*[37]

The first claim—that "philosophy is the love of a rational being for the highest ends of human reason"[38]—virtually *equates* philosophy and morality, in the manner of *Pure Reason* ("we are led . . . to entitle anyone a philosopher who appears to exhibit self-control under the guidance of reason").[39] The second claim, part of a line found in classical writers including Symmachus and Plautus *(homo homini deus, homo homini lupus*—"man is a god to man, man is a wolf to man")[40] was also used by Leibniz in his *Méditation sur la Notion Commune de la Justice,*[41] though Leibniz quotes the whole line, while Kant, always more cautious, excises *deus* and keeps only *lupus*. Plainly Kant's own politics must be placed in the space between these antipodes: if men were *merely* wolves, and not "at the same time" capable of acting to (legally) realize ends that Kant himself calls *göttlich,* then no politics would be possible; if on the other hand men sufficiently "loved" (or more exactly willed) "the highest ends of human reason," then no politics would be necessary. In the first case eternal Hobbesianism, not eternal peace, would prevail; in the second the kingdom of ends would overrule the kingdom of the earth. But the highest ends (moral ends) *can* be observed by "wolves"—even by devils, as one recalls— from the legal motives that would persuade republican citizens (who are neither wolves nor philosophers). The whole of Kant's politics, insofar as its possibility *depends* on there being moral ends that shape a republican and peaceful public legal justice, could be found in the area between the antipodal lines of the *Opus Posthumous*—between "rational ends" and "wolves."

V

If, finally, one contrasts Kant *als Politiker* with his principal modern competitors, it is hard to resist the judgment that he is both the most important and the most attractive of political philosophers.[43] For at the crucial juncture he is simply right: if politics is not given a republican and peaceful shape by objective moral ends, then public legal justice will be public and legal but not just—one will have Hobbesianism at best and the Gestapo at worst; but if politics tries to impose moral incentives for legal obedience, it will generate a despotism in which every witness-box becomes a confessional.

Kant's mastery of the details of government, to be sure, cannot touch Hobbes's or Hegel's; but then he also avoided saying, with Hobbes, that nothing is definitively right until there is a sovereign-ordained positive law and, with Hegel, that war preserves the ethical health of nations from the "foulness" that eternal peace would cause.[45] His understanding of *Realpolitik*, while considerable, was no match for Machiavelli's; but then he never said that the attainment of historical "greatness" excuses crimes such as Romulus's murder of Remus.[46] His comprehension of social psychology (and especially of the painfulness of inequality) cannot touch Rousseau's; but then he also refrained from saying that "the general will is always right" and that men can be "forced to be free."[47] His "friendship for the human race" was matched by Mill's; but then he never fell into claiming that the only proof that something is "desirable" is that people "do actually desire it."[48] His hope that men would never be used as mere means to relative ends was equalled by Marx's; but then he never allowed himself the sanguine belief that a "dictatorship of the proletariat" would flower into a *Reich der Freiheit*.[49] His careful treatment of politics as the legal realizer of moral ends is paralleled by Locke's notion that "judges" should simply execute an already known "natural law"; but then he avoided grounding that natural law in theology, in the will of God as laboring Creator.[50] His sense of the fragility of social institutions is matched by Burke's; but, then he avoided Burke's contempt for the "nakedness and solitude" of "metaphysical abstraction."[51] His notion of the necessity of coercive institutions, given the facts of human psychology, is equalled by Hume's; but then he never fell into reducing practical ideas to "feelings of a particular kind."[52] His awareness that civilization and culture involve a double-edged "glittering misery" is echoed and amplified by Freud; but then he never asserted that "judgments of value" are merely efforts to "prop up . . . illusions with arguments."[53] His devotion to culture is equalled, possibly exceeded, by Nietzsche's; but then he never crossed the *Grenzen der Menschheit* in search of an *Übermensch*.[54]

On any single point, Kant can be matched (and sometimes exceeded) by a rival, and his reflections on revolution, legal punishment and inequality are sometimes unworthy of his own better thinking; but his total conception of a republican and peaceful politics, slowly attained through "infinite approximation," seems to be the most nearly adequate non-sanguine, non-apocalyptic one, for the modern world. It is a politics "within the limits of reason" that mediates between utopian fantasy and unworthy quietism.

Notes

CHAPTER ONE

1. Immanuel Kant, *Fundamental Principles of the Metaphysic of Morals* [Grundlegung], trans. T. K. Abbott (Indianapolis: Library of Liberal Arts Press, 1949), p. 52: "The rational being [is] a member of a possible kingdom of ends . . . by his own nature as being an end in himself."

2. Immanuel Kant, *Religion within the Limits of Reason Alone,* trans. T. M. Greene and Hoyt Hudson (New York: Harper & Row, 1960), pp. 85-86.

3. Immanuel Kant, *Critique of Pure Reason,* trans. N. K. Smith (London: Macmillan Co., 1963), p. 637 (A808/B836).

4. Kant, *Religion,* trans. Greene and Hudson, p. 87: "A *juridico-civil* (political) *state* is the relation of men to each other in which they all stand socially under *public juridical laws* (which are, as a class, laws of coercion)."

5. Immanuel Kant, *The Conflict* [Contest] *of the Faculties,* in *Kant's Political Writings,* ed. H. Reiss (Cambridge: Cambridge University Press, 1970), p. 185.

6. Immanuel Kant, *Eternal* [Perpetual] *Peace,* in *Kant's Political Writings,* ed. Reiss, pp. 117-18.

7. Ibid., p. 125 (translation slightly altered).

8. Immanuel Kant, *Critique of Practical Reason,* trans. T. K. Abbott (London: Longmans, 1923), p. 164.

9. Kant, *Conflict of the Faculties,* in *Kant's Political Writings,* ed. Reiss, pp. 187-188.

10. Immanuel Kant, *Rechtslehre* [The Metaphysical Elements of Justice], trans. J. Ladd (Indianapolis: Library of Liberal Arts, 1965), pp. 20-21.

11. Immanuel Kant, *Critique of Judgment,* trans. J. C. Meredith (Oxford: Clarendon Press, 1952).

12. Ibid.

13. Kant, *Religion,* trans. Greene and Hudson, p. 6: "An objective end (i.e., the end which we ought to have) is that which is proposed to us as such by reason alone." The term *continuity* is borrowed from Yirmiahu Yovel's *Kant and the Philosophy of History* (Princeton, N.J.: Princeton University Press, 1980), p. 180. It is a work that does much to give *telos* its due weight in Kant, but that diminishes that weight at the crucial point of determining the content of the categorical imperative, by insisting that "human reason must abide only by those universal rules it sets up by itself" (p. 13). For a full treatment of Yovel, see Chapter 4.

14. Kant, *Judgment,* trans. Meredith, p. 14. This is preceded by one of *Judgment's* key passages: "The concept of freedom is meant to actualize in the sensible world the end proposed by its laws; and nature must consequently also be regarded in such a way that in the conformity to law of its form it at least harmonizes with the possibility of the ends to be effected in it according to the laws of freedom."

15. Kant, *Fundamental Principles,* trans. Abbott, p. 54: "Rational nature is distinguished from the rest of nature by this, that it sets before itself an end. This end would be the matter of every good will. But since in the idea of a will that is absolutely good without being limited by any condition . . . we must abstract from every end to be *effected* . . . it follows that in this case the end [personality or 'rational nature'] must be conceived, not as an end to be effected, but as an *independently* existing end."

16. Ibid.

17. Kant, *Religion,* trans. Greene and Hudson, pp. 15-39.

18. Kant, *Eternal Peace*, in *Kant's Political Writings*, ed. Reiss, p. 121n: "Government . . . not only gives the whole of a veneer of morality *(causae non causae)*, but by putting an end to outbreaks of lawless proclivities, it genuinely makes it much easier for the moral capacities of men to develop into an immediate respect for right."

19. George Armstrong Kelly, *Idealism, Politics and History: Sources of Hegelian Thought* (Cambridge: Cambridge University Press, 1969), pp. 116–17: "In effect, it should be impossible for citizenship or public law-abidingness to make men moral."

20. Kant, *Practical Reason*, trans. Abbott, p. 171.

21. Immanuel Kant, *Erläuterungen zu A. G. Baumgartens Initia philosophiae practicae primae*, in *Kants Handschriftlicher Nachlass*, vol. 6, ed. Prussian Academy (Berlin: Walter de Gruyter, 1934), [19 of *Kants Gesammelte Schriften*], No. 6566, p. 82.

22. Kant, *Practical Reason*, trans. Abbott, p. 88n.

23. Immanuel Kant, *On the Common Saying: This May Be True in Theory, but It Does Not Apply in Practice*, in *Kant's Political Writings*, ed. Reiss, p. 73: "Right is the restriction of everyone's freedom so that it harmonizes with the freedom of everyone else (insofar as this is possible within the terms of a general law)." (Cited hereafter as *Theory and Practice*.)

24. Immanuel Kant, *Critique of Practical Reason*, trans. L. W. Beck (Indianapolis: Library of Liberal Arts, 1956), p. 3.

25. Kant, *Practical Reason*, trans. Abbott, p. 136: "The moral law is given as a fact of pure reason of which we are *a priori* conscious, and which is apodictically certain."

26. Kant, *Fundamental Principles*, trans. Abbott, pp. 72–80.

27. Kant, *Practical Reason*, trans. Beck, p. 29.

28. Kant, *Theory and Practice*, in *Kant's Political Writings*, ed. Reiss, p. 77.

29. Lewis White Beck, *A Commentary on Kant's Critique of Practical Reason* (Chicago: University of Chicago Press, 1960), pp. 199–200.

30. John Rawls, "Kantian Constructivism in Moral Theory," *Journal of Philosophy 77*, 9 (September 1980): 554–72.

31. Thomas Hobbes, *Leviathan*, ed. Michael Oakeshott (Oxford: Basil Blackwell, 1957), p. 307.

32. John Locke, *Two Treatises of Government*, ed. P. Laslett (New York: Mentor, 1965), part 173, p. 430.

33. Kant, *Fundamental Principles*, trans. Abbott, p. 46.

34. Ibid., p. 45.

35. Beck, *Commentary*, pp. 199–200.

36. Kant, *Pure Reason*, trans. Smith, pp. 653–65 (A832/B860).

37. Beck, *Commentary*, pp. 179, 199.

38. Kant, *Pure Reason*, trans. Smith, p. 22 (Bxvi).

39. Ibid., p. 148 (A127).

40. Cited in Kelly, *Idealism, Politics and History*, p. 92.

41. T. D. Weldon, *Kant's Critique of Pure Reason*, 2nd ed. (Oxford: Clarendon Press, 1958), p. 224.

42. Kant, *Judgment*, trans. Meredith, p . 36.

43. Michael Oakeshott, *On Human Conduct* (Oxford: Clarendon Press, 1975), pp. 25–27.

44. Immanuel Kant, *Philosophical Correspondence*, ed. and trans. A. Zweig (Chicago: University of Chicago Press, 1967), p. 132.

45. Charles Taylor, *Hegel* (Cambridge: Cambridge University Press, 1975), pp. 371–72.

46. Kant, *Fundamental Principles*, trans. Abbott, p. 11.

47. This formulation is a conflation of the entire *Fundamental Principles*.

48. Immanuel Kant, *Eternal Peace*, in *The Philosophy of Kant*, ed. C. J. Friedrich (New York: Modern Library, 1949), p. 469.

49. Ibid., p. 459.

50. Kant, *Rechtslehre*, trans. Ladd, p. 13.

51. Cf. Hobbes, *Leviathan*, ed. Oakeshott, p. 103: "For he that should . . . perform all he promises, in such time, and place, where no man else should do so, should but make himself a prey to others, and procure his own certain ruin."

52. Kant, *Eternal Peace,* in *Kant's Political Writings,* ed. Reiss, p. 121n.

53. Immanuel Kant, *Anthropology from a Pragmatic Point of View,* trans. M. J. Gregor (The Hague: Martinus Nijhoff, 1974), p. 140.

54. Immanuel Kant, *Idea for a Universal History with a Cosmopolitan Purpose,* in *Kant's Political Writings,* ed. Reiss, pp. 44–45.

55. Kant, *Anthropology,* trans. Gregor, p. 140.

56. Kelly, *Idealism, Politics and History,* pp. 116–17.

57. Kant, *Conflict of the Faculties,* in *Kant's Political Writings,* ed. Reiss, pp. 187–88.

58. Immanuel Kant, *Tugendlehre* [The Metaphysical Principles of Virtue], trans. J. Ellington (Indianapolis: Library of Liberal Arts, 1964), pp. 154–55.

59. Kant, *Pure Reason,* trans. Smith, p. 312 (A316/B373).

60. Aristotle, *Politics,* trans. Ernest Barker (New York: Oxford University Press, 1962), p. 1: "This most sovereign and inclusive association . . . directed to the most sovereign of all goods . . . is the polis, as it is called, or the political association."

61. Kant, *Practical Reason,* trans. Abbott, p. 171.

62. Kant, *Rechtslehre,* trans. Ladd, pp. 20–21.

63. Kant, *Practical Reason,* trans. Abbott, p. 164.

64. One uses this term because for Kant the most important laws (e.g., against murder) are "natural" laws; since they are natural, and not merely "positive" or created, it is reasonable to view them simply as *sustained* by public legal justice.

65. Cited by Sheldon Wolin in *Politics and Vision* (Boston: Little, Brown, 1960), p. 389.

66. Kant, *Religion,* trans. Greene and Hudson, pp. 404–5.

67. Kant, *Rechtslehre,* trans. Ladd, p. 100.

68. Immanuel Kant, *Reflexionen zur Rechtsphilosophie,* in *Kants Gesammelte Schriften,* vol. 19, ed. Prussian Academy, pp. 489, 560.

69. Kant, *Pure Reason,* trans. Smith, p. 644 (A819/B847). The parallel to Plato's *Euthyphro,* 9E–10E, is very striking.

70. Kant, *Fundamental Principles,* trans. Abbott, p. 26.

71. Kant, *Theory and Practice,* in *Kant's Political Writings,* ed. Reiss, p. 79: "An original contract . . . is the test of the rightfulness of every public law."

72. Kant, *Rechtslehre,* trans. Ladd, pp. 109–14.

73. Kant, *Eternal Peace,* in *The Philosophy of Kant,* ed. Friedrich, pp. 434–36.

74. Kant, *Judgment,* trans. Meredith, pp. 95–96.

75. Kant, *Conflict of the Faculties,* in *Kant's Political Writings,* ed. Reiss, pp. 187–88.

76. Ibid.

77. Kant, *Fundamental Principles,* trans. Abbott, p. 12.

78. Kant, *Theory and Practice,* in *Kant's Political Writings,* ed. Reiss, p. 73.

79. Kant, *Eternal Peace,* in *Kant's Political Writings,* ed. Reiss, p. 100.

80. Ibid.

81. Kant, *Rechtslehre,* trans. Ladd, pp. 18–21. That the *ends* (though not of course the incentives) of legality must be moral is best explained by Mary J. Gregor in her fine *Laws of Freedom* (Oxford: Basil Blackwell, 1963), p. 31: "Law [for Kant] is independent of ethics in the sense that it has no need of ethical obligation in determining its duties. But it cannot be independent of the supreme moral principle; for if its laws were not derived from the categorical imperative, then the constraint exercised in juridical legislation would not be legal obligation but mere arbitrary violence."

82. Kant, *Fundamental Principles,* pp. 42 ff.

83. Kant, *Theory and Practice,* in *Kant's Political Writings,* ed. Reiss, p. 79.

84. Kant, *Fundamental Principles,* trans. Abbott, pp. 11–12.

85. Kant, *Practical Reason,* trans. Beck, p. 45.

86. Cited by Mary J. Gregor in *Laws of Freedom* (Oxford: Basil Blackwell, 1963), p. 206: "He who subjects his reason to the inclinations acts contrary to the essential ends of humanity." (Kant's original is in the *Lectures on Ethics.*)

87. Kant, *Religion,* trans. Greene and Hudson, p. 86.

88. Ibid.

89. Kant, *Conflict of the Faculties,* in *Kant's Political Writings,* ed. Reiss, p. 188.

CHAPTER TWO

1. Kant, *Fundamental Principles*, trans. Abbott, pp. 11–12.
2. The notion that the "ethical commonwealth" of *Religion within the Limits* should be viewed as Kant's "utopia" was suggested *en passant* by Judith Shklar.
3. St. Augustine, *De Libero Arbitrio* [The Free Choice of The Will], trans, R. P. Russell (Washington, D. C.: Catholic University of America Press, 1968), pp. 95–96.
4. Ibid., p. 97.
5. Plato, *Phaedrus*, trans. R. Hackforth, in *Plato: Collected Dialogues*, ed. E. Hamilton and H. Cairns (New York: Bollingen Foundation, 1961), pp. 499–502 (253b–257b).
6. A quasi-Augustinian sublimated erotism runs through Pascal; two striking examples are to be found in the *Lettres Provinciales* and in the *Écrits sur la Grace*. In the 18th *Provinciale*, Pascal argues that "Dieu change le coeur de l'homme par une douceur céleste qu'il y repand, qui fait que l'homme . . . conçoit du dégout pour les délices du peché qui le separent du bien incorruptible; trouvant sa plus grande joie dans le Dieu qui le charme, it s'y porte infailliblement de lui-meme." And in the *Deuxième Écrit sur la Grace* Pascal says that divine grace "n'est autre chose qu'une suavité et une délectation dans la loi de Dieu, repandue dans le coeur par le Saint-Esprit," so that "le libre arbitre, charmé par les douceurs et par les plaisirs que le Saint-Esprit lui inspire, plus que par les attraits du peché, choisit infailliblement lui-meme la loi de Dieu." Both passages are modern paraphrases of *De Libero Arbitrio*, and both are cited and discussed by A. W. S. Baird in his excellent *Studies in Pascal's Ethics* (The Hague: Martinus Nijhoff, 1975), pp. 61–73.
7. Jean-Jacques Rousseau, *Lettres Morales*, no. 5, in *Oeuvres Complètes*, vol. 4, edition Pléiade (Paris: Gallimard, 1969), p. 1107. One thinks specially of this passage from the fifth of the *Lettres Morales*: "Si quelque acte de clemence ou de générosité frap[p]e nos yeux quelle admiration, quel amour il nous inspire. Qui est-ce qui ne se dit pas à lui-meme: j'en voudrois avoir fait autant? Les ames les plus corrompues ne sauroient perdre tout à fait ce premier penchant."
8. Kant, *Fundamental Principles*, trans. Abbott, pp. 55–56: "The mere dignity of man as a rational creature, without any other end or advantage to be attained thereby, in other words, respect for a mere idea, should yet serve as an inflexible precept of the will."
9. Kant, *Practical Reason*, trans. Beck, pp. 76–79: "Respect for the moral law . . . is a feeling produced by an intellectual cause . . . [it] is therefore produced solely by reason . . . respect always applies to persons only, never to things."
10. Jean-Jacques Rousseau, *Première Version du Contrat Social* (Geneva MS), in *Rousseau: Political Writings*, vol. I, ed. C. E. Vaughan (Oxford: Basil Blackwell, 1962), p. 499.
11. Jean-Jacques Rousseau, *Discourse on the Origins of Inequality*, in *The Social Contract and Discourses*, trans. G. D. H. Cole (New York: Everyman, 1950), p. 208.
12. Ibid., pp. 208, 194.
13. Kant, *Fundamental Principles*, trans. Abbott, p. 29: "It is clear that all moral conceptions have their seat and origin completely *a priori* in the reason . . . that they cannot be obtained by abstraction from any empirical, and therefore merely contingent, knowledge."
14. Cited by Ernst Cassirer in *Rousseau, Kant and Goethe*, trans. J. Gutmann, P. O. Kristeller, and J. H. Randall, Jr. (New York: Harper, 1963), pp. 1–2.
15. Kant, *Pure Reason*, trans. Smith, pp. 464–73 (A533/B561).
16. Jean-Jacques Rousseau, *La Nouvelle Héloise*, ed. R. Pomeau (Paris: Garnier Frères, 1960), p. 671.
17. Kant, *Pure Reason*, trans. Smith, pp. 464–73 (A533/B561).
18. Rousseau, *Lettres Morales*, no. 5, in *Oeuvres Complètes*, vol. 4, p. 1107.
19. Jean-Jacques Rousseau, *Du Contrat Social*, in *Rousseau: Political Writings*, vol. 2, ed. Vaughan, pp. 42–50. On the importance of "generality" in Rousseau, see Patrick Riley, "The General Will before Rousseau," *Political Theory* 6, no. 4 (November 1978): 485–516.

20. Jean-Jacques Rousseau, *Émile*, vol. 4, edition Pléiade (Paris: Gallimard, 1969), p. 588: "Le mal général ne peut être que dans le desordre, et je vois dans le sisteme du monde un ordre qui ne se dement point." On the significance of *order* in *Émile*, see André Robinet, "Lexicographie philosophique et paléographie: à propos d'ORDRE dans la *Profession de Foi du Vicaire Savoyard*," in *Studi Filosofici*, ed. A. Postigliola (Naples: Istituto Universitario Orientale, 1978), pp. 39–76.

21. Rousseau, *Émile*, pp. 303–6.

22. Jean-Jacques Rousseau, *Lettres Écrites de la Montagne* (Amsterdam: Rey, 1764), Part II, p. 57.

23. Cassirer, *Rousseau, Kant and Goethe*, trans. Gutmann, pp. 1–2.

24. Kant, *Fundamental Principles*, trans. Abbott, p. 30.

25. Ibid., pp. 17, 58–59.

26. Ibid., p. 29: "Since moral laws ought to hold good for every rational creature, we must derive them from the general concept of a rational being . . . although for its *application* to man morality has need of anthropology."

27. David Hume, *A Treatise of Human Nature*, vol. 2, intro. A. D. Lindsay (London: Everyman, 1911), pp. 177–78.

28. Kant, *Pure Reason*, trans. Smith, pp. 472–73 (A547/B575).

29. Hume, *A Treatise of Human Nature*, vol. 2, p. 179.

30. Kant, *Fundamental Principles*, trans. Abbott, p. 59.

31. Hume, *A Treatise of Human Nature*, vol. 2, p. 180.

32. Ibid., p. 179.

33. Immanuel Kant, *Lectures on Philosophical Theology*, trans. A. W. Wood and G. M. Clark (Ithaca: Cornell University Press, 1978), p. 111.

34. Rousseau's "general will" is "the will one has as a citizen" of Sparta, of Rome, of Geneva: it is generally, not universally, good. For Rousseau's own insistence on the general-universal distinction, see *Première Version du Contrat Social*, in *Rousseau: Political Writings*, vol. 1, ed. Vaughan, pp. 449–54.

35. It is conceivable (though not demonstrable) that Hume's penchant for *generality* comes from the notion that while divine providence is "particular" (perfectly suited to each particular case), human imperfection necessitates merely "general" rules which work "on average"; see David Hume, *An Enquiry Concerning the Principles of Morals*, in *Hume's Moral and Political Philosophy*, ed. H. D. Aiken (New York: Hafner, 1948), pp. 192–98.

36. Kant, *Practical Reason*, trans. Abbott, p. 171.

37. Kant, *Tugendlehre*, trans. Ellington, pp. 154–55.

38. Kant, *Judgment*, trans. Meredith, pp. 37–38.

39. Kant, *Fundamental Principles*, trans. Abbott, pp. 27–28.

40. Ibid., pp. 44, 63.

41. Kant, *Practical Reason*, trans. Abbott, p. 222.

42. Kant, *Fundamental Principles*, trans. Abbott, p. 65.

43. Plato, *Gorgias*, in *Plato: Collected Dialogues*, ed. Hamilton and Cairns, 481a ff., pp. 264 ff.

44. Kant, *Fundamental Principles*, trans. Abbott, p. 63: "The will is a kind of causality belonging to living beings in so far as they are rational, and freedom would be this property of such causality that it can be efficient, independently on foreign causes determining it."

45. Hobbes, *Leviathan*, ed. Oakeshott, p. 38.

46. Kant, *Practical Reason*, in *The Philosophy of Kant*, ed. Friedrich, p. 238.

47. Kant, *Fundamental Principles*, trans. Abbott, pp. 27–30.

48. Kant, *Practical Reason*, trans. Beck, p. 49: "The moral law, itself needing no justifying grounds . . . is, in fact, a law of causality through freedom."

49. J. S. Mill, *Utilitarianism*, in *The Philosophy of John Stuart Mill*, ed. Marshall Cohen (New York: Modern Library, 1961), pp. 366–67: "There is in reality nothing desired except happiness. . . . Those who desire virtue for its own sake, desire it either because the consciousness of it is a pleasure, or because the consciousness of being without it is a pain, or for both reasons united."

50. Kant, *Practical Reason*, trans. Beck, p. 48.

51. Friedrich Nietzsche, *Beyond Good and Evil*, trans. W. Kaufmann (New York: Vintage, 1966), pp. 12–13.

52. Blaise Pascal, *Pensées*, in *Oeuvres de Blaise Pascal*, vol. 13, ed. Léon Brunschvicg (Paris: Librairie Hachette, 1904), p. 201.

53. Kant, *Practical Reason*, trans. Beck, p. 29.

54. Jeremy Bentham, *Principles of Morals and Legislation*, intro. L. Lafleur (New York: Hafner, 1948), pp. 1–2.

55. Hume, *A Treatise of Human Nature*, vol. 2, p. 127.

56. Kant, *Fundamental Principles*, trans. Abbott, pp. 44–45: "That which serves the will as the objective ground of its self-determination is the *end*, and if this is assigned by reason alone, it must hold for all rational beings. . . . Now I say: man and generally any rational being *exists* as an end in himself."

57. Immanuel Kant, *Über den Gebrauch Teleologischer Prinzipien in der Philosophie*, in *Immanuel Kants Werke*, vol. 4, ed. Ernst Cassirer (Berlin: Bruno Cassirer, 1922), p. 514.

58. Kant, *Fundamental Principles*, trans. Abbott, pp. 12–13.

59. Kant, *Judgment*, trans. Meredith, pp. 77–81.

60. Martin Heidegger, *The Essence of Reasons*, trans. T. Malick (Evanston: Northwestern University Press, 1969), p. 127. Much of this work, of course, is a commentary on Kant.

61. Kant, *Fundamental Principles*, trans. Abbott, pp. 14, 54–56.

62. Kant, *Pure Reason*, trans. Smith, p. 379 (B425).

63. Kant, *Fundamental Principles*, trans. Abbott, p. 14 (a neglected passage).

64. Ibid., p. 72.

65. Ibid., pp. 72–74.

66. Ibid., p. 73.

67. Kant, *Pure Reason*, trans. Smith, p. 425 (A468/B496).

68. Kant, *Eternal Peace*, in *Kant's Political Writings*, ed. Reiss, pp. 116–25.

69. Immanuel Kant, *Rechtslehre*, [The Philosophy of Law], trans. W. Hastie (Edinburgh: T. & T. Clark, 1887), p. 116. (This important passage is omitted in both the Ladd and Reiss editions.)

70. Kant, *Pure Reason*, trans. Smith, p. 464 (A533/B561).

71. Ibid.

72. Ibid., pp. 318–19 (A327/B384).

73. Ibid., p. 465 (A534/B562).

74. Ibid., pp. 495 ff. (A584/B612).

75. Ibid., p. 465 (A534/B562).

76. Ibid.

77. Ibid., p. 27 (Bxxvi).

78. Ibid.

79. Ibid., p. 28 (Bxxviii).

80. Ibid.

81. Beck, *Commentary*, p. 191.

82. Benedict de Spinoza, *Ethics*, part 2, proposition xxxv, in *Spinoza: Selections*, ed. J. Wild (New York: Scribners, 1930), p. 180: "Men are deceived because they think themselves free, and the sole reason for thinking so is that they are conscious of their own actions, and ignorant of the causes by which those actions are determined."

83. Kant, *Pure Reason*, trans. Smith, p. 433 (A480/B508).

84. Ibid., p. 28 (Bxxviii).

85. Ibid., p. 29 (Bxxix).

86. Ibids. p. 466 (A536/B564).

87. Ibid.

88. Ibid., pp. 466–67 (A537/B565).

89. Ibid., p. 467 (A537/B565).

90. Ibid.

91. Ibid., p. 472 (A547/B575).

92. Ibid., p. 473 (A549/B577).

93. Ibid., pp. 474–75 (A550/B578).
94. Ibid., p. 476 (A554/B582).
95. Ibid., p. 475 (A551/B579).
96. Ibid., p. 476 (A554/B582).
97. Ibid.
98. Ibid., p. 425 (A468/B496). For a more explicit statement, see Immanuel Kant, *Opus Posthumous*, in *Kant's Gesammelte Schriften*, vol. 21, ed. Prussian Academy, p. 62: "Man should (and therefore also can) make a good man of himself through the categorical imperative."
99. For a fair-minded account of Pelagianism, see R. F. Evans, *Pelagius: Inquiries and Reappraisals* (New York: Seabury Press, 1968), pp. 66–89.
100. Kant, *Religion*, trans. Greene and Hudson, p. 179: "Whatever good man is able to do through his own efforts, under laws of freedom . . . can be called nature."
101. Ibid., pp. 178–79: "Now we at least know the laws of freedom (the moral laws) . . . but we cannot know anything at all about supernatural aid. . . . The true (moral) service of God . . can consist solely in the disposition of obedience to all true duties as divine commands."
102. Blaise Pascal, *Écrits sur la Grace*, in *Oeuvres de Blaise Pascal*, vol. 11, ed. Brunschvicg, p. 129.
103. Kant, *Lectures on Philosophical Theology*, trans. Wood and Clark, p. 148. In their fine Introduction the translators argue persuasively that the *Lectures* date from 1783–1784—well into Kant's critical period.
104. Immanuel Kant, *Religion within the Limits of Reason Alone*, in *The Philosophy of Kant*, ed. Friedrich, pp. 388–89.
105. Ibid., p. 389.
106. Ibid., p. 388.
107. Ibid.
108. Ibid.
109. Ernst Cassirer, *Kant's Life and Thought*, trans. J. Haden (New Haven: Yale University Press, 1981), pp. 392–97. (This magnificent work is, at last, available in a fine translation.)
110. Kant, *Religion*, in *The Philosophy of Kant*, ed. Friedrich, pp. 393–94.
111. Ibid., p. 367.
112. Kant, *Rechtslehre*, trans. Hastie, p. 116.
113. Kant, *Rechtslehre*, in *Kant's Political Writings*, ed. Reiss, pp. 173–74.
114. Kant, *Pure Reason*, trans. Smith, pp. 422 ff. (A462/B490).
115. Kant, *Lectures on Philosophical Theology*, trans. Wood and Clark, p. 111.
116. Hobbes, *Leviathan*, ed. Oakeshott, p. 111.
117. Kant, *Practical Reason*, trans. Beck, p. 105.
118. On this difficulty see the brilliant short essay by Michael Oakeshott, "Logos and Telos," in *Government and Opposition*, Spring 1974, pp. 237–44.
119. Hobbes, *Leviathan*, ed. Oakeshott, p. 307.
120. Kant, *Fundamental Principles*, trans. Abbott, p. 68.
121. Ibid.
122. Ibid., p. 69.
123. Ibid., pp. 70–71.
124. Kant, *Pure Reason*, trans. Smith, p. 379 (B425).
125. Kant, *Über den Gebrauch Teleologischer Prinzipien in der Philosophie*, in *Immanuel Kants Werke*, vol. 4, ed. Cassirer, p. 514.

CHAPTER THREE

1. Kant, *Fundamental Principles*, trans. Abbott, pp. 11–12.
2. Ibid., pp. 30 ff.
3. Ibid., p. 74: "Man . . . thinks of himself as an intelligence endowed with a will, and consequently with causality."

4. Kant, *Eternal Peace*, in *Kant's Political Writings*, ed. Reiss, pp. 116–21.

5. Kant, *Fundamental Principles*, trans. Abbott, p. 48.

6. Ibid., pp. 54–55.

7. This is argued particularly in Chapter 4.

8. W. B. Gallie, "Kant's View of Reason in Politics," in *Philosophy* 54 (1979): 25. But even Gallie grants that when Kant "expounds the universality of moral rules in terms of . . . an ideal 'kingdom of ends,' the perspective is entirely changed." Unfortunately Gallie makes no effort to find a relation between "universality" and "ends" in Kant; he simply calls the former wrong and the latter right.

9. Kant, *Practical Reason*, trans. Abbott, p. 204.

10. Kant, *Practical Reason*, trans. Beck, pp. 28–29.

11. Ibid., p. 28.

12. Ibid.

13. Ibid, pp. 96–97: "Since all determining grounds of the will (except the one and only pure practical law of reason, i.e., the moral law) are empirical and as such belong to the principle of happiness, they must be separated from the supreme practical principle and never be incorporated with it as a condition, for this would destroy all moral worth." This, obviously, permits the moral law to be the "determining ground" of the will. And therefore the will does not "give" the law, *ex nihilo*.

14. Kant, *Fundamental Principles*, trans. Abbott, pp. 44–57.

15. For a fine account of Hegel's criticisms of Kant, see Judith Shklar, *Freedom and Independence: A Study of the Political Ideas of Hegel's Phenomenology of Mind* (Cambridge: Cambridge University Press, 1976), pp. 180–203.

16. G. W. F. Hegel, *Natural Law*, trans. T. M. Knox (Philadelphia: University of Pennsylvania Press, 1975), p. 76.

17. Ibid.

18. Ibid., p. 77.

19. Ibid., pp. 77–78.

20. Ibid., pp. 78–79.

21. Ibid., p. 132.

22. Ibid., pp. 132–33.

23. G. W. F. Hegel, *The Philosophy of Right*, trans. T. M. Knox (Oxford: Clarendon Press, 1942), p. 89.

24. Ibid., p. 48.

25. Ibid., p. 90.

26. Ibid., "additions," p. 252.

27. Ibid., pp. 83–84.

28. Ibid., pp. 167–70.

29. F. H. Bradley, *Ethical Studies* (Oxford: Clarendon Press, 1927), pp. 148–49.

30. Georg Lukács, *The Young Hegel: Studies in the Relations between Dialectics and Economics*, trans. R. Livingstone (Cambridge, Mass.: MIT Press, 1975), p. 160.

31. Mill, *Utilitarianism*, in *The Philosophy of John Stuart Mill*, ed. Cohen, pp. 326–27.

32. Kant, *Practical Reason*, trans. Abbott, p. 165.

33. Kant, *Fundamental Principles*, trans. Abbott, pp. 54–55: "This principle: So act in regard to every rational being . . . that he may always have place in thy maxim as an end in himself, is accordingly essentially identical with this other: Act upon a maxim which, at the same time, involves its own universal validity for every rational being."

34. Ibid.

35. Ibid., p. 44.

36. Ibid., p. 45.

37. Ibid.

38. Ibid., p. 46.

39. Ibid.

40. Ibid. Kant italicizes the whole sentence to stress its importance.

41. Ibid., p. 48.

42. Ibid.

43. Ibid., p. 49.

44. Ibid., pp. 49–50.
45. Ibid., p. 50.
46. Ibid., p. 51.
47. Ibid., p. 53.
48. Ibid.
49. Ibid.
50. Ibid., p. 54.
51. Kant, *Tugendlehre*, trans. Ellington, pp. 42–43. See also p. 54: "The supreme principle of the doctrine of virtue is this: 'Act according to a maxim whose ends are such that there can be a universal law that everyone have these ends.' According to this principle a man is an end to himself as well as to others . . . making mankind in general one's end is in itself a duty of every man." Here universality and *telos* blend.
52. On the central place of the *Critique of Judgment* in the critical philosophy, see particularly George Schrader, "The Status of Teleological Judgment in the Critical Philosophy," in *Kant-Studien* 45 (1953–1954): 204–35.
53. Kant, *Fundamental Principles*, trans. Abbott, p. 46.
54. Ibid., p. 49.
55. Kant, *Pure Reason*, trans. Smith, p. 473 (A548/B576).
56. Ibid., p. 428 (A472/B500).
57. Cited in Kelly, *Idealism, Politics and History*, p. 92. Kant also insisted, in an equally celebrated saying, that "Rousseau straightened me out . . . I learned to honor mankind." But the term *mankind* shores up a teleological notion of persons as objective ends at least as well as it supports the idea that what Kant inherited from Rousseau was the conviction that "self-imposed law" is the only real liberty. *Exactly* what Kant learned from Rousseau is not immediately clear.
58. Kant, *Religion*, trans. Greene and Hudson, p. 6n.
59. Kant, *Fundamental Principles*, trans. Abbott, p. 50.
60. Ibid., p. 46.
61. Ibid., p. 55.
62. Ibid., p. 49.
63. Kant, *Practical Reason*, trans. Beck, pp. 48, 78–80.
64. Kant, *Fundamental Principles*, trans. Abbott, p. 52. The German is taken from *Immanuel Kants Werke*, vol. 4, ed. Cassirer, p. 294.
65. Kant, *Rechtslehre*, trans. Ladd, pp. 18–30.
66. Kant, *Tugendlehre*, trans. Ellington, pp. 43 ff.
67. Ibid., p. 155. In this passage Kant complains of "ethical gymnastics," which consists in "strife against the natural impulses."
68. Kant, *Religion*, trans. Greene and Hudson, pp. 3–4.
69. Ibid., p. 4.
70. Kant, *Fundamental Principles*, trans. Abbott, p. 45.
71. Kant, *Religion*, trans. Greene and Hudson, p. 6n.
72. Ibid., p. 21n.
73. Ibid.
74. Kant, *Practical Reason*, trans. Beck, p. 13: "Only objective validity affords the ground of a necessary universal agreement."
75. Kant, *Fundamental Principles*, trans. Abbott, p. 53.
76. Ibid., pp. 54–55.
77. Ibid., p. 29.
78. Ibid., pp. 55–56.
79. Kant, *Practical Reason*, trans. Beck, p. 72.
80. Ibid., p. 136.
81. Kant, *Lectures on Philosophical Theology*, trans. Wood and Clark, pp. 14–15.
82. Ibid., p. 140.
83. Kant, *Pure Reason*, trans. Smith, p. 318 (A327/B384).
84. Ibid., pp. 318–19 (A327/B384).
85. Ibid., p. 319 (A328/B385).

86. Ibid., pp. 310–313 (A314/B371). The importance of this passage has been stressed by Ernst Cassirer in his magistral *Kants Leben und Lehre*, in *Immanuel Kants Werke*, vol. 11, pp. 268–70.

87. Ibid., p. 319 (A328/B385).

88. Ibid., p. 472 (A547/B575).

89. Ibid., pp. 472–73 (A547/B575).

90. Ibid., p. 472 (A547/B575).

91. Ibid.

92. Ibid.

93. Ibid., p. 473 (A548/B576).

94. Ibid., pp. 633–34 (A802/B830).

95. Rawls, "Kantian Constructivism in Moral Theory," pp. 554, 564: "the idea of approximating to moral truth has no place in a constructivist doctrine."

96. Ibid., p. 557.

97. Ibid., pp. 558–59.

98. Ibid., p. 559.

99. Ibid.

100. Ibid., pp. 518–19, 560.

101. John Rawls, *A Theory of Justice* (Cambridge, Mass: Harvard University Press, 1971), p. 251.

102. Rawls, "Kantian Constructivism in Moral Theory," p. 568.

103. Rawls, *A Theory of Justice*, p. 18. It was this phrase above all that distressed R. M. Hare in his rather vitriolic review of *A Theory of Justice* (reprinted, with small changes, in *Reading Rawls*, ed. N. Daniels (Oxford: Basil Blackwell, 1975), pp. 84 ff.

104. Ibid., p. 256. See also John Rawls, "The Basic Structure as Subject," in *American Philosophical Quarterly* 14, no. 2 (April 1977): 159–65. "To develop a viable Kantian conception of justice the force and content of Kant's doctrine must be detached from its background in transcendental idealism and given a procedural interpretation by means of the construction of the original position." This is a necessary enterprise, of course, only if Kant's own development of Kantian justice is inadequate; and one can wonder how far Kant's transcendental idealism is a "background" that can be "detached" from his practical thought.

105. Ibid., p. 256n.

106. Lewis White Beck, "Was haben wir von Kant gelernt?," in *Kant-Studien* (1981) vol. 1, p. 5.

107. Rawls, "Kantian Constructivism in Moral Theory," p. 559.

108. G. W. Leibniz to the Electress Sophie, in *Textes Inédits*, vol. 1, ed. Gaston Grua (Paris: Presses Universitaires de France, 1948), p. 379.

109. "The [proper] treatment of justice and that of charity cannot be separated." G. W. Leibniz, *Elementa Iuris Naturalis*, in *Sämtliche Schriften und Briefe* (Berlin: Akademi-Verlag, 1923–), Reihe VI, Band I, No. 12, p. 481. For a full treatment see Patrick Riley, ed., *The Political Writings of Leibniz* (Cambridge: Cambridge University Press, 1972), pp. 3 ff.

110. G. W. Leibniz, *Opinion on the Principles of Pufendorf*, in *The Political Writings of Leibniz*, ed. Riley, p. 5.

111. Kant, *Religion*, trans. Greene and Hudson, pp. 22–23: "The predisposition to *personality* is the capacity for respect for the moral law as *in itself a sufficient incentive of the will*."

112. Kant, *Practical Reason*, trans. Beck, p. 48.

113. Ibid. But some other formulations of the fact of reason supply Rawls and Beck with a reason to doubt that Kant is a rational intuitionist: at one point in *Practical Reason* Kant insists that "the consciousness of this fundamental [moral] law may be called a fact of reason, since one cannot ferret it out from any antecedent data of reason and since [the law] forces itself upon us as a synthetic proposition *a priori* based on no pure or empirical intuition." The seeming rejection—at least in this passage—of "pure intuition" supplies Rawls and Beck with a reason to interpret Kant as "deepened"

Rousseau. But if, as Kant insists in *Religion*, trans. Greene and Hudson, p. 6n, "an objective end (i.e., the end which we ought to have) . . . is proposed to us as such by reason alone," what can one call this if *not* "rational intuitionism"?

114. Kant, *Fundamental Principles*, trans. Abbott, pp. 78–80: "To explain how pure reason can of itself be practical . . . is beyond the power of human reason."

115. Kant, *Practical Reason*, in *The Philosophy of Kant*, ed. Friedrich, p. 238.

116. Kant, *Practical Reason*, trans. Beck, p. 48.

117. Kant, *Pure Reason*, trans. Smith, pp. 636–37 (A807/B835).

118. Kant, *Fundamental Principles*, trans. Abbott, pp. 29–30.

119. Ibid., p. 32.

120. Ibid., p. 29.

121. Ibid., p. 46.

122. Ibid., p. 29.

123. Ibid., p. 46.

124. Rawls, "Kantian Constructivism in Moral Theory," p. 559.

125. Kant, *Fundamental Principles*, trans. Abbott, p. 29.

126. All the same, the fact that persons are "there" is what keeps Rawls's theory from becoming a "radical choice" theory. As he himself says, "we take moral persons to be characterized by two moral powers and by two corresponding highest-order interests," etc. ("Kantian Constructivism in Moral Theory," p. 525). The only question is where such persons come from.

127. Rawls, "Kantian Constructivism in Moral Theory," pp. 521, 522, 523, 544, 545.

128. Kant, *Practical Reason*, trans. Beck, p. 4: "We do not understand it [freedom], but we know it as the condition of the moral law which we do know. . . . Had not the moral law already been distinctly thought in our reason, we would never have been justified in assuming anything like freedom."

129. Vacillation on this point is imputed to Kant (not wholly groundlessly) by Robert Paul Wolff in *The Autonomy of Reason* (New York: Harper & Row, 1973), pp. 181 ff.

130. H. B. Acton, *Kant's Moral Philosophy* (London: Macmillan & Co., 1970), p. 38.

131. Plato, *Euthyphro*, in *Plato: Collected Dialogues*, ed. Hamilton and Cairns, pp. 178–79 (9E–10E).

132. Kant, *Fundamental Principles*, trans. Abbott, p. 46.

133. Kant, *Judgment*, trans. Meredith, pp. 50–51.

134. Ibid., p. 88 (translation slightly altered).

135. Kant, *Fundamental Principles*, trans. Abbott, p. 30.

136. Ibid., p. 46.

137. Kant, *Judgment*, trans. Meredith, p. 99.

138. Ibid.

139. Ibid., p. 100.

140. Ibid., p. 100n.

141. Aristotle, *Metaphysica*, in *The Works of Aristotle*, vol. 8, ed. W. D. Ross (Oxford: Clarendon Press, 1928), 983a: "Evidently we have to acquire knowledge of the original causes . . . and causes are spoken of in four senses." Cf. *Physics* ii, 3, 7.

142. Immanuel Kant, *Prolegomena to Every Future Metaphysics that may be Presented as a Science*, in *The Philosophy of Kant*, ed. Friedrich, p. 45. Here, of course, Kant speaks of being awakened from his own dogmatic slumbers by Hume.

143. Kant, *Pure Reason*, trans. Smith, pp. 65–74 (A19/B34).

144. Ibid., pp. 152 ff. (B131 ff).

145. Kant, *Judgment*, trans. Meredith, p. 71: "If it happens that objects of nature present themselves, whose possibility is incapable of being conceived by us on the principle of mechanism . . . unless we rely on teleological principles . . . we may confidently study natural laws on lines following both principles."

146. Hobbes, *Leviathan*, ed. Oakeshott, entire work.

147. Ibid., pp. 80 ff.

148. T. Spragens, *The Politics of Motion: The World of Thomas Hobbes* (Lexington: University of Kentucky Press, 1973).

149. For all of this see the argument of Chapter 1.

150. Edmund Burke, *Reflections on the Revolution in France*, in *Burke's Politics: Selected Writings and Speeches*, ed. R. Hoffman and P. Levack (New York: Knopf, 1959), p. 305.
151. Kant, *Judgment*, trans. Meredith, pp. 38 40.
152. Ibid., pp. 116–17.
153. A. O. Lovejoy, *The Great Chain of Being* (New York: Harper & Row, 1960), pp. 240–41, 268–70. Admittedly, the passages on Kant are not the finest thing in this wonderful book.
154. Protagoras's famous saying is cited by George Sabine in *A History of Political Theory* (New York: Henry Holt, 1950), p. 27.
155. Nicholas Malebranche, *Conversations Chrétiennes*, in *Oeuvres Complètes*, vol. 4, ed. André Robinet (Paris: Librairie Vrin, 1959), p. 60. Malebranche adds, indeed, that God "preserves" human beings only "pour le connaitre, et . . . pour l'aimer."
156. Kant, *Judgment*, trans. Meredith, p. 100.
157. Cassirer, *Kant's Life and Thought*, trans. Haden, pp. 376–97.
158. Mill, *Utilitarianism*, in *The Philosophy of John Stuart Mill*, ed. Cohen, p. 333. One can wonder, of course, whether Mill's argument works. In view of his principle that "the sole evidence it is possible to produce that any thing is desirable, is that people do actually desire it," it must be the case that the exercise of "higher" faculties is desirable only if actually desired. If Socratic virtue is not desired, Mill has no way of saying that it *ought* to be, since desirability is the heart of utility and utility is (in its turn) "the ultimate appeal on all ethical questions." This is perhaps a more serious difficulty for Mill than tumbling into the "naturalistic fallacy."
159. Karl Marx, "The British Rule in India," in *Karl Marx on Colonialism and Modernization*, ed. Shlomo Avineri (New York: Anchor, 1969), p. 94.
160. Strictly speaking, Kant calls man the *"betitelter Herr der Natur."* In Kant, *Kritik der Urteilskraft*, in *Immanuel Kants Werke*, vol. 5, ed. Cassirer, p. 510.
161. Kant, *Judgment*, trans. Meredith, p. 86: "By extrinsic finality I mean the finality that exists where one thing in nature subserves another as means to an end."
162. Ibid.
163. Samuel Johnson, "Review of a Free Enquiry into the Nature and Origin of Evil," in *The Works of Samuel Johnson*, vol. 6 (Oxford: Talboys and Wheeler, 1825), p. 53.
164. Kant, *Fundamental Principles*, trans. Abbott, p. 54.
165. Kant, *Conflict of the Faculties*, in *Kant's Political Writings*, ed. Reiss, pp. 187–189.
166. Kant, *Judgment*, trans. Meredith, pp. 3–5, 206–225.
167. Cassirer, *Kant's Life and Thought*, trans. Haden, p. 360: "Kant's original conception of knowledge has undergone an extension and deepening [in the *Critique of Judgment*] that only now makes it feasible to survey the *whole* of natural and spiritual life and to conceive it as intrinsically a single organism of 'reason'." Though this pushes Kant in Hegel's direction, it is still a splendid summary statement.

CHAPTER FOUR

1. Kant, *Fundamental Principles*, trans. Abbott, p. 46.
2. Kant, *Judgment*, trans. Meredith, pp. 98–114.
3. Kant, *Pure Reason*, trans. Smith, pp. 658–59 (A840/B868).
4. Cited in Cassirer, *Rousseau, Kant and Goethe*, trans. Gutmann, p. 64.
5. Kant, *Prolegomena*, in *The Philosophy of Kant*, ed. Friedrich, pp. 42–47.
6. Kant, *Pure Reason*, trans. Smith, p. 560 (A687/B715).
7. Ibid., pp. 560/61 (A688/B716).
8. Ibid.
9. Ibid., p. 472 (A547/B575).
10. Ibid., p. 653 (A832/B860).
11. Ibid., p. 658 (A840/B868).
12. Kant, *Fundamental Principles*, trans. Abbott, pp. 43–46.
13. Kant, *Pure Reason*, trans. Smith, pp. 658–59 (A840/B868).
14. J. W. von Goethe, "Einwirkung der Neueren Philosophie," in *Goethes Werke*

[Goethes Naturwissenschaftliche Schriften] vol. 11 (Weimar: Hermann Böhlau, 1893), p. 51. For a helpful commentary—which also shows the limits of Goethe's reverence for Kant—see Hans-Georg Gadamer, "Goethe und die Philosophie," in *Kleine Schriften*, vol. 2 (Tübingen: J.C.B. Mohr, 1967), pp. 87–90.

15. Kant, *Judgment*, trans. Meredith, pp. 12–13.
16. Ibid., p. 14.
17. Karl Baedeker, *Northern Germany* (Leipzig: Karl Baedeker, 1910), p. 366.
18. Kant, *Practical Reason*, trans. Beck, p. 166.
19. Kant, *Judgment*, trans. Meredith, p. 14.
20. Ibid., p. 14.
21. Ibid.
22. Ibid., pp. 36–37.
23. Ibid., p. 38.
24. Ibid. Through *whose* "intellectual faculty"? God's, no doubt, if he were knowable; since he is not, the world is only *interpreted* (by us) as "purposive."
25. Ibid.
26. Immanuel Kant, *First Introduction to the Critique of Judgment*, trans. James Haden (Indianapolis: Library of Liberal Arts, 1965), p. 44.
27. Kant, *Pure Reason*, trans. Smith, p. 472 (A547/B575).
28. Kant, *Judgment*, trans. Meredith, p. 53.
29. Ibid., pp. 98–99.
30. Cited in Yirmiahu Yovel, *Kant and the Philosophy of History* (Princeton, N.J.: Princeton University Press, 1980), p. 83.
31. Kant, *Judgment*, trans. Meredith, pp. 114–115.
32. This is still clearer in the original German. In the *Fundamental Principles* Kant insists that we must derive the moral law "aus dem allgemeinen Begriffe eines vernünftigen wesens überhaupt"; in *Judgment* he says that we must find the moral law "in dem Begriffe eines . . . vernünftigen wesens überhaupt." Plainly *Judgment* is borrowing the language of the *Grundlegung*. (For the text of the *Fundamental Principles*, see *Immanuel Kants Werke*, vol. 4, ed. Cassirer, p. 269; for that of *Judgment* see Ibid., vol. 5, p. 528.)
33. Kant, *Judgment*, trans. Meredith, p. 115.
34. Ibid., p. 14.
35. Ibid., p. 123.
36. Kant, *Rechtslehre*, trans. Ladd, pp. 20–21.
37. Kant, *Judgment*, trans. Meredith, pp. 93–97.
38. Ibid., p. 209.
39. Ibid., p. 215.
40. Ibid., p. 208. This sentence has been given its due weight particularly by Ernst Cassirer; see his "Critical Idealism as a Philosophy of Culture," in *Symbol, Myth and Culture*, trans. Donald Verene (New Haven: Yale University Press, 1979), p. 88.
41. Kant, *Pure Reason*, trans. Smith, p. 379 (B425).
42. Kant, *Judgment*. trans. Meredith, pp. 224–25.
43. Cited in George Armstrong Kelly, *Hegel's Retreat from Eleusis* (Princeton, N.J.: Princeton University Press, 1978), pp. 22–23. This book contains fine passages on Hegel's reading of Kant.
44. Kant, *Judgment*, trans. Meredith, p. 223–25. To be sure, Kant is here discussing the *beautiful*. But he is treating it as the symbol of the morally good.
45. Ibid., p. 224.
46. Ibid., p. 54.
47. Ibid., p. 66.
48. Ibid., pp. 50–51.
49. Ibid., p. 53.
50. Ibid., p. 38.
51. Ibid., pp. 71–73.
52. Ibid., p. 73.
53. Jean-Jacques Rousseau, "Institutions Chymiques," in *Annales de la Société Jean-Jacques Rousseau*, vol. 12 (Geneva: A. Jullien, 1919), pp. 46–47.

54. Kant, *Judgment*, trans. Meredith, pp. 86–87.

55. Ibid., p. 86.

56. Kant, *Fundamental Principles*, trans. Abbott, pp. 45–48.

57. Kant, *Judgment*, trans. Meredith, p. 87.

58. Ibid., p. 88.

59. Kant himself sometimes forgets this fine distinction—see section 82 of *Judgment*, trans. Meredith, p. 88.

60. Kant, *Judgment*, trans. Meredith, p. 92.

61. Ibid., p. 88.

62. Ibid., p. 94.

63. Gerard Lebrun, *Kant et la Fin de la Métaphysique* (Paris: Librairie Armand Colin, 1970), pp. 467 ff. An extraordinarily imaginative, if slightly chaotic, book, beginning with its artful title. But Lebrun would have done better not to quote Nietzsche ("to create values is the true droit du seigneur") as a clue to Kant, since Kant (correctly) confines "creativity" to the "genius" in art. It is only Sartre who views art and morality *equally* as creations.

64. Kant, *Judgment*, trans. Meredith, pp. 92–95.

65. Ibid., p. 92.

66. Kant, *Fundamental Principles*, trans. Abbott, pp. 35–36, 59.

67. Kant, *Judgment*, trans. Meredith, pp. 93–94.

68. Ibid.

69. Ibid., p. 97n.

70. Ibid., pp. 47–48.

71. Ibid., p. 94.

72. Kant, *Fundamental Principles*, trans. Abbott, p. 45.

73. Kant, *Religion*, trans. Greene and Hudson, p. 179.

74. Immanuel Kant, *Reflexionen zur Anthropologie*, in *Kants Gesammelte Schriften*, vol. 15, ed. Prussian Academy, p. 891.

75. Kant, *Judgment*, trans. Meredith, pp. 94–95.

76. Ibid., pp. 92–97.

77. Ibid., p. 95.

78. Kant, *Fundamental Principles*, trans. Abbott, p. 44: "The will is conceived as a faculty of determining oneself to action in accordance with the conception of certain [moral] laws."

79. Kant, *Judgment*, trans. Meredith, p. 95.

80. Ibid.

81. Ibid.

82. Ibid.

83. Kant, *Idea for a Universal History*, in *Kant's Political Writings*, ed. Reiss, p. 44.

84. Kant, *Judgment*, trans. Meredith, p. 97. Civilization, Kant argues, does "much to overcome the tyrannical propensities of sense, and so prepare man for a sovereignty in which reason alone shall have sway."

85. Ibid., p. 96.

86. Ibid.

87. Ibid.

88. Kant, *Eternal Peace*, in *Kant's Political Writings*, ed. Reiss, p. 112 (translation slightly altered). Kant adds (p. 113), in a passage that shows that he views public legal justice as the legal realization of moral ends, that "we cannot expect . . . moral attitudes to produce a good political constitution; on the contrary, it is only through the latter that the people can be expected to attain a good level of moral culture. . . . A problem of this kind must be soluble. For such a task does not involve the moral improvement of man; it only means finding out how the mechanism of nature can be applied to men in such a manner that the antagonism of their hostile attitudes will make them compel one another to submit to coercive laws." Coercion, however, must not be *mere* coercion; the point of law is "the reign of established right."

89. Kant, *Judgment*, trans. Meredith, p. 97.

90. Ibid.

91. Rousseau, *Discourse on the Origins of Inequality*, in *The Social Contract and*

Discourses, trans. Cole, pp. 251–52: "Society and law . . . bound new fetters on the poor, and gave new powers to the rich . . . [they] converted clever usurpation into unalterable right, and, for the advantage of a few ambitious individuals, subjected all mankind to perpetual labor, slavery and wretchedness."

92. Kant, *Judgment*, trans. Meredith, p. 97.

93. Immanuel Kant, "Conjectural Beginning of Human History," in *Kant on History*, ed. L. W. Beck (Indianapolis: Library of Liberal Arts, 1963), pp. 60–61.

94. Kant, *Eternal Peace*, in *Kant's Political Writings*, ed. Reiss, p. 130. More exactly, Kant speaks of "an infinite process of gradual approximation."

95. Kant, *Judgment*, trans. Meredith, p. 97.

96. Ibid., pp. 223. Is it merely accidental that this crucial passage opens with the same three words (*Nun sage ich*) as the still more important first statement of the doctrine that persons are ends in the *Fundamental Principles*?

97. Ibid., p. 225.

98. Ibid., p. 227. Kant goes on to offer the following bridge between aesthetic judgment and teleological judgment: "Humanity signifies, on the one hand, the universal feeling of sympathy, and, on the other, the faculty of being able to communicate universally one's inmost self—properties constituting in conjunction the befitting social spirit of mankind, in contradistinction to the narrow life of the lower animals."

99. Ibid., p. 224.

100. Kant, *Eternal Peace*, in *Kant's Political Writings*, ed. Reiss, p. 121n.

101. Yovel, *Kant and the Philosophy of History*, p. 189.

102. Kant, *Conflict of the Faculties*, in *Kant's Political Writings*, ed. Reiss, pp. 187–88.

103. Yovel, *Kant and the Philosophy of History*, p. 13.

104. Beck, *Commentary*, pp. 199–200.

105. Yovel, *Kant and the Philosophy of History*, pp. 13–42.

106. Kant, *Judgment*, trans. Meredith, p. 14. The subtitle of Section III of the Introduction to *Judgment* is "The *Critique of Judgment* as a Means of Connecting the Two Parts [Theoretical and Practical] of Philosophy in a Whole."

107. Yovel, *Kant and the Philosophy of History*, p. 180.

108. Kant, *Judgment*, trans. Meredith, p. 118.

109. Yovel, *Kant and the Philosophy of History*, p. 180.

110. Kant, *Judgment*, trans. Meredith, p. 98.

111. Ibid., pp. 98–99.

112. Ibid.

113. Ibid., p. 99.

114. Ibid.

115. Ibid., p. 108.

116. Ibid., p. 109.

117. Ibid., pp. 116n–117n.

118. Ibid.

119. Kant, *Fundamental Principles*, trans. Abbott, pp. 45ff.; Kant, *Practical Reason*, trans. Beck, p. 48.

120. Kant, *Pure Reason*, trans. Smith, p. 475 (A552/B580): "The real morality of actions . . . remains entirely hidden from us."

121. Kant, *Judgment*, trans. Meredith, p. 153.

122. Ibid., p. 13.

123. The purpose of this chapter is to *show* that this is true. It is the best antidote to viewing Kant's politics as a mere quasi-Rousseauean appendix to his "serious" work.

124. Kant, *Rechtslehre*, in *Kant's Political Writings*, ed. Reiss, p. 166.

125. Ibid.

126. Ibid.

127. Ibid., pp. 166–67.

128. Kant, *Eternal Peace*, in *Kant's Political Writings*, ed. Reiss, p. 100.

129. Ibid., p. 117.

130. Kant, *Judgment*, trans. Meredith, p. 137.

131. Hobbes, *Leviathan*, ed. Oakeshott, p. 5: "The art of man . . . can make an

artificial animal . . . by art is created that great Leviathan called a Commonwealth, or State."

132. Kant, *Eternal Peace*, in *Kant's Political Writings*, ed. Reiss, p. 119.

133. Ibid.

134. Kant, *Conflict of the Faculties*, in *Kant's Political Writings*, ed. Reiss, p. 178.

135. Kelly, *Idealism, Politics and History*, p. 156: "Kant is preeminently gifted at taking back with one hand the dangerous doctrines extended in the other."

136. Kant, *Eternal Peace*, in *Kant's Political Writings*, ed. Reiss, p. 120.

137. Ibid.

138. Ibid., p. 123.

139. W. B. Gallie, *Philosophers of Peace and War: Kant, Clausewitz, Marx, Engels and Tolstoy* (Cambridge: Cambridge University Press, 1978), p. 11.

140. Kant, *Eternal Peace*, in *Kant's Political Writings*, ed. Reiss, p. 125 (translation slightly altered).

141. For a contrasting view that grants that "ends of various sorts and descriptions have an important place in Kant's philosophy," but then *minimizes* that place, see John Atwell, "Objective Ends in Kant's Ethics," in *Archiv für Geschichte der Philosophie* 56 (1974): 156–171. This is a very important article that should be read as a corrective to the present teleological reading of Kant.

142. G. W. F. Hegel, *Faith and Knowledge* [Glauben und Wissen], trans. W. Cerf and H. S. Harris (Albany: State University of New York Press, 1977), pp. 85–92.

143. Ibid., p. 92.

144. Ibid., p. 143. Cf. G. W. F. Hegel, *The Spirit of Christianity and its Fate*, in *Early Theological Writings*, trans. T. M. Knox (Philadelphia: University of Pennsylvania Press, 1971), pp. 210–15.

145. Hegel, *Faith and Knowledge*, trans. Cerf and Harris, p. 92.

146. Hegel, *Philosophy of Right*, trans. Knox, p. 12.

147. Ibid., p. 215. The very passage in which the phrase "ethical substance" appears shows how very far Hegel is from the Kantian state as the legal realization of moral ends: "At one time the opposition between morals and politics, and the demand that the latter should conform to the former, were much canvassed. . . . The ethical substance, the state . . . can only be this concrete existent and not one of the many universal thoughts supposed to be moral commands." This is plainly aimed at Kant, inter alia.

148. Friedrich Nietzsche, *Twilight of the Idols*, in *The Portable Nietzsche*, trans. W. Kaufmann (New York: Viking, 1954), p. 509.

149. Ibid.

150. Ibid., pp. 508–9.

151. Friedrich Nietzsche, *The Will to Power*, trans. W. Kaufmann (New York: Random House, 1967), pp. 366–70.

152. Nietzsche, *Twilight of the Idols*, p. 509. The phrase "creative mastery" is from *Beyond Good and Evil*.

153. Nietzsche, *The Will to Power*, pp. 366–70.

154. It is plainly better to be an aesthete than a crypto-Fascist or a Nazi *avant la lettre*—to recall a few of the more extravagant accusations.

155. Rousseau, *Discourse on the Arts and Sciences*, in *The Social Contract and Discourses*, trans. Cole, p. 156: "Before [the advent of Greek philosophy], the Romans were satisfied with the practice of virtue; they were undone when they began to study it."

156. Friedrich Nietzsche, *Beyond Good and Evil*, trans. W. Kaufmann (New York: Vintage, 1966), pp. 204 ff.

157. Kant, *Judgment*, trans. Meredith, pp. 168–72: "Genius is the talent (natural endowment) that gives the rule to art."

158. Ibid., p. 97.

159. Heinrich Rickert, *Kant als Philosoph der Modernen Kultur* (Tübingen: J.C.B. Mohr, 1924).

160. Wilhelm Windelband, *A History of Philosophy*, vol. 2, trans. J. H. Tufts (New York: Harper & Row, 1958), p. 561.

161. Ibid., p. 558.

162. H. J. Paton, "Review of H. W. Cassirer's *A Commentary on Kant's Critique of Judgment*," in *Philosophy* 13, no. 52 (1938): 486.

163. Paul Guyer, *Kant and the Claims of Taste* (Cambridge, Mass.: Harvard University Press, 1979), pp. 347–48. See also Ted Cohen, "Why Beauty Is a Symbol of Morality," in *Essays in Kant's Aesthetics*, ed. Ted Cohen and Paul Guyer (Chicago: University of Chicago Press, 1982), pp. 221–36, particularly p. 235: "Moral experience is a matter of engaging people, oneself and others . . . this experience is paralleled in depth and complexity only by the experience of beauty. If we take Kant at his word . . . we must suppose him to hold that *only* the experience of beauty has the kind of richness needed to stand for moral experience."

164. Ibid., p. 348.

165. Ibid., p. 382.

166. Ibid., pp. 347 ff.

167. J. D. McFarland, "The Bogus Unity of the Kantian Philosophy," in *Actes du Congrès d'Ottowa sur Kant* (Ottawa: University of Ottowa Press, 1976), p. 280.

168. Ibid., pp. 292–93.

169. Ibid.

170. Ibid., p. 292.

171. Malebranche, *Conversations Chrétiennes*, in *Oeuvres Complètes*, vol. 4, p. 60.

172. McFarland, "Bogus Unity of the Kantian Philosophy," in *Actes du Congrès d'Ottowa sur Kant*, p. 296.

173. Kant, *Judgment*, trans. Meredith, p. 224.

174. Hannah Arendt, *The Life of the Mind: Willing*, ed. Mary McCarthy (New York: Harcourt Brace Jovanovich, 1978), pp. 255–72. In her "editor's postface," McCarthy says that it is "mournful that there is not more" of Arendt's thoughts on the *Critique of Judgment;* but Arendt's *Judgment* manuscript has been cut, to judge from ellisions and discontinuities in the printed text. Apparently there could have been "more." For an interpretation of Arendt's reading of *Judgment*, see Elisabeth Young-Bruehl, "Reflections on Hannah Arendt's *The Life of the Mind*," *Political Theory* 10, no. 2 (May 1982): 297–301.

175. Ibid., p. 270.

176. Ibid., p. 256.

177. Ibid., pp. 258–59.

178. Ibid., pp. 259–60.

179. Ibid., pp. 271–72.

180. Hegel, *Faith and Knowledge*, trans. Cerf and Harris, p. 85.

181. Cassirer, "Critical Idealism as a Philosophy of Culture," in *Symbol, Myth and Culture*, pp. 87–88.

182. Ibid.

183. Kant was perfectly aware that his various limitations of philosophy could lead to (what would now be called) Hegelian objections; see, for instance, his response to Garve's charge of formalism in *Theory and Practice*, in *Kant's Political Writings*, ed. Reiss, pp. 65–68.

184. Lebrun, *Kant et la Fin de la Métaphysique*, pp. 480–81.

185. Ibid., p. 481.

186. Kant, *Idea for a Universal History*, in *Kant's Political Writings*, ed. Reiss, p. 42.

187. Ibid., p. 44.

188. Ibid., pp. 44–45.

189. Kant, *Religion*, trans. Greene and Hudson, p. 86.

190. Kelly, *Idealism, Politics and History*, pp. 116–17.

191. Leonard Krieger, *The German Idea of Freedom* (Boston: Beacon Press, 1957), p. 106.

192. Ibid., p. 116.

193. Aristotle, *Metaphysica*, in *The Works of Aristotle*, vol. 8, ed. W. D. Ross (Oxford: Clarendon Press, 1928), pp. 8-16 (994b).

194. Kant, *Judgment*, trans. Meredith, p. 99.

195. Ibid., pp. 52–53, 98–100.

196. Aristotle, *Physics*, in *Aristotle: Selections*, ed. W. D. Ross (New York: Scribners, 1927), p. 119, 199a 15–b28.

197. Ibid., p. 118.

198. Kant, *Pure Reason*, trans. Smith, p. 428 (A472/B500). In this passage Kant is actually discussing Plato and Epicurus; but the distinction between "knowing" and "saying" can apply equally well to Aristotle.

199. Aristotle, *Politics*, trans. Ernest Barker (New York: Oxford University Press, 1962), p. 5 (1252b).

200. Kant, *Judgment*, trans. Meredith, p. 224.

201. Aristotle, *Politics*, trans. Barker, p. 5 (1252b).

202. Aristotle, *Nicomachean Ethics*, trans. John Warrington (London: Everyman, 1963), pp. 107 ff. (1135a ff.).

203. Ibid., pp. 229–30 (1177b–1178a).

204. Kant, *Fundamental Principles*, trans. Abbott, pp. 11 ff.

205. Aristotle, *Politics*, trans. Barker, p. 5 (1252b).

CHAPTER FIVE

1. Kant, *Judgment*, trans. Meredith, pp. 94–97.

2. Kant, *Religion*, trans. Greene and Hudson, pp. 87–91.

3. Kant, *Judgment*, trans. Meredith, p. 14.

4. Morris R. Cohen, "A Critique of Kant's Philosophy of Law," in *The Heritage of Kant*, ed. G. T. Whitney (New York: Russell and Russell, 1962), p. 291. Amazingly, Cohen insists that "the inevitable sufferings from the maladministration of the laws do not concern Kant."

5. Kant, *Judgment*, trans. Meredith, pp. 94–97.

6. Jeremy Bentham, *The Book of Fallacies*, in *The Works of Jeremy Bentham*, vol. 2, ed. J. Bowring (Edinburgh: William Tait, 1843), p. 441.

7. Kant, *Pure Reason*, trans. Smith, p. 312 (A316/B373).

8. Kant, *Rechtslehre*, trans. Ladd, pp. 18–21.

9. Kant, *Eternal Peace*, in *Kant's Political Writings*, ed. Reiss, p. 121n.

10. Ibid., pp. 100–102.

11. Kant, *Rechtslehre*, trans. Ladd, p. 78.

12. Beck, *Commentary*, pp. 199–200.

13. Kant, *Rechtslehre*, trans. Ladd, pp. 78–79.

14. Kant, *Theory and Practice*, in *Kant's Political Writings*, ed. Reiss, p. 79: "If it is at least *possible* that a people could agree to [a public law], it is our duty to consider the law as just."

15. Kant, *Rechtslehre*, trans. Ladd, pp. 18–21.

16. Jeffrie G. Murphy, *Kant: The Philosophy of Right* (London: Macmillan & Co., 1970), p. 134.

17. Kant, *Rechtslehre*, trans. Ladd, pp. 18–21.

18. Ibid., p. 78.

19. Ibid., p. 82.

20. Rousseau, *Du Contrat Social*, in *Rousseau: Political Writings*, vol. 2, ed. Vaughan, p. 44.

21. Kant, *Rechtslehre*, trans. Ladd, pp. 78–81.

22. Ibid., p. 97: "Subjects who want to be more than just citizens . . . have crept into the machinery of government in ancient times (under feudalism, which was almost entirely organized for making war)."

23. Ibid., p. 110.

24. Cassirer, *Kant's Life and Thought*, pp. 379–95.

25. Kant, *Rechtslehre*, trans. Ladd, p. 110.

26. Ibid.

27. Ibid., p. 113: "Every true republic is and can be nothing else than a representative system of the people."

28. David Hume, "Idea of a Perfect Commonwealth," in *Hume: Theory of Politics*, ed. F. Watkins (Edinburgh: Nelson, 1951), pp. 242–43.

29. Immanuel Kant, *Reflexionen zur Rechtsphilosophie*, in *Kants Gesammelte Schriften*, vol. 19, ed. Prussian Academy, p. 595.

30. Kant, *Rechtslehre*, trans. Ladd, p. 113.

31. Ibid., pp. 111–12.

32. Ibid.

33. Ibid., p. 112.

34. Ibid.

35. Charles Secondat, Baron de Montesquieu, *De l'Esprit des Lois*, ed. Robert Dérathé (Paris: Garnier Frères, 1973) pp. 64–66, 143.

36. Kant, *Conflict of the Faculties*, in *Kant's Political Writings*, ed. Reiss, pp. 182n–183n.

37. Ibid., p. 183n.

38. Cohen, "A Critique of Kant's Philosophy of Law," p. 290.

39. Kant, *Conflict of the Faculties*, in *Kant's Political Writings*, ed. Reiss, p. 187.

40. Kant, *Theory and Practice*, in *Kant's Political Writings*, ed. Reiss, p. 83n.

41. G. W. F. Hegel, *Encyclopedia*, trans. W. Wallace (Oxford: Clarendon Press, 1894), p. 269.

42. Kant, *Conflict of the Faculties*, in *Kant's Political Writings*, ed. Reiss, p. 184.

43. Kant, *Eternal Peace*, in *Kant's Political Writings*, ed. Reiss, pp. 98–102.

44. Ibid.

45. Ibid., p. 100.

46. Ibid.

47. Ibid.

48. Kant, *Idea for a Universal History*, in *Kant's Political Writings*, ed. Reiss, pp. 50–51.

49. Kant, *Eternal Peace*, in *Kant's Political Writings*, ed. Reiss, p. 100.

50. Ibid., pp. 95 ff.

51. Wilhelm von Humboldt, *The Limits of State Action*, ed. J. W. Burrow (Cambridge: Cambridge University Press, 1969), p. 76.

52. Ibid., p. 81.

53. For example, Lewis White Beck, "Kant and the Right of Revolution," *Essays on Kant and Hume* ((New Haven: Yale University Press, 1978), p. 185. Even Beck insists that the "moral aspirations of mankind are not satisfied by punctilious obedience to the powers that be."

54. Kant, *Conflict of the Faculties*, in *Kant's Political Writings*, ed. Reiss, pp. 182–83.

55. Kant, *Rechtslehre*, trans. Ladd, p. 86.

56. Kant, *Pure Reason*, trans. Smith, pp. 464 ff. (A533/B561).

57. Cf. Kant, *Rechtslehre*, trans. Ladd, p. 78: "These three parts [of the state] are like the three propositions in a practical syllogism: the law of the sovereign will is like the major premise," etc..

58. Kant, *Pure Reason*, trans. Smith, p. 476 (A554/B582).

59. Kant, *Philosophy of Law*, trans. Hastie, p. 256.

60. Cited in Beck, "Kant and the Right of Revolution," p. 173.

61. Kant, *Rechtslehre*, trans. Ladd, p. 82.

62. Ibid., p. 87n.

63. Ibid., pp. 87n–88n.

64. Ibid.

65. Arendt, *Life of the Mind: Willing*, pp. 258–60.

66. Thomas Seebohm, "Kant's Theory of Revolution," in *Social Research* 48, no. 3 (Autumn 1981): 586–87.

67. Cf. Kant, *Theory and Practice*, in *Kant's Political Writings*, ed. Reiss, p. 82; "Achenwall, who is extremely cautious, precise and restrained . . . concludes: 'The people, in dethroning its ruler, thus returns to the state of nature' . . . But it is clear

that these peoples have done the greatest degree of wrong in seeking their rights in this way." It is doubtful that Seebohm's reading of Kant could incorporate this passage.

68. Kant, *Rechtslehre*, trans. Ladd, pp. 34–35.

69. Ibid., p. 102.

70. Ibid.

71. Kant, *Rechtslehre*, in *Kant's Political Writings*, ed. Reiss, p. 134.

72. Kant, *Rechtslehre*, trans. Ladd, pp. 102–3.

73. Sometimes, to be sure, Kant gives due weight to intentionality; cf. *Rechtslehre*, trans. Ladd, pp. 29–30: "The degree of imputability of actions must be estimated by the magnitude of the obstacles that have to be overcome." But this is only true *subjectively* considered.

74. Kant, *Pure Reason*, trans. Smith, p. 475n (A552/B580).

75. Kant, *Rechtslehre*, trans. Ladd, pp. 102–5.

76. Kant, *Philosophy of Law*, trans. Hastie, pp. 243–44.

77. Kant, *Pure Reason*, trans. Smith, p. 475n (A552/B580).

78. Kant, *Tugendlehre*, trans. Ellington, pp. 82–85.

79. Kant, *Anthropology*, trans. Gregor, pp. 126–27.

80. Kant, *Pure Reason*, trans. Smith, p. 475n (A552/B580).

81. Kant, *Rechtslehre*, trans. Ladd, p. 89.

82. Kant, *Tugendlehre*, trans. Ellington, pp. 82–85.

83. Kant, *Theory and Practice*, in *Kant's Political Writings*, ed. Reiss, p. 75.

84. Anatole France, *L'Ile des Pingouins* (Paris: Levy, 1905).

85. Kant, *Theory and Practice*, in *Kant's Political Writings*, ed. Reiss, p. 75.

86. See John Schaar, "Equality of Opportunity and Beyond," in *Nomos IX: Equality*, ed. J. R. Pennock and J. Chapman (New York: Atherton, 1967), pp. 228–49.

87. Rousseau, *Première Version du Contrat Social*, in *Rousseau: Political Writings*, vol. 1, ed. Vaughan, 392–93.

88. Kant, *Judgment*, trans. Meredith, pp. 95–97.

89. Kant, *Theory and Practice*, in *Kant's Political Writings*, ed. Reiss, pp. 77–78.

90. Ibid., p. 78.

91. Rousseau, *Du Contrat Social*, in *Rousseau: Political Writings*, Vol. 2, ed. Vaughan, pp. 44 ff.

92. Kant, *Theory and Practice*, in *Kant's Political Writings*, ed. Reiss, p. 78.

93. Kant, *Rechtslehre*, trans. Ladd, p. 80.

94. Manfred Riedel, "Transcendental Politics? Political Legitimacy and the Concept of Civil Society in Kant," *Social Research* 48, no. 3 (Autumn 1981): 588–613.

95. Kant, *Religion*, trans. Greene and Hudson, pp. 176–177n.

96. Kant, *Eternal Peace*, in *Kant's Political Writings*, ed. Reiss, pp. 100–102.

97. Rousseau, *Du Contrat Social*, in *Rousseau: Political Writings*, Vol. 2, ed. Vaughan, pp. 37–39.

CHAPTER SIX

1. Kant, *Eternal Peace*, in *Kant's Political Writings*, ed. Reiss, pp. 98 ff.

2. Kant, *Rechtslehre*, trans. Ladd, p. 100.

3. Carl J. Friedrich, "Federal Constitutional Theory and Emergent Proposals," in *Federalism Mature and Emergent*, ed. A. W. MacMahon (New York: Columbia University Press, 1956), pp. 510–33.

4. Kant, *Idea for a Universal History*, in *The Philosophy of Kant*, ed. Friedrich, pp. 123–24.

5. Ibid.

6. Ibid.

7. Ibid., pp. 123–26.

8. Kant, *Rechtslehre*, trans. Ladd, pp. 76–77.

9. Kant, *Idea for a Universal History*, in *The Philosophy of Kant*, ed. Friedrich, pp. 124 ff.

10. Ibid. Cf. Kant, *Judgment*, trans. Meredith, pp. 93–96.

11. Immanuel Kant, *Theory and Practice*, in *Eternal Peace and other International Essays*, trans. W. Hastie (Boston: World Peace Foundation, 1914), pp. 62–63.

12. Hobbes, *Leviathan*, ed. Oakeshott, pp. 84–85: "It is a precept, or general rule of reason, that every man ought to endeavour peace."

13. Kant, *Theory and Practice*, in *Kant's Political Writings*, ed. Reiss, pp. 90–91 (translation slightly altered).

14. Kant, *Theory and Practice*, in *Eternal Peace and other International Essays*, trans. Hastie, pp. 62–63.

15. Siegfried Brie, *Der Bundesstaat* (Leipzig: Engelmann, 1874), p. 31.

16. Kant, *Eternal Peace*, in *The Philosophy of Kant*, ed. Friedrich, p. 441.

17. Ibid., p. 442.

18. Ibid., pp. 441–46.

19. Montesquieu, *De l'Esprit des Lois*, ed. Dérathé, pp. 141 ff.

20. Carl J. Friedrich, *Inevitable Peace* (Cambridge, Mass.: Harvard University Press, 1948), p. 46. This is a fine study of *Eternal Peace* by the best modern historian of federal theory.

21. Kant, *Eternal Peace*, in *The Philosophy of Kant*, ed. Friedrich, p. 443.

22. Ibid., p. 445.

23. Ibid., pp. 431–36.

24. Ibid., pp. 431–32.

25. Ibid.

26. Ibid., pp. 435–36.

27. Kant, *Eternal Peace*, in *Kant's Political Writings*, ed. Reiss, p. 118n.

28. On this point see J. B. Scott, *Law, the State, and the International Community* (New York: Columbia University Press, 1939), pp. 310 ff.

29. Kant, *Eternal Peace*, in *The Philosophy of Kant*, ed. Friedrich, p. 446.

30. F. H. Hinsley, *Power and the Pursuit of Peace* (Cambridge: Cambridge University Press, 1963), p. 66. This is certainly the finest of all histories of international relations theory.

31. Kant, *Idea for a Universal History*, in *The Philosophy of Kant*, ed. Friedrich, p. 126.

32. Kant, *Eternal Peace*, in *The Philosophy of Kant*, ed. Friedrich, p. 444.

33. Ibid.

34. Ibid., p. 437 (translation slightly altered).

35. Ibid., p. 438.

36. Kant, *Idea for a Universal History*, in *The Philosophy of Kant*, ed. Friedrich, pp. 122–31.

37. Kelly, *Idealism, Politics and History*, p. 139.

38. Ibid., p. 140.

39. Kant, *Judgment*, trans. Meredith, p. 94.

40. Ibid., p. 96.

41. Kant, *Idea for a Universal History*, in *The Philosophy of Kant*, ed. Friedrich, p. 118.

42. Ibid., pp. 120–21.

43. Ibid., pp. 124–25.

44. Ibid., p. 127.

45. Kant, *Eternal Peace*, in *The Philosophy of Kant*, ed. Friedrich, p. 454.

46. Ibid., p. 430.

47. Leibniz to Grimarest, June 1712, in *The Political Writings of Leibniz*, ed. Riley, pp. 183–84.

48. G. W. Leibniz, *Codex Iuris Gentium (Praefatio)*, in *The Political Writings of Leibniz*, ed. Riley, p. 166. In this passage Leibniz quotes some lines attributed to Leo van Aitzema (d. 1669):

> *Qui pacem quaeris libertatemque, viator*
> *Aut nusquam aut isto sub tumulo invenies.*
> [O passerby who seeks peace and liberty,
> You will find it either in this tomb, or nowhere.]

49. Kant, 'Conjectural Beginning of Human History," in *Kant on History*, ed. Beck, p. 66. Cf. Kant's "The End of All Things," in same work, p. 79: "Chinese philosophers strive in dark rooms with eyes closed to experience and contemplate their nihility."

50. Hegel, *Philosophy of Right*, trans. Knox, p. 210.

51. Cf. particularly Jean-Jacques Rousseau, "Jugement sur la Paix Perpétuelle," in *Rousseau: Political Writings*, vol. 1, ed. Vaughan, pp. 388–96.

52. Immanuel Kant, *Lectures on Ethics*, trans. Louis Infield (London: Methuen, 1930), pp. 252–53. To be sure, no interpretation of Kant should be made to depend on these *Lectures*, but they can legitimately be used to shore up an interpretation grounded in "critical" works.

53. Hinsley, *Power and the Pursuit of Peace*, pp. 20 ff.

54. Ibid.

55. Ibid.

56. Ibid.

57. Charles Irenée Castel, Abbé de St. Pierre, *A Project for Settling an Everlasting Peace in Europe* (London, 1714), pp. iii, 1. A good modern edition of this work is urgently needed.

58. Ibid., p. 12.

59. Ibid., p. viii. Cf. Kant, *Theory and Practice*, in *Kant's Political Writings*, ed. Reiss, p. 92: "A permanent universal peace by means of a so-called *European balance of power* is a pure illusion, like Swift's story of the house which the builder had constructed in such perfect harmony with all the laws of equilibrium that it collapsed as soon as a sparrow alighted on it." Kant then goes on to praise St. Pierre, whose ideas, Kant says, have been "ridiculed" as "pedantic" and "childish."

60. Ibid., pp. iii–iv.

61. Ibid., p. 24.

62. Ibid., p. 32. The inaccurate character of St. Pierre's account of German constitutional history was pointed out as long ago as 1715 by Leibniz, in his "Observations on the Abbé de St. Pierre's Project for Perpetual Peace" in *The Political Writings of Leibniz*, ed. Riley, pp. 178–83: "It seems that he [St. Pierre] conceives the German union as having begun with some treaty; but this cannot be reconciled with history . . . If, in France, the Capetian family had been extinguished, and if the crown had passed from family to family, and if the other great families had been preserved, France would apparently be today a body similar to the German body, although it would never have had a single treaty of union which formed it, just as there has never been one in Germany."

63. Kant, *Idea for a Universal History*, in *The Philosophy of Kant*, ed. Friedrich, pp. 129–31.

64. St. Pierre, *Project for . . . Everlasting Peace*, p. 45.

65. Ibid., pp. 45 ff.

66. The classic statement of the argument that federalism works only as a tie between "small republics" is to be found in Montesquieu, *De l'Esprit des Lois*, ed. Dérathé, Book IX.

67. St. Pierre, *Project for . . . Everlasting Peace*, pp. v, 46.

68. Ibid., p. 47.

69. Ibid., pp. 48–49.

70. Ibid., pp. 56–96.

71. Ibid., p. 106.

72. Ibid., p. 107.

73. Rousseau, "Judgment sur la Paix Perpétuelle," in *Rousseau: Political Writings*, vol. 1, ed. Vaughan, pp. 388–96.

74. St. Pierre, *Project for . . . Everlasting Peace*, p. 107.

75. Ibid., p. 16.

76. Ibid., p. 109.

77. Ibid., pp. 110 ff.

78. Ibid., p. 119.

79. Ibid., pp. 119–20.

80. Ibid., p. 122.

81. Hinsley, *Power and the Pursuit of Peace*, pp. 43–44.

82. Ibid., p. 45.

83. Ibid. Frederick's witticism is contained in a letter to Voltaire (1742). See Thomas Carlyle, *Frederick the Great*, vol. 4 (London: Chapman and Hall, 1873), p. 80.

84. Rousseau, "Jugement sur la Paix Perpétuelle," in *Rousseau: Political Writings*, vol. 1, ed. Vaughan, p. 388.

85. François Marie Arouet de Voltaire, "Commentaire sur l'Esprit des Lois," in *Oeuvres Complètes*, vol. 34, (Brussels: Ode et Wodon, 1828), pp. 95 ff.

86. Voltaire, "Idées Républicaines," in *Oeuvres Complètes*, vol. 33, pp. 199 ff.

87. Voltaire, "De la Paix Perpétuelle," in *Oeuvres Complètes de Voltaire*, vol. 29, (Paris, 1785), pp. 35 ff.

88. Ibid., p. 35n.

89. Ibid., p. 36n.

90. Ibid., p. 72: "Let every just man work, then, each according to his power, to crush fanaticism, and to bring back the peace which this monster had banished from kingdoms, from families, and from the hearts of unhappy mortals." Cf. the article entitled *Guerre*, from Voltaire's *Dictionnaire Philosophique*, in *Oeuvres Complètes de Voltaire*, vol. 19, (Paris: Garnier Frères, 1879), pp. 318–22.

91. See J. B. Bury, *The Idea of Progress* (New York: Dover, 1955), pp. 148 ff., particularly p. 149: "If Montesquieu founded social science, Voltaire created the history of civilization."

92. Kant, *Idea for a Universal History*, in *The Philosophy of Kant*, ed. Friedrich, pp. 123–24.

93. Kant, *Theory and Practice*, in *Kant's Political Writings*, ed. Reiss, p. 92.

94. Montesquieu, *De l'Esprit des Lois*, ed. Dérathé, p. 141.

95. This is not to say, of course, that Locke thought of himself as a republican—only that the institutions defended in the *Second Treatise* would have been countenanced by Kant.

96. Rousseau, *Du Contrat Social*, in *Rousseau: Political Writings*, vol. 2, ed. Vaughan, pp. 71–76.

97. Kant, *Theory and Practice*, in *Eternal Peace and other International Essays*, trans. Hastie, pp. 40—41.

98. Jean-Jacques Rousseau, *Projet de Constitution pour la Corse*, in *Rousseau, Political Writings*, vol. 2, ed. Vaughan, pp. 306 ff.

99. On the distinction between *functional* and *territorial* power division in federal theory, see Arthur Maass, *Area and Power* (Glencoe, Ill.: Free Press, 1959), pp. 9-26.

100. Kant, *Rechtslehre*, trans. Ladd, pp. 111–14.

101. Kant, *Reflexionen zur Rechtsphilosophie*, in *Kants Gesammelte Schriften*, vol. 19, ed. Prussian Academy, p. 555.

102. A. R. Turgot, *Discours sur les Progres Succéssifs de l'Esprit Humain* (Paris, 1750).

103. Kant, *Rechtslehre*, trans. Ladd, pp. 97–98.

104. Ibid., pp. 95 ff.

105. Ibid., p. 91.

106. Ibid., pp. 94–95.

107. G. W. Leibniz, *On Natural Law*, in *The Political Writings of Leibniz*, ed. Riley, p. 77.

108. Michael Oakeshott, *On Human Conduct* (Oxford: Clarendon Press, 1975), pp. 185 ff.

109. Kant, *Theory and Practice*, in *Eternal Peace and other International Essays*, trans. Hastie, p. 34.

110. Franz Neumann, "Federalism and Freedom: A Critique," in *Federalism Mature and Emergent*, ed. MacMahon, pp. 44 ff.

111. Kant, *Fundamental Principles*, trans. Abbott, p. 12.

CHAPTER SEVEN

1. Alexandre Kojève, *Kant* (Paris: Gallimard, 1973).
2. Lucien Goldmann, *Immanuel Kant*, trans. R. Black (London: NLB, 1971).
3. Robert Paul Wolff, *In Defense of Anarchism* (New York: Harper & Row, 1970).
4. Susan M. Shell, *The Rights of Reason: A Study of Kant's Philosophy and Politics* (Toronto: University of Toronto Press, 1980).
5. Hans Saner, *Kant's Political Thought*, trans. E. B. Ashton (Chicago: University of Chicago Press, 1973).
6. John Charvet, *A Critique of Freedom and Equality* (Cambridge: Cambridge University Press, 1981).
7. Alexandre Kojève, *Introduction à la Lecture de Hegel: Leçons sur la Phénomenologie de l'Esprit* (Paris: Gallimard, 1947) pp. 19 ff., 172 ff.
8. Ibid., p. 173.
9. Ibid., p. 20.
10. Ibid., p. 174.
11. Ibid., p. 179.
12. Ibid., pp. 179–80.
13. Alexandre Kojève, "Hegel, Marx et le Christianisme," *Critique* (Paris, August–September 1946), p. 356.
14. Kojève, *Lecture de Hegel*, p. 180.
15. Ibid.
16. Ibid.
17. Ibid.
18. Ibid., pp. 182 ff., particularly p. 260.
19. Ibid., pp. 190–91.
20. Ibid., pp. 184–85.
21. Ibid., p. 494.
22. Ibid., pp. 20–23.
23. Ibid., p. 465.
24. Kojève, "Hegel, Marx et le Christianisme," pp. 355–56.
25. Kojève, *Lecture de Hegel*, p. 465.
26. Kelly, *Idealism, Politics and History*, p. 338.
27. Hegel, *Philosophy of Right*, trans. Knox, pp. 12–13.
28. Kojève, *Kant*, p. 10.
29. Ibid.
30. Kant, *Fundamental Principles*, trans. Abbott, p. 65.
31. Kant, *Eternal Peace*, in *The Philosophy of Kant*, ed. Friedrich, pp. 459 ff.
32. Kojève, *Kant*, p. 30.
33. Ibid.
34. Ibid., p. 39. Also cf. p. 197: "Kant ne veut pas admettre l'éfficacité de l'Action-libre dans la durée-étendue de l'Éxistence-empirique et c'est pourquoi il a consciemment et volontairement exclu la Sub-Categorie de la Téleologie (= Liberté) de son Systeme categorical developpable discursivement sans contra-diction dans le mode de la Vérité." (This is a fair example of Kojève's style.)
35. Kojève, *Lecture de Hegel*, p. 150. There is, of course, something in this objection, as one can see by reading Kant's *Conflict of the Faculties*.
36. Kant, *Pure Reason*, trans. Smith, p. 425 (A468/B496): "If our will is not free . . . moral ideas and principles lose all validity."
37. To be sure, in the section of *Pure Reason* called "Natural Dialectic of Human Reason" (trans. Smith, p. 559 [A685/B713]), Kant says that when "reason itself is regarded as the determining cause, as in [the sphere of] freedom, that is to say, in the case of practical principles, we have to proceed as if we had before us an object, not of the senses, but of the pure understanding." However, this passage is exceptional, and should not be allowed to color Kant's more usual view that "our reason has causality."
38. Hans Vaihinger, *The Philosophy of 'As If,'* trans. C. K. Ogden (London: K. Paul, Trench, Trubner, 1935), p. 319: "The As-if view plays an extraordinarily important part

in Kant." Cf. p. 293, where Vaihinger calls "the dignity of man" and "the realm of purposes" in Kant "concepts without any reality," "heuristic fictions," "something unreal," etc. This simply destroys Kant's moral philosophy.

39. Kojève, *Kant*, p. 87.
40. Ibid.
41. Cited in Lukács, *Young Hegel*, p. 339.
42. Kant, *Judgment*, trans. Meredith, pp. 163: "By right it is only production through freedom, i. e., through an act of will that places reason at the basis of its action, that should be termed art. For, although we are pleased to call what bees produce (their regularly constructed cells) a work of art, we only do so on the strength of an analogy with art; that is to say, as soon as we call to mind that no rational deliberation forms the basis of their labor, we say at once that it is a product of their nature (instinct)." Marx' passage in *Kapital* certainly *seems* to be a meditation on this part of *Judgment*.
43. Ibid.
44. Kojève, *Kant*, p. 90.
45. Kant, *Judgment*, in *Philosophy of Kant*, ed. Friedrich, p. 354.
46. For this argument, see the whole of Chapter 4. For a striking counter-argument, denying that *Judgment* succeeds in unifying all the Kantian realms, see Lebrun, *Kant et la Fin de la Métaphysique*, pp. 467–97.
47. Kant, *Practical Reason*, trans. Abbott, p. 180.
48. Kant, *Judgment*, trans. Meredith, pp. 108 ff.
49. Kojève, *Kant*, pp. 35 ff.
50. See the passages on the "moral proof" cited by Norman Kemp Smith in Appendix C of his *A Commentary to Kant's Critique of Pure Reason* (London: Macmillan & Co., 1923), pp. 636 ff.
51. Kant, *Fundamental Principles*, pp. 10 ff.
52. On "cancelling and preserving," see Hegel, *Phenomenology*, trans. Baillie, pp. 223 ff.
53. Kojève, "Hegel, Marx et le Christianisme," pp. 355–56.
54. Hegel, *Philosophy of Right*, trans. Knox, entire work.
55. Goldmann, *Immanuel Kant*, trans. Black, p. 176.
56. Kant, *Theory and Practice*, in *Kant's Political Writings*, ed. Reiss, pp. 75–78.
57. Lukács, *Young Hegel*, pp. 150–60. How a distinction between "mind" and "the senses" drawn at least since Plato can suddenly become an epiphenomenon of "the capitalist division of labor" is left rather unclear by Lukács.
58. Ibid.
59. Goldmann, *Immanuel Kant*, trans. Black, pp. 176–77.
60. Cassirer, "Critical Idealism as a Philosophy of Culture," in *Symbol, Myth and Culture*, pp. 87–88.
61. Kant, *Religion*, trans. Greene and Hudson, pp. 86–89.
62. Karl Marx, *Capital*, vol. 3, trans. Moore and Aveling (New York: International Publishers, 1967), p. 820.
63. Ibid.
64. Goldmann, *Immanuel Kant*, trans. Black, p. 220.
65. Ibid.
66. Ibid., pp. 221–22.
67. Arendt, *Life of the Mind: Willing*, pp. 259–60.
68. Wolff, *In Defense of Anarchism*, pp. 18–19.
69. Ibid., p. ix.
70. Ibid., pp. 21 ff.
71. Ibid., pp. 18–19, 21 ff.
72. Ibid., p. ix.
73. Kant, *Pure Reason*, trans. Smith, pp. 464 ff. (A533/B561).
74. Kant, *Rechtslehre*, trans. Ladd, pp. 75 ff.
75. Wolff, *In Defense of Anarchism*, pp. 12–19; Kant, *Fundamental Principles*, trans. Abbott, pp. 46–49.

76. Cf. Donald Stewart, "A Pseudo-Anarchist Belatedly Replies to Robert Paul Wolff," *Journal of Critical Analysis 4*, no. 2 (July 1972) 60: "Wolff's insistence upon moral autonomy as the *primary obligation* of man commits him to something very much more radical than mere anarchism; it commits him . . . to a morally aggressive state of nature from which there is no escape, [to a] *bellum morale omnium contra omnes.*"

77. Kant, *Fundamental Principles*, trans. Abbott, pp. 44–56.

78. Robert Paul Wolff, *Autonomy of Reason* (New York: Harper and Row, 1973), p. 178.

79. Ibid.

80. Ibid.

81. Ibid., pp. 178–79. The exclamation mark is Wolff's.

82. Kant, *Tugendlehre*, trans. Ellington, pp. 42 ff.

83. Wolff, *Autonomy of Reason*, p. 181.

84. Beck, *Commentary*, pp. 199–200.

85. Jean-Jacques Rousseau, *Social Contract*, in *Political Writings*, trans. F. Watkins (Edinburgh: Nelson, 1953), p. 31.

86. Kant, *Rechtslehre*, trans. Ladd, p. 26.

87. Robert Nozick, *Philosophical Explanations* (Cambridge, Mass.: Harvard University Press, 1981), p. 551.

88. Kant, *Religion*, trans. Greene and Hudson, p. 21n.

89. Wolff, *Autonomy of Reason*, p. 181.

90. Ibid., p. 174.

91. Ibid., p. 175.

92. Ibid., pp. 175–176.

93. Kant, *Fundamental Principles*, p. 47: "He who transgresses the rights of men intends to use the person of others *merely* as means, without considering that as rational beings they ought always to be esteemed *also* as ends" (emphasis added).

94. Ibid., p. 54: "Consequently it [the person as 'independently existing end'] is conceived only negatively, that is, as that which we must never act against."

95. Cf. Wolfgang Bartuschat, *Zum systematischen Ort von Kants Kritik der Urteilskraft* (Frankfurt: Klostermann, 1972), pp. 246–66.

96. Wolff, *Autonomy of Reason*, p. 4.

97. Susan M. Shell, "Kant's Theory of Property," *Political Theory 6*, no. 1 (February 1978): 75–90.

98. Ibid., p. 78.

99. Ibid.

100. Ibid. The identical sentence is to be found in Shell, *Rights of Reason*, p. 185.

101. Shell, "Kant's Theory of Property," p. 79–80.

102. Ibid., p. 87. See also Shell, *Rights of Reason*, p. 179: "Both Kant's metaphysics and his jurisprudence are theories of property. Both knowing and having are ways of appropriating or securing a right to the use of a thing, be it a concept or an object in the world." This is strained; but at least it does not, with Lukács, view Kant's metaphysics as an *epiphenomenon* of property. In Shell's interpretation, "knowing" and "having" stand in a parallel, not a causal, relationship.

103. Kant, *Pure Reason*, trans. Smith, pp. 120–25 (A84/B117).

104. Kant, *Philosophical Correspondence*, ed. Zweig, p. 105.

105. "Negation" is a term that Kant uses mainly in his theory of legal punishment, calling punishment the negation of a negation; see Kant, *Rechtslehre*, trans. Ladd, pp. 35–36. For a fuller treatment, see Chapter 5.

106. Kelly, *Idealism, Politics and History*, p. 338.

107. Kant, *Philosophical Correspondence*, ed. Zweig, p. 254.

108. Shell, "Kant's Theory of Property," p. 79.

109. What Kant thought of Fichte on this point can be readily deduced from J. S. Beck's letter to Kant (June 24, 1797), in Kant, *Philosophical Correspondence*, ed. Zweig, pp. 231–34.

110. Shell, *Rights of Reason*, p. 134; repeated *verbatim* from Shell, "Kant's Theory of

Property," p. 80. Certainly this is an effective passage. But it is also a "passage" in another sense: it transports Kant from Königsberg to Albert Camus's Algeria. Apparently there can be wrongs, as well as rites, of passage.

111. Shell, "Kant's Theory of Property," p. 80.

112. As Kant himself knew perfectly well. See Kant, *Philosophy of Law*, trans. Hastie, pp. 61 ff.

113. Immanuel Kant, *Kritik der Reinen Vernunft*, in *Immanuel Kants Werke*, vol. 3, ed. Cassirer.

114. Ibid., pp. 105–137. It is perfectly true, however, that in the 1787 edition (B) Kant once speaks of "representations" as "belonging to me": "Der Gedanke: diese in der Anschauung gegebenen Vorstellungen gehören mir insgesamt zu, heisst demnach soviel, als ich vereinige sie in einem Selbstbewusstsein," and so on (pp. 115–16 [B134]). But Shell, though she appeals to a nonexistent *das Meine*, does not cite this passage.

115. As far as diligent searching will reveal.

116. Shell, "Kant's Theory of Property," p. 78; repeated with trifling changes in Shell, *Rights of Reason*, p. 185.

117. Shell, "Kant's Theory of Property," p. 86.

118. Shell, *Rights of Reason*, pp. 176 ff.

119. Kant, *Rechtslehre*, trans. Ladd, p. 100.

120. Kant, *Eternal Peace*, in *Kant's Political Writings*, ed. Reiss, pp. 93 ff.

121. For this argument see Chapter 5.

122. Shell, *Rights of Reason*, p. 185: "Kant's philosophic development, and his critical thought in particular, can be understood as an explanation and defense of man's appropriation of the world."

123. Shell, *Rights of Reason*, pp. 109 ff.

124. Kant, *Practical Reason*, trans. Beck, p. 48.

125. Kant, *Judgment*, trans. Meredith, p. 127. As Cassirer says in *Kant's Life and Thought*, p. 261, "in words like these we are in touch with Kant whole and entire."

126. Kant, *Judgment*, trans. Meredith, p. 128.

127. Ibid.

128. Shell, *Rights of Reason*, p. 122.

129. Nietzsche, *Twilight of the Idols*, in *The Portable Nietzsche*, trans. Kaufmann, p. 484.

130. Hans Saner, *Kants Weg vom Krieg zum Frieden: Widerstreit und Einheit* (Munich: Piper Verlag, 1967), title page.

131. Saner, *Kant's Political Philosophy*, pp. 7–49.

132. Ibid., pp. 230, 313.

133. Ibid., p. 259.

134. Ibid., p. 212.

135. Roughly half of Saner's book is given over to Kant's "polemics."

136. Ibid., p. 134.

137. Ibid., pp. 73–107. On p. 92 of the English translation, there is a bit of unintended comic relief: "Kant himself never made these assignations."

138. Ibid., p. 193.

139. Ibid., p. 152.

140. Ibid., pp. 26, 35.

141. Ibid., p. 281.

142. Ibid., p. 15.

143. Kant, *Fundamental Principles*, trans. Abbott, pp. 30–31.

144. Saner, *Kant's Political Philosophy*, trans. Ashton, pp. 298–99.

145. On this point see Chapter 5.

146. Kant, *Judgment*, trans. Meredith, pp. 82–108.

147. Saner, *Kant's Political Philosophy*, trans. Ashton, p. 263.

148. Saner, *Kants Weg vom Krieg zum Frieden*, title page.

149. Charvet, *Critique of Freedom and Equality*, pp. 41–68, 117–55. Charvet's Kant chapter is perhaps the least persuasive part of a book whose *general* thesis is important and striking.

150. See Quentin Skinner, *The Foundations of Modern Political Thought* (Cambridge:

Cambridge University Press, 1978), and John Dunn's various Locke studies (his finest work).

151. Charvet, *Critique of Freedom and Equality*, p. 69.
152. Ibid., pp. 70–71.
153. Kant, *Practical Reason*, trans. Beck, pp. 33–35.
154. Charvet, *Critique of Freedom and Equality*, p. 71.
155. Kant, *Fundamental Principles*, trans. Abbott, pp. 53–56.
156. Charvet, *Critique of Freedom and Equality*, p. 71.
157. Ibid., p. 72.
158. Hegel, *Philosophy of Right*, trans. Knox, p. 90.
159. Kant, *Fundamental Principles*, trans. Abbott, pp. 53–56.
160. Charvet, *Critique of Freedom and Equality*, p. 72.
161. Kant, *Religion*, trans. Greene and Hudson, p. 6n.
162. Charvet, *Critique of Freedom and Equality*, p. 74.
163. Ibid., pp. 79–80.
164. On this point see Chapter 5.
165. Charvet, *Critique of Freedom and Equality*, p. 80.
166. On this point see Chapters 1, 5 and 6.
167. Kant, *Practical Reason*, trans. Beck, p. 105.
168. Charvet, *Critique of Freedom and Equality*, p. 80.
169. For this argument, see Chapter 4.
170. Charvet, *Critique of Freedom and Equality*, p. 80.
171. Kant, *Pure Reason*, trans. Smith, p. 475n (A552/B580).
172. Kant, *Religion*, trans. Greene and Hudson, pp. 86–89.
173. Charvet, *Critique of Freedom and Equality*, p. 78.
174. Kant, *Practical Reason*, trans. Beck, pp. 48–49.
175. On this point see Chapters 3 and 4.
176. Kant, *Pure Reason*, trans. Smith, p. 560 (A687/B715).

CHAPTER EIGHT

1. Kant, *Religion*, trans. Greene and Hudson, pp. 86–90.
2. Kant, *Judgment*, trans. Meredith, pp. 14–15, 38–39, 116–17.
3. Kant, *Pure Reason*, trans. Smith, pp. 642–43 (A816/B844).
4. W. B. Gallie, "Kant's View of Reason in Politics," in *Philosophy* 54 (1979): 20 ff.
5. Morris R. Cohen, "Critique of Kant's Philosophy of Law," in *The Heritage of Kant*, p. 290.
6. Charles Taylor, *Hegel*, p. 372.
7. Kant, *Eternal Peace*, in *Kant's Political Writings*, ed. Reiss, p. 100.
8. Ibid.
9. Ibid., p. 99.
10. Kant, *Rechtslehre*, in *Kant's Political Writings*, ed. Reiss, p. 174. For the German text, see *Immanuel Kants Werke*, vol. 7, ed. Cassirer, pp. 161–62.
11. Kant, *Fundamental Principles*, trans. abbott, p. 54.
12. Ibid., pp. 49, 55.
13. Ibid., pp. 45 ff.
14. Kant, *Tugendlehre*, trans. Ellington, pp. 42–43.
15. Kant, *Religion*, trans. Greene and Hudson, p. 6n.
16. Kant, *Judgment*, trans. Meredith, p. 99.
17. Kant, *Fundamental Principles*, trans. Abbott, pp. 79–80.
18. Kant, *Practical Reason*, trans. Beck, p. 48.
19. Kant, *Opus Posthumous*, in *Kants Gesammelte Schriften*, vol. 21, ed. Prussian Academy, p. 36: "Der Begriff der Freiheit gründet sich auf ein Factum: den catg. Imperativ."
20. G. W. Leibniz to the Electress Sophie, in *Textes Inédits*, vol. 1, ed. Grua, p. 379 (quoted in Chapter 3). Leibniz was, apparently, much affected by Plato's *Phaedo* ("that

excellent dialogue on the immortality of the soul or on the death of Socrates"); and it is in *Phaedo* above all that Plato assimilates practical knowledge to mathematical knowledge: "We must have . . . knowledge . . . not only of equality and relative magnitudes, but of all absolute standards. Our present argument applies no more to equality than it does to absolute beauty, goodness, uprightness, holiness and . . . all those characteristics which we designate in our discussions by the term 'absolute' " (75 d). For Leibniz's comments on *Phaedo*, see the so-called *Lettres sur Descartes et le Cartésianisme*, in *Nouvelles Lettres et Opuscules Inédits de Leibniz*, ed. A. Foucher de Careil (Paris: Didot Frères, 1857), p. 4. For a fuller treatment of Leibniz's Platonism, see Patrick Riley, "An Unpublished Lecture of Leibniz on the Greeks as Founders of Rational Theology," *Journal of the History of Philosophy* 14, no. 2 (April 1976): 205–16.

21. The phrase appeared in a note to a Hegel paper presented at the Boston Area Conference for the Study of Political Thought, c. 1970, 1971.

22. Kant, *Fundamental Principles*, p. 80.

23. Cassirer, *Kant's Life and Thought*, pp. 261–62.

24. Karl Ameriks, "Kant's Deduction of Freedom and Morality," *Journal of the History of Philosophy*, 19, no. 1 (January 1981): 72. It is on p. 53 of this article that Ameriks asserts that "it has always been recognized that within Kant's philosophy the problem of a justification of freedom and the moral law has a central significance." But when virtually the whole text of "Kant's Deduction" was republished as chapter VI of Ameriks's *Kant's Theory of Mind* (Oxford: Clarendon Press, 1982), the notion that the moral law needs "justifying" was dropped.

25. Kant, *Pure Reason*, trans. Smith, pp. 464 ff. (A533/B561).

26. Kant, *Fundamental Principles*, trans. Abbott, p. 79.

27. Kant, *Judgment*, trans. Meredith, p. 100: "Only in man, and only in him as the individual being to whom the moral law applies, do we find unconditional legislation in respect of ends. This legislation, therefore, is what alone qualifies him to be a final end to which entire nature is teleologically subordinated."

28. Kant, *Tugendlehre*, trans. Ellington, pp. 96–97.

29. Kant, *Conflict of the Faculties*, in *Kant's Political Writings*, ed. Reiss, p. 185 (translation slightly altered).

30. Kant, *Eternal Peace*, in *Kant's Political Writings*, ed. Reiss, p. 121n.

31. Kant, *Rechtslehre*, trans. ladd, pp. 18–21.

32. Howard Warrender, "A Postscript on Hobbes and Kant," in *Hobbes-Forschungen*, ed. R. Koselleck and R. Schnur (Berlin: Duncker und Humblot, 1969), pp. 155–57.

33. G. W. F. Hegel, *Lectures on the History of Philosophy*, vol. 3, trans. E. S. Haldane and F. H. Simson (London: Kegal Paul, 1896).

34. Kant, *Fundamental Principles*, trans. Abbott, p. 48.

35. Yovel, *Kant and the Philosophy of History*, pp. 137 ff.

36. Oakeshott, *On Human Conduct*, p. 174.

37. Kant, *Opus Posthumous*, in *Kants Gesammelte Schriften*, vol. 21, ed. Prussian Academy, pp. 120–21.

38. Ibid. Cf. Plato, *Phaedrus* 256b, for the best account of philosophy as *philo-sophia*.

39. Kant, *Pure Reason*, trans. Smith, p. 658 (A840/B868).

40. Symmachus, *Epistolae* IX, 114; Plautus, *Asinaria* II, 88. Both cited in *The Political Writings of Leibniz*, ed. Riley, p. 57n.

41. Ibid.

42. Kant, *Opus Posthumous*, in *Kants Gesammelte Schriften*, vol. 21, ed. Prussian Academy, p. 120.

43. Michael Oakeshott—a remarkable and generous scholar—once said to the author *en passant* that Kant is "important but not attractive." This elegant half-jest, which probably refers mainly to Kant's style (or lack of it), half-inspired the author to write this book.

44. Hobbes, *Leviathan*, ed. Oakeshott, pp. 82–84.

45. Hegel, *Philosophy of Right*, trans. Knox, pp. 209–10.

46. Niccolò Machiavelli, *The Discourses*, in *The Prince and Discourses*, ed. M. Lerner (New York: Modern Library, 1950), pp. 138–39.

47. Rousseau, *Du Contrat Social*, in *Rousseau: Political Writings*, vol. 2, ed. Vaughan, pp. 50–51.

48. Mill, *Utilitarianism*, in *The Philosophy of John Stuart Mill*, ed. Cohen, pp. 362–63.

49. Marx, *Capital*, vol. 3, trans. Moore and Aveling, p. 820.

50. Locke, *Two Treatises of Government*, ed. Laslett, p. 311.

51. Burke, *Reflections on the Revolution in France*, in *Burke's Politics*, p. 284.

52. Hume, *Treatise of Human Nature*, ed. Lindsay, p. 179.

53. Sigmund Freud, *Civilization and its Discontents*, in *Civilisation, War and Death*, ed. J. Rickman (London: The Hogarth Press, 1968), p. 80.

54. J. W. Goethe, "Grenzen der Menschheit," in *Goethe, the Lyrist*, intro. E. H. Zeydel (Chapel Hill, N.C.: University of North Carolina Press, 1955), pp. 64–67. Despite Nietzsche's reverence for Goethe, he may have undervalued these lines:

> Denn mit Göttern
> Soll sich nicht messen
> Irgend ein Mensch.
> [For with the gods
> No man should ever
> Seek to compare.]

Index